# OUR MOTHERS' LAND

## CHAPTERS IN WELSH WOMEN'S HISTORY,

### 1830–1939

# OUR MOTHERS' LAND

## CHAPTERS IN WELSH WOMEN'S HISTORY,

## 1830–1939

*Edited by*

Angela V. John

CARDIFF
UNIVERSITY OF WALES PRESS
1991

*British Library Cataloguing in Publication Data*

Our Mothers' land : chapters in Welsh women's
history 1830–1939.
I. John, Angela V.
305.4209429

ISBN 0–7083–1120–2
ISBN 0–7083–1129–6 pbk

Jacket and cover design by Rhiain M. Davies, Carmarthen
Typeset by Megaron, Cardiff
Printed in Great Britain by Billings Book Plan Ltd., Worcester

*In memory of*
*the Welsh writer*
*Menna Gallie*
*1920–1990*

# Contents

# Illustrations

# Contributors

DEIRDRE BEDDOE is Professor of Women's History at the Polytechnic of Wales, Pontypridd. She is the author of several books on women's history, the latest being *Back to Home and Duty: Women Between the Wars 1918–1939* (London, Pandora, 1989).

KAY COOK has just completed her degree in History and Sociology at the University of Warwick. A native of Barry, she did a variety of jobs, including working in a supermarket and bringing up a family, before going to Coleg Harlech (where she undertook the research for her contribution to this volume) in 1986.

RUSSELL DAVIES was educated in schools in Ffair Fach and Llandeilo, and at the University College of Wales, Aberystwyth. He was awarded a Ph.D. for a study of culture and society in south-west Wales between 1870 and 1920. He is now an administrator at the University College of Wales, Aberystwyth.

NEIL EVANS is Tutor in History and Co-ordinator of the Centre for Welsh Studies at Coleg Harlech. He has published in a wide variety of journals and edited collections and is currently writing a book, *Darker Cardiff:The Underside of The City, 1840–1960*. He is Vice-Chairperson of Llafur:The Welsh Labour History Society.

ANGELA V. JOHN, originally from Port Talbot, is Professor of History and an Associate Head of the School of Humanities at Thames Polytechnic, London, and Chairperson of Llafur. Her published work includes *By the Sweat of Their Brow: Women Workers at Victorian Coal Mines* (London, Croom Helm, 1980; Routledge, 1984), and the award-winning *Coalmining Women* (Cambridge, Cambridge Educational, 1984). She edited *Unequal Opportunities: Women's Employment in England 1800–1918* (Oxford, Basil Blackwell, 1986) and also wrote (with Revel Guest)

*Lady Charlotte: A Biography of the Nineteenth Century* (London, Weidenfeld and Nicolson, 1989).

DOT JONES is currently working as a Research Assistant in the Department of Economics at the University College of Wales, Aberystwyth. She has written articles on workmen's compensation and the south Wales miner, the Poor Law and women's friendly societies in Wales. She is Membership Secretary for Llafur.

ROSEMARY A. N. JONES is a native of Cricieth, Gwynedd, and works for the Royal Commission on Ancient and Historical Monuments in Wales. She has a BA in history and an MA (on the political history of mid-nineteenth-century Cardiff) from the University College of Wales, Aberystwyth. She has recently published an article in *Ceredigion* on the *ceffyl pren* in Cardigan and is currently completing a more detailed study of popular protest and politics in mid-nineteenth-century Cardiganshire.

CERIDWEN LLOYD-MORGAN was brought up in Tregarth, Caernarfonshire, and was educated at the Universities of Oxford, Poitiers and Wales (Aberystwyth); since 1981 she has been an archivist in the Department of Manuscripts, National Library of Wales. She has published widely in Welsh, French and English. One of her main research interests is women's writing in Welsh.

SIAN RHIANNON WILLIAMS read History at University College of Wales, Aberystwyth, and was awarded a Ph.D. in 1985 for her study of the social history of the Welsh language in industrial Monmouthshire. A book based on her research is soon to be published by the University of Wales Press. Previous publications include articles in *Llafur*, *Planet* and *Y Traethodydd*.

# Acknowledgements

We are grateful to the following for permission to use their work/ records: the Masters and Fellows of Girton College, Cambridge, the archivists at Cyfarthfa Castle Museum, Glamorgan Record Office, Powys Record Office, the Imperial War Museum, Viscount Wimborne, Philip N. Jones, Hywel Francis, Ann Williams, Ryland Wallace, Thalia Campbell, Diana Atkinson and the editors of the journal *Llafur* (where an earlier English version of Sian Rhiannon Williams's article originally appeared). Thanks also go to members of Llafur (The Welsh Labour History Society) for their support via a day school. We are especially grateful to Susan Jenkins and Ceinwen Jones at the University of Wales Press. The editor would like to thank the reader for constructive comments and all the contributors for being so co-operative and committed.

Photographs appear by kind permission of the following: in chapters 1, 3, 6, 7 the National Library of Wales, in chapter 2 John Owen, in chapter 4 the University College of Wales, Aberystwyth, in chapter 5 the National Museum of Wales, in chapter 8 the Imperial War Museum.

# Abbreviations

| | |
|---|---|
| BWTA | British Women's Temperance Association |
| CCWE | Central Committee for Women's Employment |
| CDWSS | Cardiff and District Women's Suffrage Society |
| ILP | Independent Labour Party |
| NVA | National Vigilance Association |
| NUWSS | National Union of Women's Suffrage Societies |
| UDMD | Undeb Dirwestol Merched y De |
| | (South Wales Women's Temperance Union) |
| UDMGC | Undeb Dirwestol Merched Gogledd Cymru |
| | (North Wales Women's Temperance Union) |
| WFL | Women's Freedom League |
| WSPU | Women's Social and Political Union |

Wales, showing the pre-1974 county boundaries.
(From T. Herbert and G. E. Jones (eds.), *People and Protest*:
*Wales 1815–1880*, by permission of the Open University.)

# Another Chronology

| | |
|---|---|
| 1832 | 'Great' Reform Act formally confirms exclusion of all women from voting. |
| 1834 | Poor Law Amendment Act. Bastardy clauses especially problematic for women. |
| | Augusta Hall (later Lady Llanofer) wins at Cardiff Eisteddfod (for essay on the preservation of the language and customs of Wales). |
| c.1839 | Female radical associations support Chartism and prisoners' families. |
| 1842 | All females banned from working in mining below ground. |
| 1847 | Commissioners' report on state of education in Wales. |
| 1849 | Lady Charlotte Guest publishes three-volume edition of *The Mabinogion*. |
| 1850 | *Y Gymraes*, first Welsh periodical specifically intended for women. |
| 1852 | Lady Charlotte Guest runs world's largest ironworks at Dowlais. |
| 1866 | First women's suffrage petition. |
| 1870 | Elementary Education Act. |
| 1871 | Rose Crawshay is the first woman in Wales to sit on one of the new School Boards. |
| 1876 | British Women's Temperance Association founded. |
| 1870s–80s | Expansion of opportunities for women in Welsh higher education. |
| 1879 | First issue of *Y Frythones*, edited by Sarah Rees ('Cranogwen'). |
| 1883–4 | Women's League for the Spread of Co-operation, renamed as Women's Co-operative Guild in 1884. |

| | |
|---|---|
| 1885 | Frances Hoggan registers as Wales's first qualified woman doctor. |
| 1886 | Association for Promoting the Education of Girls in Wales founded. |
| 1889 | Welsh Intermediate and Technical Education Act. |
| *c.*1890 | Welsh Liberal women become organized. |
| 1892 | Undeb Dirwestol Merched Gogledd Cymru (North Wales Women's Temperance Union) founded. |
| 1896 | *Y Gymraes* reappears under the editorship of Ceridwen Peris. |
| 1897 | National Union of Women's Suffrage Societies formed. |
| 1901 | Undeb Dirwestol Merched Y De (South Wales Women's Temperance Union) formed. |
| 1903 | Women's Social and Political Union formed. |
| 1907 | Women's suffrage becomes organized in north Wales. |
| 1912 | Llanystumdwy incident involves suffrage and Lloyd George. |
| 1914–18 | First World War. Vast increase in numbers of women in waged work. |
| 1915 | Publication of Co-operative Women's Guild letters. |
| 1918 | Limited vote for women over thirty. |
| 1919 | Sex Discrimination Removal Act. Elizabeth Andrews becomes Labour Party's women's organizer in Wales. |
| 1923 | *Price* v. *Rhondda* court case helps institutionalize marriage bar for teachers. |
| 1926 | General Strike. Pilgrimage of Peace. |
| 1928 | Votes for all women. |
| 1930s | Women take part in hunger marches. |
| 1939 | Outbreak of Second World War. |

# Introduction

I

The history of Welsh people has often been camouflaged in British history yet women have also been rendered inconspicuous within their own Welsh history. The icons of the making of modern Wales are powerful and familiar: coal-mining and slate-quarrying dominate the images of work in south and north respectively whilst rugby and male-voice choirs have frequently been made synonymous with recreation. The emphasis has been placed on celebrating the land of our fathers rather than viewing Welsh history from the equally valid perspectives of women. A powerful labour tradition has meant an emphasis on the institutional, organizational aspects of modern Welsh history, occluding women's activities or casting their often tangential relationship to active trade unionism in terms of deficiency. The strength of Nonconformity has reinforced domestic values whilst the low female rates of participation in the formal economy until comparatively recently have further exacerbated women's neglect by historians.

The under-recording of women's paid work in census returns makes a realistic assessment of their employment very difficult. Nevertheless, it is still possible to compare women's recorded work for Wales with the English equivalent and for the time-span of this book the participation rates for women in Wales consistently remain significantly lower than in England. The contrast is especially evident when considering married women's work in the labour market. The kinds of work performed by women and men in Wales also reinforce the association of the male sex with heavy industry and the female sex with servicing and domesticity. At every decennial census except

1851, the proportion of women in domestic service (with its many varieties) in Wales was at least 10 per cent higher than in England.[1] Between 1871 and 1901 domestic service alone accounted for over half the total number of women employed in Wales. The last quarter of the nineteenth century and years up to 1914 also witnessed a staggering concentration of male employment. By 1911 one in three of the entire male occupied population of Wales was a miner or quarryman.[2]

Some specific groups, especially those Welsh women who most challenged dominant ideals of femininity — for example convicts and pit women — were examined some years ago and articles on Welsh women's history have appeared regularly in one journal, *Llafur*, the journal of the Welsh Labour History Society. Yet this is the first book devoted to a historical examination of Victorian and early twentieth-century women in Wales despite the steady output in England and recently a number of important studies in both Scotland and Ireland.[3] Moreover debates current in feminist historical theory which have stimulated discussion elsewhere over issues such as the significance of equality/difference arguments and the public/private dichotomy appear as yet to have had little resonance within Welsh historiography.

Yet such omission becomes more understandable when we consider the sex ratio of History departments in the University of Wales. At present there are *no* women lecturers working on women's history/ gender of the nineteenth or twentieth centuries in the University Colleges' History departments and only one (at the Polytechnic of Wales) in higher education in Wales. Such a situation is hardly conducive to encouraging undergraduates, postgraduates and staff to undertake work in this field.[4] When Welsh history publications include women they tend to be reserved for a separate chapter. This is an improvement from the neglect of the past but it does not recognize that the historical construction of femininity and masculinity constitutes a problematic central to any study of society in the past.

The chapters in this book cover the period from the 1830s to the outbreak of the Second World War in 1939. Taken together they amount to a history of the period, providing a rather different reading of the chronology and developments of the time from that of most books about the period. We cover different classes and regions and deploy a variety of sources, both English and Welsh, ranging from newspaper accounts and formal statistical records to diaries and oral testimonies.

## II

The book opens with an exploration of women's involvement in nineteenth-century community sanctions. Rosemary Jones shows how women helped structure popular culture, identities and loyalties at the local level through a public shaming ritual known as the *ceffyl pren* ('wooden horse') which punished moral transgressors. Such community sanctions, especially common in south-west Wales, can be seen as part of the 'rough music' or *charivari* tradition which has been explored in other countries.[5] Since rural Wales witnessed the persistence of such customs into a period of increased literacy in the Victorian period, it is possible to obtain from Welsh sources rare insights into rituals most commonly associated with pre-industrial societies with less written testimony.

This chapter illustrates how women might exercise some informal control outside the home via the drama of community action and at the same time reinforce moral codes. It helps us to discern shifting attitudes towards sexuality, marriage and patriarchal control as well as showing how the *ceffyl pren* punished those who threatened the political integrity of the community. Tracing the increased feminization (and marginalization) of such activities over time also involves questioning some of the distinctions between rural and urban, pre-industrial and industrial society through, for example, the persistence of community sanctions in south-east Wales earlier this century. During the miners' strike of 1984–5 remnants of women's earlier tactics could still be found: one group of miners' wives carried a big drum to beat as a warning to any potential strike-breakers.

The second chapter focuses on industrial south Wales and the heartland of the early nineteenth-century iron trade, Merthyr Tydfil. In place of the familiar concentration on masters and men it centres on two influential women, Lady Charlotte Guest and Rose Crawshay. Both were of English birth and their ideas and activities were not confined to their adopted homes despite Lady Charlotte's propensity for things Welsh. They were married to ironmasters and helped to cement social relations in their community. Yet they did this in their own ways and subverted traditions as much as they reinforced them. Although such ladies were supposed to be interested in good works rather than *the* works, Lady Charlotte combined motherhood (she had five boys and five girls) with Welsh translation work which made her an international figure, and also effectively deputized for her husband for many years before taking over the running of the largest ironworks in the world. The early feminist Rose Crawshay continually undermined gender stereotyping. Were they simply exceptional women? If we probe further and ask questions about the operation of gender and power relations within families, might we not find other women whose lives have previously been represented (if at all) in one-dimensional ways, refracted through their husbands' aspirations?

Both women seem a far cry from the Welshwoman of prescriptive literature though they were familiar with its tenets. The third chapter traces the development of *Y Gymraes* (*The Welshwoman*), the first Welsh periodical aimed specifically at women (portrayed as potential or actual wives and mothers). Edited by a Baptist minister it shaped an ideal rather than reflecting a reality though, as the chapter shows, the magazine's popularity was not amongst those for whom it was intended. Neither did its successor, edited by the Methodist Sarah Rees ('Cranogwen'), really manage to appeal to the working-class women it sought to enlighten. Even at the end of the century a revived *Y Gymraes*, now edited by a woman, still maintained the fiction of the ideal Welshwoman, albeit one subtly adapted to fit different times.

One grim reality could be found in the high incidence of suicide. Chapter 4 points out the disjuncture between the perceptions of the Victorian male as the one constantly under pressure in society, coping with the demands of the public world, and the literary image of the female as the one who succumbed and surrendered her life. Much of this was, as Lynda Nead has argued in relation to visual representation, linked to the concept of the fallen woman consigned to her fate, the penalties of sin being death for those who had become public women — and it was usually a death by drowning.[6] Yet, as Russell Davies shows, statistics of actual suicides for 1911 to 1919 for Carmarthenshire, the largest county in Wales, reveal that male suicides actually outnumbered female in both rural and urban districts.

The following chapter uses mortality statistics and census returns to demonstrate the toll coal-mining took on the women of the Rhondda in the late Victorian and Edwardian periods. By 1911 almost 63 per cent of the population of Wales was concentrated in Glamorgan and Monmouthshire. Yet although history books tell of the vast employment opportunities provided by the development of the steam-coal trade from the 1870s, this was not the case for women.

Their job prospects were extremely limited in the Valleys: Merthyr Tydfil and the Rhondda had the lowest rates of employment for married women in the whole of Great Britain and only 14 per cent of females over ten were recorded as being 'gainfully employed' in the Rhondda district at the beginning of the twentieth century.[7] Dot Jones shows how the women were nevertheless inextricably linked to the demands of labour and, using powerful autobiographies along-side the chilling evidence of statistics, she demonstrates how being a collier's wife constituted a health hazard.

For many men, the pub offered a welcome release from work and a central focus of their recreation. Not so for women who wished to be known as respectable. Some found Friendly Societies a way of furthering communal activities and providing vital support in times of especial need.[8] For many women in Wales (as in Finland), the temperance movement provided a valuable outlet in a culture where leisure patterns were clearly gendered. Chapter 6 challenges the notion that the temperance movement was in decline in Wales at the end of the nineteenth century and discusses the significance of women creating their own space and organizations via temperance unions in north and south Wales. Whilst Chapter 3 emphasizes the constraints inherent in the messages to women emanating from the Welsh periodical press, Ceridwen Lloyd Morgan's chapter nevertheless detects some liberating influences in the specific organization of temperance. On the one hand it clearly espoused Christian morality and domesticity, shunning the *public* house. On the other hand it enabled women to participate in a life beyond their homes, providing a network of organization for rural and urban women of different classes, giving them some space of their own and a structure of organization which allowed them to turn to advantage their own limited opportunities in an approved way without overtly rocking the boat.

Others were only too anxious to rock the boat as the following chapter by Kay Cook and Neil Evans shows. They demolish the claim that the women's suffrage movement did not have much impact in Wales. They briefly examine the background to Welsh women's suffrage, especially the work of Liberal women, but show that, despite the commitment of women throughout Wales, the movement's organization and leadership were inextricably linked to organizations outside Wales, notably the major suffrage societies formed in England.[9] The authors deliberately emphasize the non-militant aspects of the movement which received less publicity at the time and, until recently, have been more muted in historical analysis.

The final chapter looks at shifting opportunities during the First World War and the inter-war period, examining the impact of war on women's employment, then the impact of unemployment for both sexes and the renewed emphasis on domestic service. Women's unpaid labour could not cease and during the 1926 strike (which lasted months not days for Welsh mining communities) and the Depression, women had to become more resourceful than ever. Not surprisingly, domestic tension and violence increased. The chapter and book closes with a wry exploration of the 'Welsh Mam', one of the popular stereotypes so powerful throughout our period. This strong mother, whose 'power' was of course severely contained and constrained, has counterparts elsewhere, for example in Catalonia's image of '*La Ben Plantada*' ('Well-Rooted Woman').[10] The Welsh Mam finally found full romantic expression in Hollywood's interpretation of the Welsh working class.

## III

These chapters highlight a number of issues which have been of concern to feminist historians in recent years. Much has been written (particularly in relation to the early Victorian English middle class) about the concept of separate spheres, the association of the male with the public world of employment and the female with the private, personal, familial domain. In Wales the difficulties facing women of all classes in obtaining and retaining decent remunerative work and the very low numbers of married women in the labour market, suggest that the divide between public and private was especially powerful. It was certainly urged in written and visual form in the magazines explored in Chapter 3.

It was underpinned more generally by religious values. Leonore Davidoff and Catherine Hall's seminal examination of gender relations in the English middle class demonstrates how chapel was ' . . . central to the articulation and diffusion of new beliefs and practices related to manliness and femininity'.[11] This was even more marked in Welsh society where so-called Nonconformity actually represented a conforming majority who did not dissent from the faith. The beliefs and practices of different Nonconformist sects included adherence to a strict delineation of gender roles and essentially linked women with domesticity. Separate sphere ideology received a specific boost in the wake of the damning 1847 inquiry into the state of education in Wales; the responsibility for refuting charges of moral, spiritual and educational laxity was firmly placed on the shoulders of the female sex.

Yet whilst education tended to reinforce gender divisions through, for example, the provision and curricula of schools, it could also be a potentially liberating force. The election of women to School Boards in the 1870s provided an important opportunity for able women to prove their worth in local government, as was demonstrated by Rose Crawshay's pioneering work on two of Wales's first School Boards. W. Gareth Evans's book on female education shows the links between educational development, the professions and feminism, though he also warns against presuming linear progress.[12] The academic orientation of late nineteenth-century girls' curricula in secondary schools in Wales was replaced by a heavy dose of domestic studies by the time of the First World War. Kay Cook and Neil Evans also show that the opening up of women's higher education in Wales provided a vital spring-board for further feminist developments. It can be no coincidence that many of Wales's suffragists, women such as Anna Morris, Clara Neal and Emily Phipps, were teachers or principals of schools or colleges.[13]

Moreover, despite the wealth of literature emphasizing the domestic ideal for women, there is also sufficient evidence in this book to suggest a gap between the theory and practice and a danger in representing too stark a dichotomy between the public and private spheres. In practice women often broke down the boundaries between the public and private and a recurrent theme is their negotiation of some limited control in the community. The communal, unofficial pressure and sanctions involved in the *ceffyl pren* had important repercussions on the regulation of individuals' private lives. Work in temperance or charity organizations (briefly considered in Chapter 7) or in the more confrontational structures of feminist activity provided more formal breaching of the divide whilst some individuals, particularly those from more privileged backgrounds, might negotiate space and time for themselves and even invert the ideology. Lady Charlotte Guest deliberately described the business world of the ironworks as 'my proper sphere' though her simultaneous wish to fulfil her duty as a loyal wife suggests the care we need to exercise in analysing motives and behaviour.

Several chapters remind us that working-class women (who were in the majority) faced continual demands and routines structured around the workplace despite the fact that they spent their time in the home. Many women in rural communities were not formally employed yet farmers' wives, for example, played a vital role in sustaining what were modest family enterprises. The recollections of a Radnorshire farmer's wife early this century could have been echoed in many other parts of the country.[14] Mona Morgan's mother moved from domestic service (for a wealthy shipping family) to a daily round of getting up before anyone else, milking the cows, feeding the animals, cleaning the fowl house and carrying water from the well before most people were out of bed. Meals involved not only feeding her four children but providing for farm workers. Cooking included big bakes, cleaning meant jobs like blackleading the grate, and responsibility for clothing entailed making and mending what the family wore. Domestic service may have been a formal and generic job description for those who worked in other people's homes, such as the thousands of young Welsh women in London described by Deirdre Beddoe and given literary form in Winifred Foley's delightful memoir *A Child in the Forest*,[15] but it also describes the daily grind of many of the subjects of this book, women and girls absent from the census and the historical record.

Historians such as Tilly and Scott have stressed the need to reflect the different stages of family life and not neglect the large numbers of widows.[16] Many widows took over the running of farms or small-holdings (38.9 per cent of widows worked in Cardiganshire in 1911 compared with 30.2 per cent on average in England)[17] yet their toil, and female farm labour more generally, is largely forgotten. It has only been in wartime that women's heavy manual labour has been made visible and acceptable. Deirdre Beddoe points to this appreci-ation of 'our gallant girls'. The First World War clearly involved unprecedented numbers of women workers yet Victorian and Edwardian society had been familiar with female farm servants all over Wales, with small numbers of pit-top workers in Denbighshire, Flintshire, Glamorgan, Monmouthshire and Pembrokeshire and, at the beginning of our period, with women and girls working in mines. There were women working in brick-making, at tin works and as 'Copar Ledis' (breaking up copperstone) on Anglesey.[18] Such work, performed by single women and widows, offended notions of an appropriately segregated labour market and either became targeted for protective legislation or disparaged, whilst domestic service (which involved hauling buckets of coal and other manual labour) was applauded as was its association with harmonious labour relations, a model relationship of deference rather than defiance.

The powerful labour tradition in Wales and emphasis on organization at the workplace has meant that women's protests of other kinds have not always been recognized. This book draws attention to some of them. Their involvement in the *ceffyl pren* and other related activities demonstrates how they could effectively exert pressure and bypass or undermine the law and state intervention. David Jones's book on the Rebecca riots of the late 1830s and early 1840s[19] confirms this, showing not only how Rebecca's brief stretched well beyond attacking toll-gates but also how it included a strong female presence. Community sanctions both provoked and replaced legal action, asserting alternative concepts of moral and just behaviour, particularly in the context of the 1834 Poor Law Amendment Act which contained clauses which were especially problematic for unmarried mothers, placing the onus for maintaining illegitimate children on them or their parents and increasing the likelihood of their having to resort to the workhouse.[20] There is evidence, for example, of single fathers being held over rivers, the burial service being read out and a choice offered between a quick marriage or an early death.

Rosemary Jones also draws attention to women resisting scabs in the coalfield. There was a tradition of women's political activity in Wales which can be seen clearly from movements such as Chartism at the beginning of our period to the Peace Movement in the 1920s (in 1924 390,296 women, 65 per cent of the female population over eighteen in Wales, signed a Peace Memorial to the women of the United States).[21] During the First World War an English police sergeant for the Ministry of Munitions[22] found the Welsh munition workers at Pembrey in south-west Wales 'very full of socialistic theories . . . perpetually getting up strikes in true Tonypandy style'. During the inter-war period women stormed offices and town halls and went on hunger marches. Women teachers were again in evidence. The Syndicalist Gwen Ray Evans helped orchestrate the Rhondda teachers' strike of 1919 whilst Mavis Llewellyn, a teacher and Communist Party member from Nantymoel, completed, after the author's death, Lewis Jones's powerful novel *We Live*.[23] Yet an area renowned for its industrial militancy was not necessarily progressive when it came to gender issues such as the marriage bar for teachers. The case brought by a group of married women teachers in the Rhondda (*Price* v. *Rhondda*, 1923) resulted in the establishment and acceptance of the principle that married women teachers could be dismissed if this was deemed to promote the efficiency of education in the area.[24]

These chapters make the point that women were especially concerned with promoting issues relevant to their own sex. Both Dot Jones and Deirdre Beddoe show how women worked for better welfare conditions, urging improved housing, health and, above all, maternity care. Although many of the women discussed by Kay Cook and Neil Evans were middle-class suffragists or suffragettes, there *were* working-class women active in the Labour Party and in suffrage. One such woman was Elizabeth Andrews who at seventeen worked in people's homes sewing for two shillings (10p) a day before marrying a Rhondda miner. She was a leading figure in the immensely popular Co-operative Women's Guild in her district, advocated votes for women and became a Labour Party women's organizer.[25]

Ceridwen Lloyd-Morgan's chapter shows how temperance supporters could urge the importance of citizenship. Nevertheless the women involved in Welsh temperance and the periodical press seem largely to have subscribed to a notion of women's worth predicated on their assumed superior moral position. If they did advocate equality it was through an equality based on difference. This was a far cry from the demands of equal-rights feminists such as the middle-class Welsh businesswoman Margaret Haigh (Viscountess Rhondda) who, as Chapter 7 shows, was a very active suffragette. She went on to form the Six Point Group in the 1920s, which was dedicated to removing women's legal inequalities, and she founded and later edited the feminist journal *Time and Tide*.[26]

The chapter on temperance also discusses the relevance of the Welsh temperance unions to the British Women's Temperance Association. Ceridwen Lloyd-Morgan's consideration of the reasons why temperance and suffrage overlapped less in Wales than in England and the United States, and appeared more marked in Anglicized areas of Wales such as coastal towns rather than in Welsh-speaking Wales, raises the wider issue of the need to examine Welsh women's history not as an adjunct to English history or simply as part of an unproblematic umbrella labelled British history.[27] We need, as these chapters show, to unpackage the specific social, economic and cultural factors operating within Welsh society as well as locating them within a wider British and European framework. Moreover, it is important to discern the differences within Wales and to be sensitive to linguistic trends and patterns of in-migration.

We also need to consider the meanings and usage of Welshness. Welsh imagery could be conveniently evoked at certain appropriate moments. For example, Mrs Mansell Moulin, founder of the London-based non-party Forward Cymric Suffrage Union, organized the making of the national Welsh costumes worn in the Women's Coronation Procession of 1911.[28] She was drawing on a romantic 'tradition' created by Lady Llanofer as recently as the 1830s and fervently advocated by her in the Welsh periodical press examined in Chapter 3. Such symbolism and the tendency to portray Wales in newspapers as a female figure clad in quaint Welsh costume represent but one aspect of a more serious and politicized heightened concern with language and nation which was crystallizing late in the nineteenth century. Sian Rhiannon Williams suggests that the Welsh ideal of woman with a renewed emphasis on motherhood was of importance to the growth of Welsh national consciousness with its emphasis on the Welsh language and upholding the character of the nation. Certainly the historical relationship between women and nationalism in Wales is a subject which would merit research by feminist historians.

The chapters in this book explore the power of domestic ideology and the ways in which women coped with it, challenged it or subverted it. Taken together they underscore the distinction between a shifting ideal of femininity continually adjusted to fit class and circumstance and a reality which fundamentally questions the notion of the 'unoccupied' Welsh woman cheerfully fulfilling her 'natural' destiny. These discrepancies require much further exploration. Russell Davies's chapter on suicide also suggests the need to look much more critically at the historical and social construction of masculinity. The male images evoked there and at the opening of the Introduction need to be examined in the same way as historians have taken apart the meanings of femininity and the expectations surrounding it. Have the standard images of the land of our fathers ever really been applicable to the aspirations of most Welsh*men*? We also need to bear in mind the potency of myths despite the fact that they may be dismissed by some as irrelevant. Only by looking behind the stereotypes and by seeing how they have consciously or otherwise shaped expectations and behaviour for both sexes can we begin any serious examination of gender relations in the past.

These chapters in modern Welsh women's history are intended as a beginning of this process, an initial stimulus to further questioning and research. Each chapter is accompanied by a bibliographical note suggesting some of the major works and sources which may be consulted by the reader and will, it is hoped, lead before too long to further publications in this badly neglected yet crucial part of the modern history of Wales.

Angela V. John

*Notes to Introduction*

1.  L. J. Williams, Dot Jones, 'Women at work in nineteenth century Wales', *Llafur*, 3 No. 3 (1982), 23.
2.  John Williams, 'The rise and decline of the Welsh economy, 1890–1930', in Deian R. Hopkin and Gregory S. Kealey (eds.), *Class, Community and the Labour Movement: Wales and Canada 1850–1930* (Aberystwyth, Llafur/CCLH, 1989), 8.
3.  Recent books include: Cliona Murphy, *The Women's Suffrage Movement and Irish Society in the Early Twentieth Century* (Hemel Hempstead, Harvester Wheatsheaf, 1989), Mary Cullen (ed.), *Girls Don't Do Honours: Irish Women in Education in the Nineteenth and Twentieth Centuries* (Dublin, Argus Press, 1987) and Maria Luddy, Cliona Murphy (eds.), *Women Surviving: Studies in Irish Women's History in the Nineteenth and Twentieth Centuries* (Dublin, Poolbeg, 1990). This last book involved members of the Feminist History Forum, part of the Irish Women's Studies Association. For Scotland, see Eleanor Gordon and Esther Breitenbach (eds.), *'The World is Ill-Divided': Women's Work in Scotland in the Nineteenth and Early Twentieth Centuries* (Edinburgh, Edinburgh University Press, 1990), Glasgow Women's Studies Group, *Uncharted Lives. Extracts from Scots Women* (Glasgow, Pressgang, 1983), Sian Reynolds, *Britannica's Typesetters: Women Compositors in Edinburgh* (Edinburgh, Edinburgh University Press, 1989) and Linda Mahood, *The Magdalenes: Prostitution in the Nineteenth Century* (London, Routledge, 1990). In the United States (College of St Catherine, St Paul, Minnesota),

Constance W. Holt is compiling *An Annotated Bibliography of Women in Wales and Women of Welsh Descent in America* (London, Scarecrow Press, forthcoming).

4. There is nevertheless currently some research being undertaken by research students, for example on women and crime in nineteenth-century Pembrokeshire and on women's mass employment in and after the Second World War. There is also a Feminist Press, *Honno*, which has reprinted Jane Williams ('Ysgafell') (ed.), 'Betsy Cadwaladyr: A Balaclava Nurse' under the title of *An Autobiography of Elizabeth Davies* with an Introduction by Deirdre Beddoe (Cardiff, Honno, 1987). For many years historical novels have been written by and for women. An interesting example of the better-researched of this genre can be found in the work of Iris Gower whose nine novels have sold over half a million copies. Her historical romantic sagas are centred on the Swansea copper trade and are carefully packaged, each displaying a strong, defiant woman on the jacket.

5. For a discussion of such traditions in Britain see John R. Gillis, *For Better For Worse: British Marriages 1600 to the Present* (Oxford, Oxford University Press, 1985), especially Chapters 2 and 4.

6. Lynda Nead, *Myths of Sexuality: Representations of Women in Victorian Britain* (Oxford, Basil Blackwell, 1988).

7. L. J. Williams, Dot Jones, op. cit., 27–8. Interestingly in Scranton, Pennsylvania, part of an American little Wales beyond England (there were seven churches with Welsh-language services there in the 1870s), few married women went out to work even though there was employment for women in the silk mills. W. D. Jones, 'Wales in America: Scranton and the Welsh c.1860–1920' (University of Wales Ph.D. thesis, 1987). I am grateful to Dr Bill Jones for discussing this.

8. At least half a million women were members of such societies by the 1870s though their numbers declined in later years. See Dot Jones, 'Self-help in nineteenth-century Wales: the rise and fall of the female friendly society', *Llafur*, 4 No.1 (1984).

9. Although local women became active, it was the English leaders, particularly the Pankhursts, who received most publicity, adulation and scorn. One Harlech woman recalling her Edwardian childhood remembers being given envelopes for her mother by a local butcher's wife. Opening them she would find tracts and pamphlets with pictures of Mrs Pankhurst. She also recollects how 'in those days the very name of Suffragette was something mysterious, even unpleasant. We'd say "Here comes a Suffragette" and run like blazes' (O. Wynne Hughes, *Every Day Was Summer: Childhood Memories of Edwardian Days in a Small Welsh Town* (Llandysul, Gomer Press, 1990), 4 — recollections from the author's aunt).

10. I am grateful to Mary Nash for this information.

11.  Leonore Davidoff and Catherine Hall, *Family Fortunes: Men and Women of the English Middle Class, 1780–1850* (London, Hutchinson, 1987), 149.
12.  See W. Gareth Evans, *Education and Female Emancipation: The Welsh Experience, 1847–1914* (Cardiff, University of Wales Press, 1990).
13.  Anna Morris was principal of a Swansea school and signed both the 1864 Cambridge Local Examinations Memorial and the 1866 Suffrage Petition. I am grateful to Ann Dingsdale for this information. Clara Neal and Emily Phipps were Swansea headmistresses: the former became a University governor and sat on the national executive of the Women's Freedom League; Emily Phipps stood (unsuccessfully) for Parliament as one of the first enfranchised women and eventually became President of the National Union of Women Teachers. Staff and students from Swansea Training College signed the Women's Liberal Association of Swansea's petition to the House of Commons on women's suffrage. By 1901 there were close to 11,000 women teachers in Wales. See Ursula Masson's research on Swansea suffrage in Luana Dee, Katell Keineg (eds.), *Women in Wales: A Documentary of Our Recent History, 1* (Cardiff, Womenwrite Press, 1987), 67–76.
14.  Mona M. Morgan, *Growing Up in Kilvert Country: Recollections of a Radnorshire Childhood* (Llandysul, Gomer Press, 1990).
15.  Winifred Foley, *A Child in the Forest* (London, Futura edition, 1978), Part 11. This describes Winifred leaving her beloved Forest of Dean to enter service in London in the 1920s. At Paddington she was met by Blodwen with her overdose of make-up, cropped hair, flapper coat, pink silk stockings and high heels. Desperate to be mistaken for an actress, she spent her free time in the gods at the Shoreditch Olympia. The porter at Paddington immediately identified her as a skivvy. Some women of course found employment within Wales in homes and hotels, especially in seaside resorts. Jobs did not, however, automatically go to the Welsh even though they tended to be favoured in England. Anne Williams's research shows that in Victorian Anglesey, for example, the gentry and aristocracy tended to recruit staff from England. Anne Williams, 'Unending labour. Working women in nineteenth-century Anglesey' (University of Wales M.Phil. thesis, 1990).
16.  Louise A. Tilly, Joan W. Scott, *Women, Work and Family* (New York, Holt, Rinehart and Winston, 1978), 51–3.
17.  John L. Williams, 'The move from the land', in Trevor Herbert and Gareth Elwyn Jones (eds.), *Wales 1880–1914* (Cardiff, University of Wales Press, 1988), 30.
18.  Angela V. John, *By The Sweat of Their Brow: Women Workers at Victorian Coal Mines* (London, Routledge and Kegan Paul edition, 1984), 39. Sheila Owen Jones, 'Women in the tinplate industry: Llanelli 1930–1950', *Oral History Journal*, 15 No.1 (Spring 1987); Anne

Williams thesis, op. cit.; Val Lloyd, 'Attitudes to women at north Wales coalmines *c*.1840–1901', *Llafur*, 5 No.2 (1989); David Pretty, 'Women and trade unionism in Welsh rural society 1889–1950', *Llafur*, 5 No.3 (1990). David Pretty's article points out that the battle to control the farmworker's day, orchestrated by the Anglesey journalist who styled himself 'Ap Ffarmwr', was a battle to control hours for men alone despite complaints in the press by a woman that her sex worked longer days and faced worse conditions.

19. David J. V. Jones, *Rebecca's Children: A Study of Rural Society, Crime and Protest* (Oxford, Clarendon Press, 1985), especially Chapters 2 and 4.

20. A modification of the law in 1844 allowed a mother to bring an affiliation order against the putative father in court (and Poor Law Guardians could sue him for maintenance) but the responsibility for instigating the court action still lay with the woman.

21. See Angela V. John, 'A miner struggle? Women's protests in Welsh mining history', *Llafur*, 4 No.1 (1984). For an example of women actively involved in Chartism, see the Chartist *Advocate and Merthyr Free Press* for June 1840 which contains a letter from Elizabeth Morgan who organized Merthyr women Chartists in a Female Association. Elizabeth and her husband Morgan (one of the local Chartist leaders) jointly ran a small web and flannel factory where women workers were in the majority. Their children included a son called Thomas Jefferson Williams. I am grateful to Kevin Littlewood for information on the Williams family. Information on the Peace Memorial is in *The Woman Citizen*, 23 February 1924. I am grateful to Constance Holt for this reference. Fifty-five years before the march from Cardiff which resulted in the women's peace camp at Greenham Common, Welsh women participated in a Pilgrimage of Peace march to London, *Western Mail*, 19 June 1926.

22. The Diaries of Miss G. M. West, 14 January 1917, Imperial War Museum. Every effort has been made to trace the copyright holder. I am grateful to Dr Deborah Thom for originally alerting me to this source.

23. Lewis Jones, *We Live* (London, Lawrence and Wishart edition, 1978), Introduction by Dai Smith. See also Sue Bruley, 'Socialism and Feminism in the Communist Party of Great Britain 1920–39' (London School of Economics Ph.D., 1980).

24. Alison Oram, '"Serving two masters?" The introduction of a marriage bar in teaching in the 1920s', in London Feminist History Group, *The Sexual Dynamics of History* (London, Pluto Press, 1983).

25. Elizabeth Andrews, *A Woman's Work is Never Done* (Ystrad Rhondda, Cymric Democrat Publishing Society [1956]), 6. For the heavy demands on women in mining see also Gertrude Harris, 'The valley of my childhood', *Llafur*, 4 No.3 (1986).

26. Viscountess Rhondda, *This Was My World* (London, Macmillan, 1933).
27. For a discussion of Welsh and British history and gender, see Angela V. John, 'Sitting on the Severn Bridge: Wales and British History', *History Workshop Journal*, 30 (Autumn 1990), 91–100.
28. There is a photograph of the Welsh women in their costume at the procession in Lisa Tickner, *The Spectacle of Women. Imagery of the Suffrage Campaign, 1907–14* (London, Chatto and Windus, 1987), 129. See also the photograph of Ellis Griffith with the 'Welsh Suffragists' in *Votes for Women*, 30 June 1911.

# Women, Community and Collective Action: The 'Ceffyl Pren' Tradition

ROSEMARY A. N. JONES

At the beginning of the nineteenth century, Welsh women often occupied a conspicuous position in their respective communities, particularly in relation to popular protest. Indeed, the militancy of women was almost proverbial: contemporary reports on food riots, enclosure disturbances and attacks on bailiffs and other officials invariably attest to the commitment and vitality of female participation. At that time, social protest (unlike the formal electoral process) was essentially a community affair; and, to a considerable extent, collective values and solidarities united the interests of women and men in political terms. During the course of the nineteenth century, however, opportunities for female participation in the public arena were gradually eroded. Demands for adult male suffrage and the advent of a more formalized, male-dominated labour movement ensured that 'traditional', community-based forms of protest were increasingly replaced by more 'modern' and institutionalized strategies. Moreover, this effective marginalization of women, in political terms, was reinforced by wider social, cultural and economic shifts: in particular, a gradual separation of the spheres of home and work assigned many women to a far less public and visible role within the community.

But while these observations may be true in general terms, important elements of continuity were also evident. A preoccupation on the part of social historians with formal political institutions has tended to distract attention from the persistence of earlier political forms and, therefore, the continued importance of women. Although most women exercised no formal public or political power, the apparent domesticity and insular nature of their lives did not preclude participation in wider neighbourhood affairs. In fact, it is clear that women were often actively involved in public displays of communal solidarity and spearheaded demonstrations against individuals who contravened established social norms. In this respect, they played a central role in structuring popular values at a neighbourhood level.

In order to assess the role of women in the day-to-day affairs of their immediate communities — as well as in more overtly political expressions of communal solidarity — historians must examine less formal strategies and networks for the regulation of community affairs and the formation and reaffirmation of collective political consciousness. This chapter seeks to discuss in detail one such network: namely, the *ceffyl pren* or 'wooden horse', a highly ritualized community sanction used to punish 'deviant' behaviour. It served as an effective moral policing mechanism in the public surveillance of sexual or marital behaviour. It also provided a useful model for popular protest movements and inspired the Rebecca riots of 1839 and 1843–4, during which bands of aggrieved farmers, dressed in female attire or other elaborate disguises, attacked one of the tangible symbols of their exploitation and impoverished condition — the infamous toll-gate system. Moreover, by studying the *ceffyl pren* over an extended period, useful pointers can be drawn to wider social forces and changes. In particular, it may be observed that 'folkloric' traditions such as the *ceffyl pren* often reflect deep-seated shifts of power, in *gender* as well as political terms, and can assist in our understanding of the means whereby gender values and relations are constructed and reinforced.

The *ceffyl pren* must be viewed as part of a wider European phenomenon, since most closely knit, face-to-face communities sanctioned some type of informal, collective denunciation of 'aberrant' behaviour. Historians usually refer to these community sanctions by the collective and, at times, amorphous label *charivari* — the French *charivari* constituting, in the main, a humiliating parade backwards on a horse or donkey.[1] Most parts of the British Isles evolved similar public shaming rituals.[2] In Scotland and the north of England a custom known as 'riding the stang' was a popular method of punishment. Offenders were mounted on a pole or plank before being subjected to a censorial and sometimes painful ride through the neighbourhood — often to the accompaniment of a 'mock' serenade, termed 'rough music'. At times, a straw effigy was carried in the intended victim's place and, in many areas, it was common for the 'stang' to be mounted by a prominent or witty member of the crowd,

Rowlandson cartoon: Dr Syntax with the Skimmington Riders.
(By permission of the National Library of Wales.)

who assumed the role of spokesperson and delivered a comic 'sermon', usually in stanza form, on the alleged offence. In some areas of southern England, particularly during the early modern period, the highly theatrical 'skimmington' procession was used to express public disapprobation. This custom was usually directed at quarrelsome couples, most notably in cases where a wife sought to dominate her husband, and featured two surrogates dressed to represent the couple in question. Seated back to back on a horse or donkey, these surrogates provided a dramatic re-enactment of the supposed misdemeanour: the 'wife', usually a man in female disguise, belaboured the 'husband', who sat facing the donkey's tail, with a large ladle termed a 'skimmington' ladle. The procession was accompanied by a band of 'rough' musicians and a number of standard-bearers who carried female articles of clothing (such as smocks, nightdresses, chemises or petticoats) mounted on poles, to symbolize or, rather, to satirize 'petticoat government'.

Wales, too, had its public, processional shaming rituals — referred to loosely, for the purposes of this chapter, as the *ceffyl pren* tradition.[3] In essence, the *ceffyl pren* was precisely what its name suggests: a 'wooden horse' upon which offenders were paraded, either in person or in straw effigy, and subjected to the jibes and jeers of the neighbourhood. The 'horse' often took the form of a makeshift pole, ladder, wheelbarrow or garden gate although, in some areas of Wales, time was spent in secretly constructing a life-size effigy of a horse made from wood and straw. This 'horse' was usually carried by a number of men who blackened their faces and otherwise disguised their appearance by dressing in women's clothes or reversed jackets. Occasionally, a 'spokesman' (often a man in female disguise) was carried on the 'horse', from which he delivered a sermon or discourse denouncing the victim's alleged offence.

As a rule, the *ceffyl pren* procession was staged at night and was repeated either for three consecutive nights or on the same night each week for three successive weeks. It was invariably accompanied by a good deal of noise and disruption, such as raucous yelling and hooting, the beating of drums, blowing of horns, firing of guns and, in particular, some form of 'rough music' — that is, a cacophony of discordant sounds produced on a variety of improvised instruments, such as pots and pans, kettles, tins and tea-trays. On occasions, a few satirical verses, ridiculing the victim's behaviour, were specially composed. If an effigy was paraded, it was usually ritually 'executed', amidst loud applause, by burning, hanging or shooting. When the offender was carried in person, he — or she, for women were often singled out for punishment and treated in an equally brutal manner — was subjected to a good deal of physical and verbal abuse. Having been forcibly dragged from their homes, the victims of such attacks were frequently pelted with mud, stones, addled eggs and manure before being severely beaten, whipped or ducked in a local pond or river.

A wide cross-section of the local community usually participated, men and women, young and old. Although in some areas youth groups assumed a conspicuous role, it seems that their actions often met with the tacit approval of (or were sometimes actually instigated by) the community at large. An element of consensus and collective acquiescence seems to have been an essential prerequisite of most *ceffyl pren* demonstrations. Such incidents were not usually provoked by personal malice or a desire for revenge. In many instances, the strength of neighbourhood approval was expressed at a formal 'mock court', which either took place prior to the event or formed an integral part of the ritual. During its deliberations the alleged offence was subjected to vigorous public scrutiny, often by means of an elaborate parody of official court procedure. At Laugharne in 1851, for example, a female farm servant suspected of poisoning her mistress and a fellow servant was subjected to just such an ordeal: once sentence had been announced, her effigy was suspended from a mock gallows and ceremonially burnt.[4]

The *ceffyl pren*'s stated purpose was usually to force offenders to reform their ways; but, in some instances, particularly when the ceremony was repeated night after night or was buttressed by a wider social boycott of the offending party, the overriding aim was to force the victim to flee the neighbourhood altogether. Betsi Gibbs, the suspected Laugharne poisoner, was forewarned that a 'mock' execution would be staged outside her home 'every night for one month' unless she consented to leave the village immediately. These threats were reinforced by a concerted campaign which ensured her total exclusion from the social and cultural life of the neighbourhood. As the local press reported:

> In the first place she has been 'sent to Coventry' by the whole village, high and low, rich and poor, and by way of getting rid of her hated presence the shopkeepers resolved to starve her out, by refusing to supply her with provisions upon any terms. Both herself and her

relations were forbid [*sic*] to go near the dwellings of any of the residents . . . [5]

Not surprisingly, Betsi Gibbs fled Laugharne a few days after these sanctions were introduced.

In small, tightly integrated, face-to-face communities, where disputes between individuals could prove disruptive to the wider social or economic unit, such sanctions proved an effective form of social control. They were the product of a highly autonomous and self-regulatory approach to community affairs and were dependent upon widespread acceptance that the 'private' behaviour of individuals should be subject to scrutiny by the neighbourhood as a whole. By resorting to these sanctions, the community dissipated potentially disruptive tensions and, in the process, helped to create a deep sense of corporate identity and loyalty.

The *ceffyl pren* has usually been associated with the tightly knit peasant communities of rural south-west Wales, most notably with those areas where Rebecca was entrenched. But the *ceffyl pren* was not the exclusive preserve of Rebecca and her 'daughters': far from it. The Vale of Glamorgan, for example, had its own indigenous tradition, often referred to as the *cwlstrin*/'coolstrin' or *cwltrin*/'cooltrin'.[6] The *ceffyl pren* also survived, with a surprising resilience, the cultural shift induced by the growth of industrialized society. In 1845, for example, a Merthyr Tydfil workman, seized after a drinking spree in the infamous Cellars region of the town, was conveyed home in a 'rude chair' mounted on the shoulders of his fellow townsmen.[7] At Aberdare, in 1856, a collier from Mountain Ash 'who had incurred the displeasure of the women, in seducing a fair demoiselle of Aberdare, concealing the fact that he was a married man with three children' was paraded on a ladder and pelted with 'every kind of filth'.[8] At Blaenau Ffestiniog, in 1877, a number of quarrymen seized a colleague suspected of adultery and paraded him for hours in a hand-barrow, 'relating his delinquencies as they went along . . . and calling him all sorts of opprobrious names'.[9] Although local magistrates, police and, in those areas where Rebecca had been active, the military engaged in concerted attempts to outlaw the custom during the middle decades of the nineteenth century, it is clear that most regions of Wales retained some form of public sanction allied to the *ceffyl pren* tradition well into the present century.

Women participated in these sanctions on a number of levels. Firstly, it seems apparent that women helped to sustain the various informal gossip channels which detected and defined 'aberrant' social behaviour and, therefore, ultimately influenced the selection of prospective *ceffyl pren* victims. 'Gossip', of course, was not an exclusively female prerogative: men, too, observed and passed judgement on the indiscretions and idiosyncrasies of their neighbours. The Glamorgan *cwlstrin*, for example, was often prompted by gossip among the male fraternity at a local tavern. But gossip networks also enabled women to play a central role in the surveillance of community affairs. Gossip, it must be stressed, was often a constructive rather than a divisive force; it was rarely 'idle'. In particular, it served to define the accepted boundaries between 'respectable' and 'deviant' conduct and could exert a devastating influence over the personal and professional lives of its victims. At Rhyl in 1857, for example, a policeman suspected of adultery was forced to resign from the police force after his effigy was paraded in public.[10] By gossiping informally in the streets, on doorsteps, at the village well or bakehouse, women helped to regulate community affairs and were thus afforded a real measure of public influence and power. Indeed, such was the importance of gossip to 'women's culture' that, on occasions, it was channelled through more formal, quasi-institutionalized networks, such as the *Clwb Te* ('Tea Club') — a gossip circle which was popular in many parts of south-east Wales during the early decades of the nineteenth century. Women were invited to join the *Clwb Te*, on the eve of their wedding, by the married women of the neighbourhood; its members were sworn to secrecy and men were entirely excluded from the proceedings.[11]

Similarly, the success of the social boycott — which exerted intense psychological as well as economic pressure on its intended victim — was dependent on the co-operation and commitment of the entire community, women included. Neither should we underestimate the importance of women in transmitting to each successive generation the oral traditions, collective 'folk wisdom' and highly theatrical popular repertoire which underpinned the *ceffyl pren* tradition and secured its broad appeal. Furthermore, the converse must also have been true, in that those women who, during the second half of the nineteenth century, increasingly distanced themselves from more 'vulgar' or 'uncouth' public activities, helped to discredit communal customs such as the *ceffyl pren* and secure their ultimate demise. A New Quay woman who, as a young child, witnessed the last *ceffyl pren*

to be paraded in that vicinity (*c*.1890) later recalled being chastised by
her mother for having watched 'such a thing'.[12]

In addition to these more covert channels of influence, women
frequently performed a conspicuous, rather than a purely passive,
spectator role in the *ceffyl pren* procession. On a number of occasions,
female members of the crowd subjected the victim to a tirade of
abuse, both verbal and physical. At Llangefni, in 1887, a man who
had deserted his wife was paraded on a ladder by a group of
neighbours who stopped at certain points 'to allow the womenkind to
wreak their vengeance upon him'.[13] Women often played an
inflammatory part, inciting their menfolk to further violence. An eye-
witness to a *ceffyl pren* attack at Tenby noted how, after seizing a
neighbour suspected of adultery, the men in the crowd 'seemed
ashamed or afraid of what they had done, and, probably, would have
abandoned their undertaking, but for the *gentler* sex, who, with
taunts and reproaches succeeded in keeping them to their post'. At
times, the women appeared more menacing than the men; as the same
writer records:

> The women were the most obstreperous. Indeed, on such occasions,
> women are the most violent — especially to the erring member of their
> own sex, whom they have occasionally been known to lacerate with
> knives and pins.[14]

Women were also reported to have been responsible for the initial
seizure of the victim. In 1845, three Cardiganshire women were
prosecuted for forcibly entering an offender's home, dragging him to
the door and, with the assistance of a number of young men, parading
him on a *ceffyl pren* to the accompaniment of a 'rough music'
serenade.[15] In 1856, two women were among a number of persons
prosecuted for a similar attack on a suspected Cwmaman wife-beater
who, after being dragged from his bed, was carried for some
considerable time on a ladder, until the ladder broke.[16] From time to
time, women added to the humiliation of a male victim by depriving
him of his clothes. In 1861, a Llanarth wife-beater was paraded
through the neighbourhood in his nightshirt until his attackers
'allowed him to alight from his uneasy perch and go home in a state of
nudity, the women who had formed part of the procession having
torn his shirt off his back'.[17] Moreover, two further Cardiganshire
examples reveal that women were often responsible for carrying the
*ceffyl pren* through the streets. During an unusually festive procession

witnessed at Llandysul in 1861, and headed by a local brass band, the 'horse' was reportedly 'borne along chiefly by females (who)... bore a conspicuous part in the affair'.[18] Likewise at Llanfair Orllwyn, during the following year, a local tailor suspected of an 'illicit connection' was confronted by a large crowd who congregated outside his home; the *ceffyl* was carried by four women who swore and shouted abuse.[19] Finally, on a few rare occasions, women assumed the most prestigious role of all: that of 'spokesperson'. As the press reported in 1850:

> A 'CEFFYL PREN' was carried through the village of St Dogmells [sic], in open daylight on Monday last. It was ridden by a female, who harangued the crowd at different places through which the exhibition was carried. This is the second instance of female oratory this town and neighbourhood has lately witnessed directed against two of the most crying evils of the times — drunkenness and adultery. A strong hope can now be entertained of their being rapidly suppressed.[20]

Although, on the whole, community sanctions reflected a co-operative effort on the part of the wider community, both male and female, several cases were reported during the last century in which the main instigators and participants were almost *exclusively* female. This was often the case in relation to the punishment of wife-beaters. During the latter months of 1843, for instance, at the height of the Rebecca disturbances, around forty Pontarddulais women, led by a woman blowing a horn, gathered outside the home of a neighbour 'who was in the habit of rather ill using his better half' and threatened to duck him in a river unless he reformed his ways.[21] In 1855, the married women of Llanrwst convened a 'mock court' which scrutinized the behaviour of a notorious wife-beater. According to the press:

> Llanrwst was... last week, the scene of great uproar, nearly the whole population having assembled to give public expression to their indignation and disgust at the conduct of a fellow-townsman who, on more than one occasion, has been guilty of castigating his wife. The town crier in the early part of the day had publicly announced that a meeting of all the married women of Llanrwst was to be held at the Town Hall, to deliberate upon some means of putting a stop to this cowardly practice. At 7 o'clock in the evening a large assembly (the majority of whom consisted of females) congregated on the square to witness the ceremony of 'burning the culprit in effigy'.[22]

Sanctions such as these reveal a marked degree of female self-determination and help to dispel notions of women as the perpetual and passive victims of male violence and oppression. Despite the pervasiveness of male power, many women were assertive and resourceful, treating the *ceffyl pren* tradition as an important collective defence mechanism to be mobilized as and when required. It cannot, however, be assumed that this had always been the case or, moreover, that the custom had always been deployed to the potential benefit of women. Indeed, if parallels are drawn with earlier centuries, it cannot even be concluded, with any great certainty, that active female participation was a feature of any great antiquity. Neither can it be assumed that women and men had always participated on equal terms nor that they necessarily viewed events from a similar perspective. There are clear indications that the custom was originally used to buttress patriarchal authority by humiliating 'scolding' or 'unruly' women. And a brief comparison between the public shaming rituals of the seventeenth and nineteenth centuries suggests that a deep-seated and qualitative change in gender relations had taken place during the intervening years. As very little is known about the *ceffyl pren* prior to the second quarter of the nineteenth century, this point can best be illustrated by referring, briefly, to the English 'skimmington' during the early modern period.

The 'skimmington' appears to have been primarily a phenomenon of the late sixteenth and seventeenth centuries and numerous examples have been recorded, particularly in the southern counties of Somerset and Wiltshire. It was a by-product of the so-called 'crisis of order' which was evident at that time; the destabilizing effects of rapid economic change, increased mobility and population growth, coupled with an attendant increase in the economic freedom and independence of women, alarmed many contemporaries. And, at a time when the patriarchal model was viewed as the corner-stone of the wider political order, the 'skimmington' was introduced as a means of reinforcing patriarchal authority. Husbands, it was felt, had a duty to chastise 'headstrong' wives who, by their 'hen-pecking', presented a threat not only to male supremacy but to the entire political infrastructure. Weak or compliant husbands were therefore ridiculed during the 'skimmington' procession, along with their 'shrewish' wives, and taunted for their lack of manhood. The extent to which women participated in such proceedings — other than as the unwilling butt — has not been established. No doubt many women acquiesced in the patriarchal ideal, thereby endorsing their own suppression, just as members of the working classes and other oppressed social groups have often espoused or condoned ideologies which condemn them to an inferior position within society. But it appears that men, rather than women, were most perturbed by the phenomenon of the domineering wife. On the whole, women were less concerned with upholding the patriarchal ideal than with protecting their sexual honour. In London, for example, women defended wives who had given their husbands a 'sound thrashing' for questioning their fidelity by parading effigies of the men in question.[23] As Susan Amussen has suggested, women seemingly modelled their own view of public 'respectability' on chastity and sexual reputation rather than on obedience to their menfolk.[24]

The history of the *ceffyl pren* during earlier centuries has yet to be charted. None the less, patchy evidence from eighteenth-century Wales suggests that the custom was, at one time, similarly used to enforce patriarchal domination and may, in fact, have been used for that purpose until the early nineteenth century — particularly in areas where women retained a marked degree of social and economic independence. The specific rituals adopted were often reminiscent of the 'skimmington' procession. The Glamorgan *cwlstrin* provides an interesting case in point. A particularly vivid description of the custom appears in Charles Redwood's *History of the Vale of Glamorgan*, published in 1839, by which time such proceedings were already a rare occurrence.[25] In Redwood's highly coloured account, the menfolk of a Vale community were aroused by the cowardly behaviour of a drinking partner whose wife resented his visits to a local tavern and had consequently beaten him: in their eyes, the man's obvious fear of his wife represented an act of 'slavery to petticoat government, and a disgrace to manhood' and was deserving of punishment. An elaborate 'mock court' was convened in the local churchyard and 'all good . . . and true men who as yet wore their own breeches' were instructed to attend. After lengthy debate a 'judge' dressed in a blanket and horse's 'collar-bone' delivered a speech on the threat posed by female tyranny: 'all the danger is from the WOMEN . . . it is no light matter keeping the breeches from them'. The court's verdict was that the village should 'hold a riding' to humiliate the 'hen-pecked' husband and his 'notorious vixen' of a wife, thereby providing other 'hectoring wenches' with a salutary warning. On the appointed day, a large procession headed by the 'judge', his 'officials' and a band of 'rough' musicians, armed with frying-pans and gridirons, perambulated the neighbouring villages. Two surrogates impersonated the couple in question: the 'wife' carried a ladle and the 'husband' a broom, a symbol of female domestic labour. The procession also included two standard-bearers who carried a petticoat on one pole and a pair of breeches — turned upside down to symbolize the subversion of male authority — on the other. Outside the home of the offending couple, the petticoat was pelted with mud, stones and addled eggs until it dropped to the ground in tatters, while the breeches were elevated in its place 'as the standard of masculine government'.

The *cwlstrin* (as described by Redwood) represented an attempt on the part of men to uphold ideal — rather than actual — relations between the sexes. In short, it sought to enforce adherence to the patriarchal model at a time when men were particularly sensitive about the behaviour of headstrong wives. Women were entirely excluded from the proceedings; indeed, they taunted the men for lending their support. As Redwood recorded, *cwlstrin* participants could meet with a mixed reception:

> The men everywhere received them with shouts and merriment, and sometimes even with bell-ringing; but the women kept within doors, and only mocked at them through the windows; . . .when at length they returned to their own village, the women there had collected to scoff at them, and poured out a din of hoots and yells, that could not be drowned even by the Coolstrin band of kitchen music . . . [26]

It would therefore appear that, up until the early decades of the nineteenth century, the primary purpose of the *ceffyl pren* and related customs was formally to discredit the behaviour of 'unruly' women by endorsing patriarchal values. By the second quarter of the nineteenth century, however, there are clear indications that a fundamental shift in gender values and relations had already taken place. Although there was a degree of continuity in the choice of prospective victims, the wife-beater had, by that time, increasingly come to replace the husband-beater as a primary target of popular disapprobation. In fact, the use of public shaming rituals against 'scolding' or domineering women was a rare occurrence by the middle decades.

But does this phenomenon reflect a widespread and fundamental improvement in the status of women as a whole? The question is open to debate but, on balance, it would appear that this was not the case. The change in selected targets partly reflects a dismantling of patriarchy as the main bulwark of political as well as social order. No doubt the patriarchal model continued to provide a desirable ideal to which many 'respectable' Victorian couples aspired; but, as the hysteria of earlier periods was dissipated and, moreover, new political tensions and challenges emerged in the wake of industrialization, the independent-minded wife no longer constituted a realistic threat to *political* stability. Furthermore, a gradual separation of the spheres of home and work ensured that women were no longer perceived as a credible threat to the social and economic power wielded by men. As the lives of women became increasingly dependent on the male wage-earner, and lost most of the outward vestiges of economic and personal independence, so men became increasingly less cautious and sensitive about signs of female assertiveness. Far from being an indication of women's improved status within society, the punishment of wife-beaters was probably symptomatic of increasing female dependency on men — their 'natural protectors' — and the widespread dissemination of beliefs about the innate passivity and vulnerability of women. And, as E. P. Thompson has observed in relation to English 'rough music' rituals, many attacks on wife-beaters were, in fact, initiated and executed primarily by *men*, who increasingly came to view women as weak, defenceless creatures in need of chivalrous protection and compassion.[27] The following example from Aberdare, which appears to reflect male gallantry and conviviality rather than female self-determination, illustrates this point; in particular, it highlights the collective and public assertion of masculine values as an important ingredient in some *ceffyl pren* attacks. During this particular incident, which took place in 1855, a collier known as 'Dai Dumpin' was punished by his fellow workmen for beating his wife 'until she lay bleeding and senseless':

> The news of Dai's violence towards his wife spread rapidly, and next morning a host of colliers and miners procured a plank, and . . . pounced upon the wife beater . . . whom they very quickly placed athwart the plank, which was carried by four men . . . In this manner he was carried from Penywaun down through . . . Llwydcoed Ironworks, accompanied by about one hundred people, many of whom had small branches of ash and other trees, with which they often flagellated the miserable man . . . Having been well paraded . . . [he was] feelingly and impressively addressed by two of his Lynching attendants . . . on the

wickedness of his conduct . . . The parties who had administered to
'Dai' this specimen of Aberdare justice, spent the remainder of the day
at the several public-houses, regaling themselves with a few extra
glasses, after the performance of what they considered their bounden
duty in the way of protecting the weaker sex.[28]

No doubt the chivalrous public gestures displayed by some working-
class men co-existed with ambivalence and guilt about their own
domestic behaviour. As recent research by A. J. Hammerton has
revealed, men who beat and otherwise abused their wives could
themselves actively encourage popular sanctions against other,
known wife-beaters.[29] But a deep-seated change in the public
enforcement of 'ideal', outward standards of marital behaviour and
gender relations had undoubtedly taken place.

Furthermore, the *ceffyl pren* clearly served as an important
collective mechanism for protecting the battered wife at a time when
many women were unable, or unwilling, to bring their husbands to
justice through official legal channels. Victims of domestic violence
could rely not only on the moral support of neighbours but also, at
times, on concerted physical intervention. Indeed, neighbours often
felt a duty to intervene in such matters, even if the consent of the
injured wife had not been obtained. A suspected wife-beater at
Cwmaman in 1856, for example, was seized by a group of irate
neighbours despite his wife's protestations of his innocence.[30]
Similarly, married men who deserted their wives and children or
embarked on adulterous liaisons could be confronted with swift and
retributive community justice. At Tregaron (*c*.1880), a notorious
adulterer and wife-deserter was paraded on the *ceffyl pren* before
being ducked in a river: ignoring the remonstrances of his neighbours,
he had apparently abandoned, in turn, his legal wife, his common-law
'wife' and his offspring by both women, in order to set up home with
yet another woman.[31] Moreover, at times, a particularly resourceful
wife could capitalize on neighbourhood support to engineer her
erring husband's public downfall. A Solva woman who suspected her
husband of adultery paid a number of local youths to watch his
movements and when his 'illicit affair' came to light the same young
men paraded the man on a ladder.[32] The *ceffyl pren* continued to
provide many vulnerable or abused women with a degree of practical
support and protection throughout the middle decades of the
nineteenth century.

Yet, in addition, women continued to be the victims of such attacks. At Llangadog in 1837, for example, a woman was forced to ride the *ceffyl pren* in the hope that the experience would make her a 'virtuous woman'.[33] At Waunfawr, in 1868, a woman who had married a man who had deserted his wife was paraded on a ladder.[34] During the late 1880s, the effigy of a horse was burnt outside the home of a New Quay woman accused of cruelty towards her stepchildren and at Pontrhydfendigaid (*c.*1870) a girl was punished for 'jilting several young men'.[35] Although by the mid nineteenth century the *ceffyl pren* was no longer used to suppress women *per se* (that is, by enforcing patriarchal values), it none the less continued to punish women who flouted current norms and imposed strict constraints on their sexual and domestic behaviour. In this respect, the *ceffyl pren* was motivated by a highly developed sense of moral rectitude. Despite the scathing accusations of sexual laxness and unbridled promiscuity which were frequently voiced against Welsh working-class women — particularly by English, middle-class critics — the *ceffyl pren* enforced adherence to a strict moral and sexual code which was defended by the entire community, women and men alike. Indeed, women of dubious reputation frequently found members of their *own* sex to be their most vociferous critics.[36]

Even so, the code of sexual morality endorsed by many Welsh communities could, at times, display a marked disparity with the moral standards set by 'respectable', middle-class commentators. Whereas extra-marital entanglements were strictly prohibited, the punishment of pre-marital sexual relations seems, on the whole, to have been omitted from the *ceffyl pren* agenda. On those rare occasions when unmarried mothers were singled out for punishment it would appear that their sexual 'indiscretion' was not the underlying reason for their unpopularity. At Aberporth, for instance, an unmarried mother was subjected in 1839 to a particularly brutal assault for allegedly attributing her condition to the wrong man.[37] Her plight does, however, illustrate the intense physical as well as psychological pressure which could be exerted against any woman seeking to establish the paternity of her child, particularly if the man in question commanded the respect and support of the community at large.

Detailed analysis of the *ceffyl pren* can, therefore, serve as a useful indicator of popular attitudes to sexual morality and to changing gender relations. The custom provided an important method of integrating the individual into collective modes of behaviour and, in view of its effectiveness in strengthening and mobilizing neighbourhood ties, it is hardly surprising that it should also have been adapted to changing *political* circumstances. In fact, it is within an almost exclusively political context that the custom's significance has usually been assessed by historians. On the eve of the Rebecca riots, for example, a period of acute social and economic dislocation in many parts of south-west Wales, the *ceffyl pren* appears to have experienced a dramatic resurgence — most notably as a means of punishing so-called 'informers' who betrayed local standards of behaviour by collaborating with the authorities against the wider interests of their neighbours.[38] The custom could also serve as a guise for direct criticism of the ruling classes by, on occasions, providing a useful model for more widespread protest. There were, after all, marked similarities between the *ceffyl pren* tradition and the repertoire deployed by the Rebecca rioters, both in the use of the female persona as the anonymous defender of customary morality and in the adoption of retributive direct action to safeguard collective interests.[39] The *ceffyl pren* was clearly a valuable defence mechanism which could be activated when the political integrity of the community was threatened. It helped to create a strong sense of communal identity, loyalty and cohesion and, in the long term, the capacity of any community to mobilize in times of crisis depended on this sense of mutual obligation and solidarity. Historians of popular protest must, therefore, examine alternative forms of collective action, such as the *ceffyl pren*, which not only mobilized popular loyalties at times of heightened political tension but also nurtured and reinforced those loyalties during periods of relative calm. In particular, a preoccupation with the dramatic 'flashpoints' of popular protest can often negate the seemingly marginal but nevertheless crucial role played by women in the long-term creation and reaffirmation of the collective loyalties and strategies which ultimately moulded and sustained that protest.

Most examples of *ceffyl pren* activity against 'political' offenders, such as informers, seem to have occurred during the highly-charged period which preceded the Rebecca riots, and during subsequent years the custom was primarily directed against 'moral' transgressions such as wife-beating and adultery. None the less, remnants of the *ceffyl pren* tradition continued to re-emerge during political disputes throughout the nineteenth century — most notably during those periodic displays of communal solidarity which accompanied anti-tithe demonstrations. In 1857, for instance, the Mumbles area witnessed a particularly heated dispute related to the tithe payable on oysters collected in the locality and when a certain Mr Knight of Ilfracombe sought to exact payment he was 'drummed out' by the oyster dredgers' families:

> The resistance was of a passive rather than an active character, and those who principally figured in it were the wives and children of the hard-working dredgers. A sort of mock procession was formed, and with the true Flemish red whittle as a banner, and accompanied by a brass kettle band, such a hubbub was raised about the ears of Mr Knight as compelled him to beat a precipitate retreat from the village.[40]

Similar disturbances were witnessed during the so-called 'Tithe War' of the 1880s and 1890s, when Nonconformist farmers registered their antipathy to the Anglican establishment by withholding the payment of tithe. In several Welsh communities — including those areas of south-west Wales where the *ceffyl pren* had remained resilient — tithe bailiffs and auctioneers were confronted by crowds of angry protesters whose tactics were frequently reminiscent of earlier shaming rituals: the parading of comic effigies dressed to represent local clergymen, the blowing of horns, the singing of anti-tithe verses and the almost obligatory 'rough music' serenade were all popular devices. At Rhydlewis in 1887, a bailiff found serving notices on tithe defaulters 'was honoured with an escort of half-a-dozen tin-kettles and pans, vigorously played upon by an enthusiastic band of amateur drummers'; according to the press, the 'half-dozen soon increased to a hundred, so that when the bailiff reached Rhydlewis the noise was deafening and the whole village turned out'.[41] Tithe officials were also subjected to a good deal of physical as well as verbal abuse; and, it must be stressed, women frequently spearheaded these attacks. In an account of a tithe auction held at Aberarth in 1887, the local press reported that there were 'some fifty or sixty women present, and they were by no means the most easily-managed portion of the crowd'. At Newport (Pembrokeshire) in 1891, a group of women made unsuccessful attempts to deprive a tithe bailiff of his clothes and, during the same year, a tithe agent visiting the Cardigan area was set upon 'by a crowd of Amazons . . . their avowed object being to duck [him] in the pond'.[42]

It is therefore apparent that, during the closing years of the nineteenth century, women continued to play an important role in the dispensation of popular 'justice' by ridiculing and haranguing the community's perceived 'enemies'. Although, by that time, the more formalized, institutionalized politics of 'rational' debate and constitutional reform endorsed by mainstream Liberal radicalism had reached hegemonic proportions in rural Wales, at a neighbourhood level the rhetoric of 'respectable' Nonconformist Liberalism often fused with more 'primitive' direct-action tactics. The persistence of earlier rituals and sanctions — in particular, the use of vivid visual imagery, symbolic gestures and other theatrical devices, such as the parading of effigies — helped to reactivate neighbourhood loyalties and provided an important element of continuity in the organizational structure of social protest. Indeed, the resilience of these earlier forms suggests that too rigid a demarcation line has sometimes been drawn between 'traditional' and 'modern' methods of protest and that, as a result, the continued centrality of community, and therefore female, support has not always been recognized.

Just as this demarcation line between 'primitive' and 'modern' political action is misleading, so the same may be said of the equally arbitrary and artificial distinction which is sometimes made between the values and networks of 'pre-industrial' and 'industrial' communities. The Industrial Revolution did not produce a sharp break in the political tactics deployed by the working classes. Despite the gradual proliferation of more modern forms of action, industrial disputes were frequently underpinned by a series of 'traditional' intimidatory tactics borrowed from this earlier 'folk' repertoire. The activities of the infamous Scotch Cattle who, between the 1820s and 1840s, terrorized strike-breakers in the south Wales coalfield, provide a particularly dramatic case in point. Dressed in women's clothes, reversed jackets and animal skins, the Scotch Cattle were themselves directly descended from the *ceffyl pren* tradition.[43] And that characteristic blend of violent direct action and vivid 'street theatre' remained an integral feature of such disputes well into the present century — even though the degree of violence deployed gradually diminished. At Maesteg in 1906, for example, miners who had refused to join the South Wales Miners' Federation were paraded in wheelbarrows, to the sound of a cornet or bugle, before being ceremonially ducked in a nearby river.[44]

Although the notion of separate spheres was more marked in the male-dominated coal and metal-manufacturing districts of south-east Wales, many women nevertheless continued to play a key role in the community sanctions which invariably accompanied industrial disputes. From a very early date, the 'rough music' serenade was a popular method of intimidating blackleg miners and their families. During the 1843 strike, miners' wives and children in the Gelligaer and Aberdare area used this tactic to humiliate blacklegs on their way to and from work. As the *Monmouthshire Merlin* reported:

> ... large numbers of women and children are in the habit of assembling together, furnished with frying pans, kettles, saucepans, and other culinary utensils, which they furiously strike with ladles, sticks, pokers ... (and) practice this ... in the ears of any recusant coal-owner or supporter of the masters whom they meet, to their great discomfort in mind and body.[45]

A few years later, similar scenes were again witnessed on the streets of Aberdare.[46] During the strike of 1850, for example, the funerals of strike-breakers and their families were callously interrupted by jeering crowds:

> ... the dead children and relatives of those who have not joined in the strike, are followed to the grave amidst the heartless laughter, the abominable hootings and exultation of hundreds, not only of men, but of women and children, who follow the melancholy procession beating frying-pans, kettles, and tea-trays ... [47]

Again, at Blaengarw, as late as 1929, women greeted blacklegs with 'the loud beating of tin cans, kettles ... frying pans, and a great deal of booing and jeering ... '[48]

At times, troops of women reportedly subjected 'political' offenders to physical abuse. In 1906, for example, a non-unionist was 'belaboured with brooms, splashed with pigs'-wash, painted with black lead, and deprived of his shirt by the Amazons of Maesteg'.[49] The social boycott also retained its popularity as an effective intimidatory tactic in which all members of the community could participate. It was deployed on a large scale within the south Wales coalfield in 1934 and among the slate quarrying communities of the north during the protracted Penrhyn quarry lock-out of 1900–3.[50] Another component derived from earlier shaming rituals was the appearance of female articles of clothing mounted on poles. This device, previously used to ridicule the 'hen-pecked' husband, was resurrected as a means of humiliating the equally 'cowardly' strike-breaker. During the 1920s, for instance, the women of Markham reportedly pinned a white nightdress to a broom whilst intimidating a local blackleg.[51] A recurring feature of such incidents, as in earlier centuries, was for the intended victim to be taunted for his lack of manhood.[52]

Even more interesting, however, were the notorious, but none the less effective, 'white shirting' processions (often associated with women) witnessed in a number of coalfield communities during the early twentieth century.[53] During these processions blackleg or non-unionist miners were forced to don a white shirt before being frog-marched through the streets, or paraded in a wheelbarrow, in true *ceffyl pren* fashion. At Maesteg, in 1906, a number of local miners were subjected to such an ordeal before being severely ducked. Again, during the 1926 strike, the women of Cwm Rhymni 'prepared white shirts and buckets of whitewash for the reception of the men who had gone to work'.[54] Similarly, at Heol-y-cyw, a working miner was 'covered with a white shirt and conveyed in a wheelbarrow to his home', while one of his attackers played a concertina.[55]

In many respects these 'white shirting' ceremonies were reminiscent of the *ceffyl pren* proper — not least in the probable simulation of ritual female disguise, which again served to highlight the victim's alleged 'unmanliness'.[56] The makeshift use of a white shirt, smock or nightdress to represent female attire was a common device in many European countries and was popular with the Rebecca rioters.[57] It would have proved particularly convenient in cases such as these where the wearer was unwilling to co-operate. Also, at Maesteg in 1906, at least one attempt was made to actually dress a blackleg in women's clothes, rather than a functional white shirt, before parading him through the streets in a wheelbarrow.[58] At times, a white hat decorated with coloured ribbons — presumably intended to represent a woman's bonnet — completed the outfit.[59]

Remnants of the *ceffyl pren* tradition therefore provided women with a continued political outlet at a time when the arena of mainstream political conflict was rapidly becoming male-dominated and class-orientated, thereby marginalizing the contribution of female non-electors and non-unionists. In a sense it may be argued that women who participated in 'rough music' or 'white shirting' processions performed a purely supportive, and somewhat anachronistic, role in relation to the more formalized, and certainly more exclusive, world of workplace politics. But the importance of female participation should not be underestimated. By upholding collective standards of behaviour and ensuring that the men did not break ranks during industrial disputes, women helped to forge and cement the mutual supportive ties and strong sense of political cohesiveness which were evident characteristics of community life in many parts of Wales and upon which the success of those disputes ultimately depended. Women who participated in these rituals were, in a very fundamental sense, helping to structure class consciousness at a grass-roots, neighbourhood level.

These community sanctions were not, of course, the *exclusive* preserve of women. Large numbers of men participated in the Maesteg 'white shirting' activities of 1906, some of whom were later prosecuted for the offence.[60] But as men became increasingly embroiled in the formal electoral system or organized trade unionism and, more importantly, 'respectable' trade union opinion distanced itself from rather more violent or licentious displays of communal solidarity, those who participated in such rituals were, to a certain extent, left stranded on the political sidelines. These rituals gradually came to be viewed rather more specifically as the prerogative of relatively powerless groups, such as women and children, who had no other formal vehicle of political expression. The prolonged popularity of the *ceffyl pren* tradition among women — as witnessed in the 'white shirting' rituals of the early decades of the twentieth century — was, in a sense, symptomatic of the increasing isolation and marginalization of women in formal political terms. It reflected a polarization of popular political expression along more rigid gender lines. Nevertheless, the commitment of women to more traditional elements in repertoire of social protest, such as effigy burnings and 'rough music' serenades, safeguarded the survival of these sanctions into recent times. And, although such rituals have not entirely disappeared, it may, in fact, be argued that these 'folkloric' expressions of communal solidarity only began to diminish, both in frequency and intensity, when women were finally enfranchised and therefore began to be assimilated into the formal, national electoral process.

*Bibliographical note*

Although a wealth of research has been undertaken on the French *charivari*, British social historians have been slow to follow suit. For those who read French, the work of E. P. Thompson is the essential starting point for further enquiry into this much-neglected topic. His pioneering article ' "Rough music": le charivari anglais', published as far back as 1972 (see *Annales ESC*, 27), is still the most detailed and valuable study of English 'rough music' rituals during the nineteenth century. Unfortunately, very little primary research (relating specifically to the nineteenth and early twentieth centuries) has since been produced and a comprehensive, comparative study of 'rough music' rituals in the British Isles is urgently required. On the other hand, the history of English shaming rituals during the early modern period has been reasonably well charted. Works by Martin Ingram are particularly useful; see, for example, his article entitled 'Ridings, rough music and the "reform of popular culture" in early modern England', published in *Past and Present*, 105 (1984) and his chapter in Barry Reay (ed.), *Popular Culture in Seventeenth Century England* (London, Croom Helm, 1985, 166–97). Readers with a specific interest in gender relations during the early modern period should also consult David Underdown, 'The taming of the scold: the enforcement of patriarchal authority in early modern England', in Anthony Fletcher and John Stevenson (eds.), *Order and Disorder in Early Modern England* (Cambridge, Cambridge University Press, 1985), 116–36.

Within a specifically Welsh context, see works cited below by David Williams and David Jones which deal with the Rebecca riots; these volumes both contain references to links between the *ceffyl pren* and Rebeccaism. See also my article, recently published in *Ceredigion* (also cited below), which deals primarily with the suppression of the custom during the post-Rebecca period.

*Notes to Chapter 1*

1. For studies of the French *charivari* see Eugen Weber, *Peasants into Frenchmen: The Modernization of Rural France, 1870–1914* (London, Chatto and Windus, 1977), Ch.22 and Natalie Zemon Davis, *Society and Culture in Early Modern France* (Oxford, Basil Blackwell, 1987 edn.), Ch.4.

2. For a discussion of English 'rough music' rituals see E. P. Thompson, '"Rough music": le charivari anglais', *Annales ESC*, 27 (1972), 285–312 and Martin Ingram, 'Ridings, rough music and the "reform of popular culture" in early modern England', *Past and Present*, 105 (1984), 79–113. Brief reference is made to Scottish shaming rituals in E. J. Guthrie, *Old Scottish Customs, Local and General* (London, Hamilton, 1885), 146–7.

3. The central motif of the *ceffyl pren* procession was, strictly speaking, some form of real or symbolic 'riding'. However, there was often no discernible difference (either in purpose or in broad content) between the *ceffyl pren* proper and other, more generalized, effigy-burning or 'rough music' incidents. For this reason, a wide range of related shaming rituals have been included within the remit of this chapter.

4. *Carmarthen Journal*, 4 April 1851.

5. Ibid.

6. See, for example, Charles Redwood, *The Vale of Glamorgan: Scenes and Tales among the Welsh* (London, Saunders and Otley, 1839), 271–95 and T. C. Evans ('Cadrawd'), *History of Llangynwyd Parish* (Llanelli, printed at the offices of the *Llanelli and County Guardian*, 1887), 162–3. The term *cwlstrin* was probably a dialect derivative of the English 'cowlstringing' or 'cowlstaffing' (i.e. to parade on a cowl/coul-staff or pole). Indeed, it is worth noting that the term 'coulstringing' was used, in 1856, to describe the parading of a man on a ladder at Aberdare (*Cardiff and Merthyr Guardian*, 3 May 1856).

7. *Cardiff and Merthyr Guardian*, 14 June 1845.

8. Ibid., 3 May 1856.

9. *Cambrian News*, 16 March 1877.

10. Clwyd Record Office, Flintshire Constabulary Papers, FP/2/7, Chief Constable's Order Book, 1857–75, 31.

11. References to the *Clwb Te* are difficult to locate. The only known references are as follows: Isaac Foulkes, *'Cymru Fu', yn Cynwys Hanesion, Traddodiadau, yn nghyda Chwedlau a Damhegion Cymreig (oddiar lafar gwlad a gweithiau y prif awduron . . . )* (Liverpool, Isaac Foulkes, 1864), 90–1; Edward Matthews, *Hanes Bywyd Siencyn Penhydd* (Wrexham, Hughes a'i Fab, 1867 edn.), 43–4.

12. Myra Evans, *Atgofion Ceinewydd* (Aberystwyth, Cymdeithas Lyfrau Ceredigion, 1961), 23.

13. *Bye-Gones*, 23 March 1887, 273.

14. Mr and Mrs Samuel Carter Hall, *Tenby: Its History, Antiquities, Scenery, Traditions, and Customs* (Tenby, Mason, c.1860), 139–40. The available evidence is inconclusive but it may well be that, on occasions, women were able to respond more violently because they expected to be treated with greater leniency by the authorities. A larger sample of incidents needs to be examined, but my initial impressions are that

women were less likely than men to suffer arrest for participating in such disturbances.

15. *Welshman*, 3 January 1845.
16. *Carmarthen Journal*, 3 October 1856.
17. Ibid., 4 October 1861.
18. Ibid., 18 October 1861.
19. Ibid., 17 October 1862.
20. *Welshman*, 26 April 1850.
21. *Carmarthen Journal*, 1 December 1843.
22. *Chester Chronicle*, 17 March 1855.
23. John Brand, *Observations on the Popular Antiquities of Great Britain: Chiefly Illustrating the Origin of our Vulgar and Provincial Customs, Ceremonies, and Superstitions* (London, Charles Knight, 1854 edn.), vol.2, 191.
24. Susan D. Amussen, *An Ordered Society: Gender and Class in Early Modern Society* (Oxford, Basil Blackwell, 1988), 118–19.
25. Redwood, op. cit., 271–95.
26. Ibid., 293–4.
27. E. P. Thompson, op. cit., 301–4.
28. *Chester Chronicle*, 29 September 1855.
29. See A. James Hammerton, 'The targets of "rough music": respectability and domestic violence in Victorian England', *Gender and History*, 2 No.3 (1991). I am grateful to Dr Hammerton for sending me a copy of this work before publication.
30. *Carmarthen Journal*, 3 October 1856.
31. National Library of Wales, David Thomas MSS, B61; notes compiled by E. G. Williams, Lampeter (*c.*1920) based on information supplied by Mrs J. C. Jones of Tregaron.
32. *Carmarthen Journal*, 7 March 1856.
33. Ibid., 6 April 1838.
34. *By-Gones*, June 1875, 248.
35. Myra Evans, op. cit., 22–3; NLW, David Thomas MS B61.
36. Hall, op. cit., 139.
37. *Cambrian*, 10 August 1839.
38. See my article 'Popular culture, policing and the "disappearance" of the *ceffyl pren* in Cardigan, *c.*1837–1850', *Ceredigion*, 11 No.1 (1988–9), 19–39 for a discussion of this theme.
39. The links between Rebecca and the *ceffyl pren* have been pointed out in David Williams, *The Rebecca Riots: A Study in Agrarian Discontent* (Cardiff, University of Wales Press, 1986 edn.), 53–6 and, more recently, in David J. V. Jones, *Rebecca's Children: A Study of Rural Society, Crime and Protest* (Oxford, Clarendon Press, 1989), 194–8.
40. *Pembrokeshire Herald*, 18 September 1857. See also *Cambrian*, 4 September 1857.

41. *Cambrian News*, 24 June 1887.
42. Ibid., 16 December 1887; *Carmarthen Journal*, 29 May 1891; *Cardigan and Tivyside Advertiser*, 1 May 1891 (supplement).
43. For a study of the Scotch Cattle see David Jones, *Before Rebecca: Popular Protests in Wales, 1793–1835* (London, Allen Lane, 1973), Ch.4.
44. For details of these Maesteg disturbances see the *W(estern) M(ail)* and *S(outh) W(ales) D(aily) N(ews)* for September 1906.
45. *Monmouthshire Merlin*, 25 March and 1 April 1843.
46. *Cambrian*, 25 January 1850.
47. *Cardiff and Merthyr Guardian*, 23 March 1850.
48. *WM*, 24 October 1929.
49. Ibid., 5 September 1906.
50. For references to the social boycott within an industrial context see David Smith, 'The struggle against company unionism in the south Wales coalfield, 1926–1939', *Welsh History Review*, 6 No.3 (1973), 369–70; *WM*, 20, 23 and 26 October 1934 and R. Merfyn Jones, *The North Wales Quarrymen, 1874–1922* (Cardiff, University of Wales Press, 1982), 232–44.
51. Angela V. John, 'A miner struggle? Women's protests in Welsh mining history', *Llafur*, 4 No.1 (1984), 78.
52. David Smith, op. cit., 367–8.
53. For references to 'white shirting', see Hywel Francis and David Smith, *The Fed: A History of the South Wales Miners in the Twentieth Century* (London, Lawrence and Wishart, 1980), 59.
54. *WM* and *SWDN*, 25 August 1926. The women of New Tredegar were reported to be similarly armed.
55. *SWDN* and *Daily Herald*, 13 August 1926. A similar attack was reported to have taken place at Pencoed.
56. In my opinion this is the most likely derivation of the white shirt, although the custom may have been influenced by a punishment once imposed by the ecclesiastical courts. This entailed forcing offenders to stand before the church congregation during divine service, dressed in a white sheet, as a form of public penance.
57. See, for example, Natalie Zemon Davis, op. cit., 148–9; *Quarterly Review*, 74 (June and October 1844), 129; NLW MS 12368E, 205, 217 and 219; and Evan D. Jones, 'A file of "Rebecca" papers', *Carmarthen Antiquary*, 1 (1943–4), 24 and 50.
58. *WM*, 10 September 1906. It is also worth citing a similar incident at Bargoed, during which two non-unionists were 'covered with print aprons' (ibid.).
59. Ibid., 1 October and *SWDN*, 10 September 1906.
60. *WM*, 1 October 1906.

# 2

# *Beyond Paternalism: The Ironmaster's Wife in the Industrial Community*

When, in 1852, Sir Josiah John Guest, owner of the largest ironworks in the world, died at Dowlais House, Merthyr Tydfil, in the south Wales valleys, the works and the community virtually came to a standstill. At Dowlais Church, built for the ironmaster, its sole incumbent depicted his patron as 'not only the high and noble-minded Master but also the kind friend and tender-hearted father of his people'.[1] Newspaper obituaries combined this paternalistic image evocative of the feudal lord with the forward-looking entrepreneurial spirit which had transformed the family concern into a major industrial business. *The Times* compared the Guests to the Arkwrights and Peels, attributing to Sir John's foresight much of the wealth and prosperity of mid nineteenth-century Britain.[2] Many of his workers might have pointed instead to their own personal industry and asked where in Dowlais was the evidence of this prosperity. Nevertheless, contemporaries commented on the 'universality of woe' in the district at the death of the ironmaster.[3]

*The Times* also made another comparison, praising Lady Charlotte, the employer's wife and noting

> . . . the moral and social improvement that has taken place in the population connected with the Dowlais works. Identifying herself with the people, she acquired their language, translated and published their national traditions and directed her well-observed influence to the establishment of schools and other instruments for the education of the working classes.[4]

A *Memoir* to Sir John for the Institute of Civil Engineers also focused on Lady Charlotte, an 'estimable lady whose literary powers are as well appreciated as her general talents and acquirements in branches of knowledge not usually presenting attractive features for ladies'.[5] It noted how she also 'administered to the wants of all around her; thus performing her Christian duty she extended the previously acquired influence and power of her husband.' This aspect of her achievements effectively reinserted her into a more familiar and traditional female role. The *Memoir* (which devoted one-third of its space to Lady Charlotte) described Sir John as being 'ably seconded' by his wife.

This chapter will examine what was meant by being 'ably seconded', that neat phrase denoting both acceptance and dismissal. What influence did — and could — the wives of ironmasters exert in Victorian south Wales at a time when the cult of domesticity combined so effectively with the power of Nonconformity? Patrick Joyce's pioneering work on the Lancashire cotton industry showed how industrial paternalism helped produce a 'rational' and largely deferential work-force by the mid nineteenth century.[6] Yet he did not examine the part played by industrialists' wives in this process of ensuring social stability in the wake of social and political upheaval by adapting older paternalistic values to the new society. Neither did David Roberts in his exploration of the persistence and pervasiveness of paternalism in early Victorian England, though he did concede that the idea 'inspired the lady bountiful to organise clothing clubs . . .'[7] Studying the early Victorian industrial community of Merthyr Tydfil, which was the heartland of the Welsh iron trade and the largest town in Wales, helps reveal how employers' wives might cement social relations. Their methods may well have been more subtle than those generally (and disparagingly) associated with the 'lady bountiful' image. Moreover, their aims and ways of fulfilling them are likely to have diverged from those of their husbands and to have been perceived and received differently. To put it another way: how important was gender in the exercising of industrial paternalism? The women who spoke (literally) in the name of their husbands and helped define the nature of industrial and class relations were at the same time denied full participation and power in the communities they helped to shape even though they might in their own ways be extremely influential.

I shall concentrate on two women associated with the Merthyr iron oligarchies, Lady Charlotte Guest (née Bertie) and Rose Mary Crawshay (née Yeates). These women married into the greatest of the iron dynasties of nineteenth-century Merthyr. Both women were

The Ladies patronize Lady Charlotte's female friendly society. This branch of the Oddfellows met at the Vulcan Inn, Dowlais. Based on a silk presentation copy presented to Lady Charlotte by the society.

joining ironmaking families which had, over several generations, consolidated their influence and wealth. Yet both women were also 'achievers' in their own right. What was the nature of their involvement in securing Merthyr's industrial supremacy and stability? By what means did these two women, both outsiders from privileged English families, insinuate themselves into their adopted communities and at what price to themselves and the local people?

Lady Charlotte (1812–95), eldest child of the ninth Earl and Countess of Lindsey, came to Dowlais in 1833 as a 21-year-old bride.[8] Her husband, John Guest, was considerably older, had been widowed and was childless. His grandfather had started one small furnace in 1759. In less than a hundred years the Dowlais works had been transformed into a gigantic industrial venture, its trade vastly stimulated by the international demand for bar iron for the laying of railways.[9] John Guest can be seen as a paternalist of the better sort. Roberts's claim[10] that typical paternalists believed in capital punishment and whipping finds little echo in this industrialist who, in his early years as Merthyr's MP, was a 'Whig in party and radical in opinion', supported the secret ballot and identified himself so closely with his home that his wife nicknamed him Merthyr. He is more recognizable as one of the paternalists who advocated religious dissent but he remained closer in outlook to the model factory owners such as Titus Salt (though Guest's record in provision of amenities such as decent housing lagged far behind). He can also be compared to one of the few 'improving' colliery owners, his friend Sir Francis Egerton at the Worsley collieries in Lancashire, or to the Birmingham manufacturers, Nettlefold and Chamberlain (with whom the Dowlais fortunes would ultimately be linked).

In contrast, Lady Charlotte is probably best remembered for her pioneering and classic three-volume English translation of the medieval Welsh tales she called *The Mabinogion*. A devoted linguist from an early age, she had taught herself Arabic and Persian as a lonely adolescent in Lincolnshire, and her learning of Welsh when she came to Dowlais helped to endear her to local radicals such as Taliesin Williams, son of Iolo Morganwg. Two years later, during the election dinner celebrating John Guest's return as Merthyr's MP, Taliesin toasted Lady Charlotte. Other English people who had settled locally had viewed 'our national habits and our indefeasible attachment to our ancient language with jealous unkindness'. Not so Lady Charlotte: 'she has adopted our costumes — and our language, from the first day that she honoured Merthyr with her residence, has been the object of her successful study; and beyond all she has visited the widow and the fatherless, and fed the poor and the needy.' The subject of the toast was, of course, absent from the dinner of electors but a letter from her was read out and half of it was in Welsh.

Yet although Lady Charlotte recognized the political expediency of the Welsh language, it seems significant that it was medieval Welsh which secured her attention. Her search for an identity and sphere of influence via the past, distinct from her husband's control over the present, was consistent with her passionate interest in Romance literature and in history and it encouraged her to romanticize Welshness. Steeping herself in a tradition abounding in myths and intrepid heroes led her to view contemporaries somewhat differently from her husband. She described the leader of the Rebecca riots (recently sentenced to twenty-one years' transportation — Sir John had sat on the Grand Jury) as 'my poor Welsh rebel with all his faults and all his grievances and all his romance'. In the immediate aftermath of the Chartist Newport Rising of 1839 she, unlike many, maintained utter faith in the work-force: 'If anything had happened I should have walked into the forges which were in full work . . . our own men are good and true.' Her upbringing had accustomed her to deferential loyalty whilst her reading supplied her with chivalric deeds defending her sex. Moreover, her personal knowledge of some Chartists, such as the flamboyant Dr William Price whose learning she respected, encouraged her to believe that something must be done *for* for the people rather than abdicating responsibility and thus making likely the possibility of the people taking action for themselves.

Lady Charlotte had involved herself in the works from the start. Deliberately defying the usual definition of separate spheres with its demarcation of 'he for the public, she for the private', she wrote of the ironworks, 'I always feel here in my proper sphere.' She studied accounts, wrote business letters, made business deals, wrote about the iron trade and, from the mid 1840s, increasingly deputized for her husband as serious illness periodically incapacitated him. Her class and her sex put her in a very different position from him in relation to the work-force. Not only was she at this stage technically not the 'boss' but her aristocratic birth marked her out from both employees and employer. She was thus in a less ambivalent relationship *vis-à-vis* the workers than her husband who was from a self-made family and felt the need to distance himself from the work-force. Not only was it customary for coal and ironworkers to make pleas for wages, clemency and so on to employers' wives, but Lady Charlotte also enjoyed the role of 'personnel officer'. It enabled her to intervene effectively and use her own judgement. On a number of occasions it was to her that senior employees appealed in the first instance. She dealt with threats of resignation, not only acting as an intermediary but on occasions sorting out grievances without informing Sir John. The sales agent Thomas Evans went straight to her with his letter of resignation. She persuaded him to remain, finding him prepared to 'quite rely upon me and do as I advised'. By contrast, her husband had known Evans since childhood and had been 'brought up in his ways and interests'.

Lady Charlotte's faith in the work-force was bolstered by her belief, shared with her husband, in education as a powerful force for harmony. The progressive Dowlais schools have been praised for their innovatory approach — using trained teachers, separate classrooms based on the Prussian system and buildings designed by Sir Charles Barry.[11] They provided a system of education for both sexes starting in infancy and lasting into adulthood. Although John Guest instigated this process in the 1820s it was Lady Charlotte who really developed the system.

In the spring of 1848 she discussed the volatile political situation in Britain and Europe with her archaeologist cousin Henry Layard, then in his most radical phase. The day after the Chartist Kennington Common demonstration in London (attended by Henry), Lady Charlotte wrote in her journal: 'Something must be done for our unemployed, the events of yesterday must not lull us into security and make us overlook this duty, this necessity.'

Despite Sir John's efforts as an MP, she understood that 'one cannot make people good and religious by Act of Parliament. The first step is to make them comfortable and happy.' She saw her task as complementing her husband's parliamentary work. Early 1848 was an especially worrying time; the future of the works hung in the balance as the Earl of Bute, who owned the land on which the Dowlais works were built, procrastinated over renewing the lease. Some furnaces had already been blown out and many workers laid off. Just three weeks after the presentation of the third Chartist petition, a settlement was finally made and the future of the works secured. The Guests' return to Dowlais resembled that of triumphant warriors coming home from battle greeted by a mile-long procession.[12] Lady Charlotte wrote in her journal:

> May we indeed be enabled to do them good, and under a reviving trade have it in our power to minister to their necessities etc not only bodily but mental. May we by our care and unceasing attention to their improvements in every respect, in some measure, justify the warmth their reception has evinced towards us. It is a heavy responsibility.

Lady Charlotte's interest in educational schemes really developed from this point. Although already involved with infant schools and Sunday schools, she now concentrated especially on adult education. In October 1848 she opened 'my new school for the girls belonging to the works'. These young women were divided into seven classes. They met in the winter months with an average attendance of 150. Lady Charlotte spent many evenings in the schools (rather more than Sir John wished), occasionally teaching, distributing prizes, introducing guest lecturers and generally supervising. It gave her an opportunity to further a cause her husband believed in but, by demarcating her own area of interest in the young women's education, she could develop her particular interest and influence. Not content with success at Dowlais she sought to inspire others in Merthyr. It was she who was largely responsible for the enlargement of the school in Georgetown, the establishment of an infant school in 1852 and the growth of adult schools. Her tactic was to use the small network of local middle-class women. She approached ministers' wives and wrote with satisfaction of a meeting with the wife of Merthyr's Anglican clergyman: 'I think I inspired her with the desire of attempting something.' Through these women she won the support of their husbands. Dining with philistine ironmasters was not her favourite occupation but it could have its uses. Lady Charlotte's journal records dining at Cyfarthfa Castle where,

> I had some talk with Mrs Crawshay and have great hopes of her as a co-operator in this work of reform in the social and educational systems of the district. She is young yet and has bad health but she seems to catch anxiously at the sound of anything that is likely to do good.

She persuaded Lady Morgan of Tredegar Park to subscribe to the adult schools and, when ironmasters such as Richard Fothergill came

to Dowlais House, she could not resist 'turning his visit to account. So
I took him up to see our schools before tea. He was pleased with them
and put himself down as a subscriber to the similar ones at Merthyr.'
Sir John, however, was less impressed: 'he thought I was putting
myself too forward about the evening schools in Merthyr.' Yet the
very next day another ironmaster, Alderman Thompson, came to
discuss railway business and 'I felt it my duty for the sake of the cause
to make the effort, and I did so, and to my great delight I did succeed.'
'Duty' could sometimes be turned to positive use. Now only Anthony
Hill remained of the local ironmasters and Lady Charlotte tackled
him. 'How frightened I was I cannot tell', she wrote in her journal.
'But I summoned all my courage and made my petition for the
Merthyr adult schools.' Not only did Hill agree to subscribe but he
soon established day and evening schools at his nearby Plymouth
works. Her advice and support were also given when middle-class
girls' schooling was developed at the Howell Schools at Llandaff and
Denbigh.

Recognizing that education was broader than schooling, Lady
Charlotte promoted temperance, helped develop a savings bank
scheme and supported friendly societies. The poster in the illustration
shows her with Rose Crawshay patronizing an Oddfellows' tea-party
in 1849. They named a local branch after Lady Charlotte. She
accompanied Dowlais ironworkers and tenants from Canford (the
Guests' Dorset estate) on a trip to the Great Exhibition in 1851.
Although this particular trip was strictly for workMEN, she nevertheless firmly believed that women could help promote social
harmony by developing educational and welfare schemes.

She sought to turn free time to good purpose — and, unlike some,
did at least set an example through her own study which was
combined with having ten children in thirteen years. Like a later
ironmaster's wife, Florence Bell in Middlesbrough, Lady Charlotte
believed that 'rational recreation' would benefit employees and the
employer.[13] A field at Dowlais was converted into a recreation area
with a bowling green, quoits, cricket pitch and gymnastic poles. The
Dowlais band practised there, seeking to emulate Crawshay's
acclaimed band, and refreshments were made available. 'I can only
pray that this one other effort to give the people quiet, rational
amusement may be blest', wrote Lady Charlotte.

It was she who executed the plans of Henry Bruce and John Guest
for evening gatherings for 'the people' in the pattern room in the

ironworks. Music was played, flowers, books, drawings and fossils were exhibited and the school children and a local choir sang. Between three and six hundred workers apparently attended these gatherings. Chartists and other radicals also held 'evenings with the people' but their events were designed to combine politics and poetry.[14] The Guest parties (hosted by Lady Charlotte) and complete with refreshments, replaced politics with culture in the increasingly conciliatory atmosphere of the early 1850s. Lady Charlotte's handwritten invitations were specifically reserved for 'sober and steady people' who had proved themselves over time. There may nevertheless have been those amongst the artisan élite, such as the puddlers, who were not willing to accept the ethos of the Guests but still welcomed the opportunity of hearing people like Henry Layard, one of Britain's mid-century heroes, talk about his discoveries at Nineveh or listen to the brilliant works of the scholar Thomas Stephens. They could recognize Lady Charlotte's efforts to 'humanize' the work-force but they did not necessarily subscribe to her views.

Although the Guests managed to fill the pattern room on a number of occasions, there must have been many others who felt that there were more basic amenities crying out for attention. Housing conditions were deplorable and in 1848 Merthyr's mortality rate was the highest in Wales and the third highest in the kingdom.[15] Under the terms of the new Public Health Act Merthyr qualified for the local authorities (on the security of the rates) to raise the necessary amount to provide an adequate water supply. The Merthyr Board of Guardians signed a petition requesting the adoption of the law and a public inquiry followed. Yet although there was no shortage of water — the River Taff ran through the town and the relentless Welsh rain gathered at the foothills of the Brecon Beacons — the lack of a sizeable residential middle class to act as a pressure group, the absence of an elected town council (Merthyr was not yet incorporated) and, above all, the oligarchy of powerful ironmasters meant that the local inhabitants were the last to benefit from natural resources. Water from the Taff was diverted to drive Crawshay's mills and supply his steam engines. Lady Charlotte knew that Crawshay, large ratepayers and local landlords wanted to maintain the status quo but she also recognized that 'there is no place where cleansing and proper regulations are more needed or have been more neglected'. Her response to a draft copy of the public inquiry is interesting as it signals both her interest in the question of a water supply and her deliberate dissociation of the Guests (or, at least, herself) from the views of the other industrialists. She wrote: 'The Ironmasters are averse to every improvement on the score of expense. However I will do my best to promote an amelioration of matters, though I fear my influence will not go far.'

The following month saw a severe outbreak of cholera in the district. It reached Dowlais in June 1849 and resulted in 500 deaths there. Yet not until 1850 did a Board of Health come into existence, with Sir John as its first chairman. Plans were mooted for a joint-stock company to solve the problem of supplying water to the community but Crawshay and Hill kept changing their minds and it came to nothing. A Merthyr Waterworks bill was passed in June 1852 but the voices of Crawshay, Hill and the Glamorgan Canal Company were soon heard objecting and an umpire (the distinguished I. K. Brunel) was appointed. By this time Lady Charlotte was personally in control at Dowlais having taken over the running of the works after her husband's death in November 1852. Fearing further pro-crastination she contemplated unilateral action which would at least secure a separate water supply for Dowlais. She sought legal advice but was in an awkward position because a Water Company did now exist in theory and anyway her interests were identified with the Merthyr Board through her late husband. Moreover the Board's consent was needed for any independent action. Anticipating their dilatoriness she tried appealing to members' consciences in a letter:

> The threatened approach of cholera, heretofore so fatal in this district, renders the Dowlais Company most anxious to do everything in their power that may tend to avert a recurrence of so fearful a visitation and believing that no precautionary measures that could be adopted would be so efficacious as a plentiful supply of water . . . [16]

Dowlais therefore proposed to supply its inhabitants with piped water at an estimated outlay of £3,000 to be refunded by the Board.

Her scheme impressed the *Cardiff and Merthyr Guardian*[17] In an effusive editorial it stressed Lady Charlotte's ability to think clearly:

> her Ladyship steps in, cuts the knot, solves the difficulty, and in the name of the 'Dowlais Company' offers the supply — and on such conditions only as it would be a reproach to those entrusted with power to refuse. For this noble act Lady Charlotte Guest deserves a

statue . . . she now adds a cubit to the moral stature by an act which must perpetuate her memory so long as water is essential to a healthy existence.

No statue was forthcoming and the praise was premature. The Board's continued intransigence forced Lady Charlotte to concede defeat.[18] The ironmasters were suspicious, fearing that Dowlais would benefit at their expense. Her request was refused and not until the end of 1860 was water available from stand-pipes for Merthyr's inhabitants. Reservoir construction was finally completed in 1863. The election to the Board of Health of the engineer G. T. Clark, who took over at Dowlais after Lady Charlotte remarried, made a vital difference to the interest and expertise in sanitary matters. Yet all this came too late since, as Lady Charlotte had warned, cholera returned and in 1854 the streets were once more 'black with funerals'.[19]

Admittedly Lady Charlotte's proposals on behalf of Dowlais had come rather late in the day but at least she had attempted to resolve the situation. Like Ibsen's symbolic character Dr Stockmann, she was isolated in her concern about the water supply. For once she had failed and, interestingly, this episode is rather less well known than her more successful ventures. Improvement had been sacrificed to the powerful interests of a small group of men who could have ameliorated an insanitary environment which shocked both visitors and government officials.[20] Lady Charlotte had, all along, been less hopeful than the local press since, as she put it, 'I am always prepared for these breaches of faith from Ironmasters.' Her desire to cleanse Dowlais both mentally and physically also shows the limits of her actual power. She was not a member of the all-male Board; her requests had to take the form of pleading letters considered in her absence. Moreover, her dealings here and in other instances with her fellow industrialists demonstrate the difficulties she faced as a lone woman at a time when women's direct participation in running industrial affairs was extremely uncommon and she was faced with negotiating with men who were experienced in working in concert (and oppositon).

When, in June 1853, the owners of the Merthyr ironworks got together to decide how best to regulate wage rises, Lady Charlotte, newly widowed, had for the first time to confront directly a group of men who were more used to seeing her as a companion at dinner than as a colleague. She in turn was shocked at their readiness to force the workers into a corner. Her journal entries describe her as 'horrified' at the 'monstrous threats' being held over 'our steady good men'. Although resisting intimidation and methods of hurrying matters 'unduly to an assumed conclusion', she felt uneasy in this arena; the politics of negotiation were new to her, 'a woman and in argument ALONE against the opinion of FIVE experienced men of business ... ' She reluctantly conceded to their demands, afraid that they might interpret her objections as 'a woman's weakness'. Yet she soon blamed herself for not speaking out more resolutely and during the strike which ensued she sought to prove to herself and to the ironmasters that she could not be dismissed as a weak, indecisive woman. Unfortunately, she abandoned in the process her previously conciliatory attitude towards the work-force whose respect she had gained over the years. Her new determination was summed up in her telling comment, 'I will be their Master'.[21]

Yet towards the end of the strike when Merthyr tradesmen met to gain support for a memorial to the ironmasters, they still exculpated Lady Charlotte from blame. One of the major speakers, William Gould a grocer, criticized the employers for not paying wages according to the market price of iron yet carefully singled out Lady Charlotte for praise: her 'claims to their good wishes could scarcely be overstated'. Gould (who had been a prominent Chartist in the 1840s) stressed that he wanted it known 'that the meeting sympathized with her, as did workmen in general'. In part this reflects traditional Victorian attitudes of flattery towards the female sex, not necessarily to be confused with genuine admiration. Furthermore, Lady Charlotte was clearly a 'lady' whilst few saw employers such as Crawshay as 'gentlemen'. Yet the statement may also suggest something beyond a genuflection towards her class and sex. It may refer to a more tangible history and the specific nature of Lady Charlotte's involvement with the community over the years, an involvement which actually concerned questions of gender and class in a more complex dialectic. Ironically, this involvement now effectively came to an end as Lady Charlotte remarried in 1855 and began a second 'career' which took her abroad for much of the year so that only very occasionally did she revisit her erstwhile home at Dowlais.

In contrast Rose Mary Crawshay (1828–1907) never evoked such enthusiasm from the population of Merthyr. In a revealing statement she once observed of the Cyfarthfa work-force: 'on many lines my thoughts and ways were not theirs, still they did not hate me, and I loved them.'[22] She did converse with a few shopkeepers, notably Thomas Norbury (who had built an observatory over his oilshop), dubbing him 'our local philosopher', but her intellectual stimulation mainly lay outside Wales. Her grandson observed that she and her husband had few familiar friends locally though literary and scientific figures visited her at Cyfarthfa Castle. They included Robert Browning, Ralph Waldo Emerson and Henry Irving.

Rose's family had been neighbours of the Crawshays in Berkshire. When she married Robert Thompson Crawshay in 1846, the eighteen-year-old bride was, like Lady Charlotte, marrying an older man (Robert was twenty-nine, John Guest forty-eight) and leaving a rural, wealthy society for the unknown, largely working-class, population of the Welsh valleys. Her new home, Cyfarthfa Castle, had been built in 1825 to demonstrate that the Crawshay family were lords of all they surveyed. Costing £30,000, it boasted seventy-two rooms and fifteen towers and was an incongruous piece of manu- factured medievalism in the midst of industrial development. Rose decided to include a sketch of her home in a pamphlet she wrote lest her English readers mistook her description for that of a castle in Spain![23]

Lady Charlotte's way of coping with an alien culture had been to try to penetrate it via its language and ancient customs. Rose did not actively seek to identify with Welshness, though she did preside at one meeting in 1872 where a lecture was given in Welsh on 'The Indebtedness of Women to the Bible'.[24] One of Rose's daughters wrote in her diary in 1868: 'the country is not the place to hear new things in the literary or scientific way, Mama Thinks, and we get very like our vegetables.'[25] Rose certainly promoted literature but it was emphatically *English* literature, endowing a poetic memorial fund for encouraging the study of poets and awarding annual prizes for the best essays on Byron, Shelley and Keats. In the 1890s she presented prizes for the best oil-paintings by women of subjects connected with these Romantic poets.

The two women differed in their concerns about women's rights. During Lady Charlotte's years at Dowlais there was no organized women's movement. Rather it was the men's struggle for democratic rights which was then to the fore. Nevertheless, although not openly allying herself with women's rights later in her life, Lady Charlotte's journal reveals her awareness of the contradictions inherent in her position. She recognized that she exercised both power and influence through her class and her marriage to one of the leading figures in

Welsh industry and politics yet she also understood how she was simultaneously circumscribed by her sex. Particularly aware of her incapacitation through illness during her numerous pregnancies, she wrote about how expectations for the two sexes differed:

> I see every day men, even though not encouraged, and though perhaps uneducated. I see men planning and carrying through enterprises — their minds have scope and they have field for action. But we are but another name for helplessness — unkindness must utterly crush us — and if we venture beyond the prescribed limits and should dare to act then comes scorn, and reproach and cruelty . . .

This was prompted by her reading Mrs Ellis's *Wives of England* (a gift from her husband!) which advised a woman to accept her position as 'a secondary being in the great business of conducting the general affairs of social life'. After reading Hannah More, Lady Charlotte commented: 'How deeply I have felt this inferiority of sex and how humiliated I am when it is recalled to my mind in allusion to myself!' Yet, though acutely aware, she tended only to consider her personal dilemma. She was also not prepared to be ambitious for her daughters though one of her grandchildren, Mildred Mansel, became an organizer of Bath suffragettes and was imprisoned in Holloway for breaking windows at the War Office.

Unlike Lady Charlotte, Rose Crawshay was demonstrably concerned with other women's rights. She was part of the early feminist movement which witnessed twenty-six signatures by women with Welsh addresses for the first women's Suffrage Petition of 1866 (including 3 from Merthyr, 8 from Denbigh and 10 from the Swansea area). She participated in the organized women's movement of the late 1850s and was less torn between duty and ambition than Lady Charlotte. The latter's husband was, by the standards of the time, supportive and appreciative of his wife's skills, though as his fatal kidney disease grew worse so his tolerance lessened. In contrast, Rose Crawshay was married to an autocratic, showy man whose (in)famous three-word epitaph chosen by himself for his gravestone was 'God Forgive Me'. He had a vicious temper, exacerbated after a paralytic stroke in 1860. This left him completely deaf and his family could only communicate with him by writing on a slate. He not only lived in a castle but practised *droit de seigneur* — it was widely believed that he employed a procurer to supply him with daughters of workmen.[26] The Crawshays had five children and Robert displayed an obsession with photographing his favourite daughter Rose Harriette, getting her to dress up as a fish seller, as a Swiss girl 'with my hair down in wild disorder, Gorgon fashion', but she dared not disobey his summons with a dog whistle. He was jealous of any suitors and, when she finally married, cut her out of his will. Her diary entry for Christmas Day 1871 seems to encapsulate the domestic atmosphere at Cyfarthfa: 'Papa and Mama were cross, the beef underdone and a squabbling kept up the whole time.'[27]

Not surprisingly, Rose favoured marriage reform. She was one of the early suffragists, a member of the London National Society for Women's Suffrage in the 1860s and by 1873 Vice-President of the Bristol and West of England National Society for Women's Suffrage.[28] She spoke at meetings in Merthyr on the benefits of the vote for women's characters and contributed to a pamphlet called 'Opinions of Women on Women's Suffrage'. Maria Rye and the Garrett sisters were her friends and Elizabeth and Millicent, better known as the doctor Elizabeth Garrett Anderson and suffragist Mrs Fawcett, spoke on women's rights for Rose Crawshay at a meeting in Merthyr. The *Woman's Herald* called Rose 'one of the most enlightened pioneers of women's emancipation' and, according to *The Queen*, her name was 'indissolubly linked with nearly every movement for the benefit of women'.[29] As early as July 1859, the month that her London friends formed a committee out of which developed the Society for Promoting the Employment of Women, she contributed £200 to the cause. Nine years later she was one of about 200 present at a conference of supporters of Emily Davies's women's college. Here the plans for what became Girton College were explained and discussed.[30]

Perhaps her best-known scheme for women and one which fused metropolitan and local involvement was her controversial promotion of what she called 'Lady Helps'. Conscious of the economic dilemmas facing large numbers of 'distressed gentlewomen' and also aware of the growing scarcity of 'good' servants by the 1870s, she advocated a scheme which would use these women in wealthy homes. She consulted with the Women's Employment Society and her paper on 'Domestic Service for Gentlewomen' was read to the Social Science Congress of 1874 and to a British Association meeting in Bristol the following year. She was a keen publicist, producing (at her own expense) a popular pamphlet explaining the scheme. She opened a 'Lady Help' registry office in the West End of London, employers being registered for five shillings. Prospective 'lady helps' could take cookery lessons as well as find jobs. Rose ran this successful scheme for eight years before turning it over to her superintendent. Although the *Pictorial World*[31] called her scheme 'one of the most interesting of modern contributions to Social Science and Political Economy', not surprisingly, plenty of cynics asked whether this really improved women's lot.[32] Her response was to demonstrate personally how it could operate successfully. Five 'lady helps' were imported into Cyfarthfa Castle and given rooms previously occupied by ordinary domestics — though only after 'thorough cleansing, whitewashing and painting'! They were expected to work hard and their job included making new house linen, clothes and even carpets. Their separation from ordinary servants such as the local scullery maid must have placed them in an extremely ambivalent position since, for example, they were neither waited upon nor permitted to dine with the family. They existed in a curious indeterminate state where, like their mistress, they both did and did not belong. When Robert complained that Cyfarthfa was becoming known as 'the Refuge for the Destitute', Rose was apparently delighted.

She was also involved in some of the local charitable work, which was an unwritten rule amongst wives of wealthy employers in poor districts, particularly if those employers sought social acceptance and emulated old paternalistic values. Rose was more systematic than many: she set up a soup kitchen for the poor of Cefncoedycymer and other nearby villages. For over thirty years about thirty people received three times weekly the food which was surplus to the requirements of the castle and its entourage. Although she operated a strict policy of admitting only the accredited poor using a system of tickets, her husband's attitude towards soup kitchens was much sterner. In 1864, for example, he stated that as wages had recently been increased and there was 'plenty of employment for every one seeking it I do not see any cause to give soup this year. Those who are not able to work are taken care of by the Parish so it is only the idle and the worthless who would avail themselves of the soup.'[33] After a colliery explosion in February 1862 killed forty-nine men employed by Crawshay, Rose personally visited every family.

She established a cutting-out class for young women, encouraging them to make their own clothes by cutting up *The Times* newspaper as a pattern and using the type to guide the line of the thread. She also held 'penny readings'. Perhaps with one eye on the success of the

Guests, Rose established free libraries. By 1872 there were four within a mile radius of Cyfarthfa and eventually seven such libraries, all open on Sundays and, as the *Athenaeum* commented, started long before the celebrated Sunday openings of the Birmingham Free Library. Rose publicized her own achievements in her letters to *The Times*.[34] Here she mentioned that books could be taken home. Her feminism enabled her to recognize that workmen's institutes tended to be, as their names suggested, for men's recreation. Rose wanted men and women to enjoy books (her written language usually mentioned both sexes) and she called her experiments cottage libraries.

Keeping libraries open on Sundays not only encouraged 'mental elevation' in leisure time, it also made a statement about her religious views. Rose's advanced notions worried some of the pious as did her support for cremation. She was one of he first members of the Cremation Society of England (formed in 1874) and a founder member of their Council. She hoped to have her body thrown into a Cyfarthfa furnace until Crawshay, afraid that his men might strike at the prospect, persuaded her to select Dresden. In 1884 Cardiff Assizes acquitted 84-year old Dr William Price. He had been accused of illegally cremating the body of his young son called Iesu Grist (Jesus Christ). Thanks therefore to Lady Charlotte's erstwhile acquaintance, the legality of cremation had been established in British law and a Cremation Act was passed in 1902 in time for Rose Crawshay to be cremated in Golders Green, London.

Her eschatological concerns went further. She wrote (and signed) a preface to a pamphlet endorsing euthanasia and her open support for this prompted anonymous criticism in a letter to the *Western Mail*, particularly deprecating such views from a member of the School Board. She ably defended her position in print and in person. Rose Crawshay, unlike Lady Charlotte, took up a very public stance.

She was made particularly accountable because she was amongst the first people ever to be elected to one of the new School Boards created by the Education Act of 1870. Not only was she also one of the first women to be in such a position but she chaired Vaynor School Board and, it would seem, was the only woman in the nineteenth century who simultaneously sat on two School Boards (and in two different counties, Glamorgan and Breconshire). She was elected to Merthyr Tydfil's Board in April 1871, gaining the second highest number of votes. She was the sole woman representative working with ten men and she remained in this position, occasionally taking the chair, for three years. A month later saw the first of the monthly Vaynor meetings, held at the Temperance Hall in Cefncoedycymer (and, from 1876, at the Cefn Board Schools). There had been thirteen nominations for this Breconshire post. The other twelve were men and included two ministers, a rector, two miners and a gentleman. In the press Rose was described as the wife of Robert Crawshay. She easily polled the highest number of votes — 481. Apart from the vice-chairman the others all got considerably fewer than half this number. She remained one of the five elected members on the Vaynor Board until 1879, being twice re-elected.

When Rose's friend Elizabeth Garrett had married the chairman of her Marylebone School Board and continued as the elected member, she had created a precedent which enabled women like Mrs Crawshay to follow her. In 1874 Rose's picture appeared in *The Graphic* as one of the pioneer women School Board members.[35] Another was Mrs Catherine Buckton, then active in Leeds but originally from Glamorgan. The *Englishwoman's Review*[36] recognized the significance of the election of women — 'For the first time in this country they have been elected to public positions of trust and importance — positions desired by men of eminence and distinction' — and Patricia Hollis's detailed study of women in local government has shown just how influential women might be through this kind of work in their local community.[37]

Dr Hollis has also demonstrated how demanding the job could be. Rose had two Boards to attend for the first three years. Not only must it have been difficult at that time for her to preside over meetings where she was the lone woman but also the Boards' minutes make it clear that she was quite prepared to dissent from majority views and register her protests. The Vaynor School Board minutes show her high attendance record.[38] She did not miss a meeting in the first year and the few she did not attend in following years tended to be at the very beginning of the year when she was in London. In addition to the monthly meetings there were special meetings (one was held at her home). Although the Board covered only a small area — in 1871 there were five elementary schools in the parish — Rose had to steer the Board as it sought to comply with the 1870 and 1876 Education Acts and to develop policies about attendance, corporal punishment, the appointment and salaries of teachers and pupil teachers, hardship cases involving the remission of fees and many other matters. Her efforts here and in Merthyr appear to have been appreciated. In 1872 at a Merthyr meeting of 800 people she spoke of her work on behalf of the Board and argued against various laws which discriminated against women, most notably a mother's inability in law to be the guardian of her child at her husband's death. A vote of confidence in her School Board work was proposed by a local vicar and this was seconded by William Gould who had in the past defended Lady Charlotte and was now one of the supporters of Merthyr's Liberal Nonconformist MP, Henry Richard.[39]

Unlike some of the members of her Boards, Rose was in a position to disseminate her views way beyond Merthyr. Readers of *The Times* were told by her that making ratepayers pay for religious teaching of which they did not approve was particularly unjust in an area where most people were Nonconformists.[40] She also told of her pleasure in carrying a motion (on Merthyr's Board) which simplified the religious diet meted out to School Board children, endorsing the daily use of the Lord's Prayer and a short designated selection from the Bible. Her proposal along the same lines was accepted by the Vaynor Board and incorporated into its by-laws.[41] She was concerned about superimposing a heavy dose of religious instruction which might offend parents.

An independent-minded woman, prepared to voice some disquiet in 1871 about compulsory attendance, she also supported improving opportunities for girls and instigating a rewards system in place of corporal punishment. Some of her ideas have a curiously modern ring, for example suggesting that decimal coinage be adopted as simpler for schoolchildren. She personally communicated with other Boards in Wales and England urging them to address memorials to the government on the subject. Rose also supported reforming the system of spelling. She played a prominent part in supporting the establishment of Swansea Training College which opened in 1872 and which for the first time enabled women to train as teachers within Wales.[42] She finally resigned from the Vaynor School Board when Robert was dying in 1879.

After his death (and for much of the time before this) Rose could be found not at Cyfarthfa but at Cathedine, the house he had bought for her near Llangorse Lake. She also spent time in London and in the south of France. Interestingly, as with Lady Charlotte, she was less ambitious for her daughters than her views and actions might

suggest. Lady Charlotte's daughters grew up at the height of
Victorian domesticity and 'good' marriages were what she sought for
them. One of Rose's daughters appears to have resented the fact that
her mother advocated higher education for women generally yet
failed to provide a decent education for her own child. Yet we are
dependent on the diaries of this daughter for such views and, quite
apart from the difficult relationship between Rose and Rose Harriette,
we do not have the mother's own feelings recorded in diary form. This
contrasts with Lady Charlotte, who kept an extensive journal
throughout her period at Dowlais and thus enables us to consider and
perhaps reconcile the disjuncture between her simultaneous public
utterances and private sentiments.

Although Lady Charlotte and Rose Crawshay overlapped in their
periods at Merthyr — both were there from the mid 1840s for a
decade — their most active periods did not quite coincide, Rose being
slightly younger than the mistress of Dowlais House. Moreover, from
the mid 1840s the Guests also owned Canford Manor and therefore
spent increasingly lengthy periods in Dorset. Here Lady Charlotte
seems to have adopted a more traditional approach to charity and
welfare, playing the part of the lady of the manor amongst a rather
more deferential and rural labouring class than was found in
Merthyr. When she left Canford in the care of her 21-year-old son,
she described his lavish coming-of-age party and added 'my reign
terminated magnificently'.

It would be foolish to suggest that either of these women was typical
of the ironmasters' wives of Wales or England. Clearly they were
women whose marked intelligence and independence of thought
struck contemporaries who met them. Yet, we are increasingly
finding that as further studies of women proceed and more strong-
minded women emerge from the historical woodwork, so the word
'extraordinary' becomes more questionable. Moreover, like all
Victorian women Rose and Lady Charlotte lacked the vote and were
legally and financially dependent on their husbands. Robert Crawshay gave Rose £50 twice monthly, separately from payment of
household and other bills. This was literally described in his cash
book as 'pin money'.[43] Nevertheless, Lady Charlotte and Rose were
also in positions of great influence in what was the largest town in
Wales.

Lady Charlotte was at Dowlais at the height of the iron trade and even became the world's leading ironmistress. Her husband had been Merthyr's first MP. The ways in which she actively participated in such a diverse range of interests related to the role of employer (quite apart from carving out her own specialisms) made her particularly influential at a time of social and political turbulence. Sir John's brand of paternalism was not, however, replicated by Lady Charlotte who had her own style, though she could complement and extend his approach. On the one hand her aristocratic background gave substance to his position at a time of industrial and political unrest. On the other hand, her particular 'humanizing' of Dowlais is recalled and singled out even today by the descendants of the Guest work-force. As a woman she was denied some of the same rights as the work-force and, although extending rather than challenging Guest paternalism, in a sense the very term excluded her; maternalism has different connotations from those of fatherly control and power associated with the paternalist. A family model, however, appears to have been crucial to both Sir John's and Lady Charlotte's conceptions of their work-force's duty towards them, with the father indubitably at the head and his wife, whilst dependent on her husband, nevertheless exercising regular control over her children. Perhaps 'familism' might therefore more accurately characterize their aims, though, whilst working towards the same ends, their means of expressing those aims tended to differ in kind and approach and remained essentially linked to class and gender.

Rose Crawshay took a slightly different route. She does not appear to have identified herself with the ironworks or the Welsh in the same way or to the same degree as Lady Charlotte. Her period at Merthyr represented one which was increasingly difficult for the iron trade.[44] Although both Guest and Crawshay were hostile to trade unions, Robert Crawshay, the fourth of the Crawshay 'dynasty', seems to have lacked the understanding that the Guests had of their work-force and, on top of worries about the plummeting price of iron, his opposition to the growth of union strength within his works led to the closing of the Cyfarthfa ironworks in 1874–5. Not until the end of 1879, after his death, did they reopen. Whereas his brand of paternalism seems to have been (in his later years at least) more akin to that exercised by the Marquess of Londonderry than the sort practiced by Titus Salt at Saltaire, his wife seems adequately to have fulfilled the expectations of her as the wife of a paternalist. Yet in

other respects she reached way beyond him, appealing to the rights of
the female sex and, through her elected public position, playing a part
in shaping the local politics of Merthyr and the future of its children,
and in the early development of organized feminism — usually
associated with middle-class ladies of London campaigning in an
environment far removed from ironworks.

In different ways both women helped to maintain social stability in
the local community. The kind of work they did has not been
sufficiently recognized by historians who have tended, for example,
either to see Lady Charlotte's interests as simply reflecting her
husband's work or, in the case of her literary efforts, to view her
considerable achievements as something totally separate from her
other activities. In fact her espousal of Welshness, just like her
position as a wife and mother, needs to be seen alongside her other
achievements. The work interests of John Guest and Robert
Crawshay eventually combined (though after their deaths) as in 1902
Crawshay Brothers became absorbed by Guest, Keen and Company.[45] Meanwhile Lady Charlotte's efforts for local education had
seen a successor in the form of Rose Crawshay. And, despite Guest's
and Crawshay's power as employers and husbands, somehow 'ably
seconded' seems, for different reasons, a singularly inadequate way of
describing either Lady Charlotte's or Rose Crawshay's 'work' in
Merthyr in relation to their respective ironmaster husbands.

Nevertheless, terms such as 'ably seconded' or 'supplementary' are
of significance. Deconstructing the word 'supplement', the French
theorist Jacques Derrida recognizes it as an independent, disruptive
and essentially ambiguous 'marker'.[46] Whilst Lady Charlotte and
Rose can be represented simply as the wives of the great ironmasters,
supplementary to their successes, the nature of their individual
interests, their own styles and their complex relationships to authority helped shape and reshape the public images of their families and
their historical legacies. At one and the same time they both helped to
supplement and reinforce the influence of the iron manufacturers'
families in Merthyr and thereby maintain the status quo, and also
became achievers in their own right, ('especially in literature and
education'), well-known in Wales and England and conscious of their
own capabilities and constraints. Finally, Rose Crawshay's efforts on
behalf of the early women's movement suggest a fascinating radical
edge beyond 'paternalism'.

*Bibliographical note*

Lady Charlotte's original journals remain in the Guest family's possession though extracts are reproduced in two volumes edited by a descendant, the Earl of Bessborough, *The Diaries of Lady Charlotte Guest* (London, John Murray, 1950) and *Lady Charlotte Schreiber 1853–1891* (London, John Murray, 1952). For her life see Revel Guest and Angela V. John, *Lady Charlotte: A Biography of the Nineteenth Century* (London, Weidenfeld and Nicolson, 1989). A selection of the Dowlais Iron Company correspondence held in the Glamorgan Record Office appears in M. Elsas (ed.), *Iron in the Making: Dowlais Iron Company Letters 1782–1860* (Cardiff, Glamorgan Record Office and Guest Keen Iron and Steel Company Ltd., 1960). See, too, Edgar Jones, *A History of GKN. Volume One: Innovation and Enterprise 1759–1918* (London, Macmillan, 1987).

Rose Crawshay has, as yet, no biographer though a family history was written by Margaret Stewart Taylor, *The Crawshays of Cyfarthfa Castle* (London, Robert Hale, 1967). The Cyfarthfa Papers are at the National Library of Wales. A visit to Rose's former home, now Cyfarthfa Castle Museum, Merthyr Tydfil, provides some sense of her position in the community (in 1908 the house was sold to Merthyr Corporation and turned into a school and museum). The museum also contains Eliot Crawshay-Williams's unpublished autobiography, 'I'm the King of the Castle', and a typescript of parts of the diaries of Rose's daughter, Rose Harriette. The bulk of these diaries cannot, however, be read before 2062. Chapter 11 of Ryland Wallace's *'Organise! Organise! Organise!': A Study of Reform Agitations in Wales, 1840–1886* (Cardiff, University of Wales Press, 1991), addresses women's rights in Victorian Wales.

For discussion of recent ideas on gender and power (though relating to England rather than Wales), see Leonore Davidoff and Catherine Hall, *Family Fortunes: Men and Women of the English Middle Class 1780–1850* (London, Hutchinson, 1987); Judy Lown, 'Not so much a factory, more a form of patriarchy: gender and class during industrialisation', in E. Garmarnikow *et al.* (eds.), *Gender, Class and Work* (London, Heinemann, 1983), 28–45 and Lown's book cited below. See also the life of the Swansea businesswoman Amy Dillwyn in David Painter, *Amy Dillwyn* (Cardiff, University of Wales Press, 1987).

*Notes to Chapter 2*

I am grateful to Dr Leonore Davidoff and Paul Stigant for comments on earlier drafts of this chapter and to Ann Dingsdale, Dr Jane Rendall and Dr Patricia Hollis for references to Rose Crawshay.

1.  Sir John's funeral sermon was published by Rees of Llandovery and ran into several editions.
2.  *The Times*, 9 December 1852. See also the *Gentleman's Magazine*, 39, 1 (1853).
3.  Revel Guest and Angela V. John, *Lady Charlotte: A Biography of the Nineteenth Century* (London, Weidenfeld and Nicolson, 1989), 165.
4.  *The Times*, op. cit.
5.  Sir Charles Manby, *Memoir of Sir Josiah John Guest, Bart., MP* (London, 1854) for the Institute of Civil Engineers.
6.  Patrick Joyce, *Work, Society and Politics* (Brighton, Harvester Press, 1980).
7.  David Roberts, *Paternalism in Early Victorian England* (London, Croom Helm, 1979), 269. For the gender-specific impact of paternalism on an English work-force with a high percentage of young women, see Judy Lown, *Women and Industrialization: Gender at Work in Nineteenth-Century England* (Oxford, Polity Press, 1990). This account of the Courtauld silk mills in Essex, famed for black mourning crape, shows how the Unitarian Courtauld family sought to reproduce the familial ideal through its segregated and vertically ranked work-force. The employers' wives increasingly identified with domesticity over the generations but, like Lady Charlotte, actively espoused mid-century rational recreation and education. A key figure in the transmission of this culture was, however, a paid employee, Mary Merryweather, who by the 1860s was moving in the same feminist London circles as Rose Crawshay.
8.  See Guest and John, op. cit., especially Part 2. Unless otherwise indicated, Lady Charlotte's words which are quoted in this chapter come from her original journals.
9.  See John A. Owen, *History of the Dowlais Iron Works* (Risca, The Starling Press, 1977 edn.).
10. Roberts, op. cit., 2–3.
11. Leslie Wynne Evans, 'Sir John Guest's education scheme'; *idem*, *Education in Industrial Wales* (Coventry, Avalon Press, 1971).
12. See *Cardiff and Merthyr Guardian*, 15 July 1848.
13. Lady Bell, *At The Works* (London, Virago Press edn., 1985); J. J. Turner, 'The People's Winter Garden, Middlesbrough', *Cleveland and Teesside Local History Society Bulletin*, 46 (1984), 30–9.
14. For example, discussion of 'Halls of the People' in the Owenite *Star in*

the East, 30 June 1838. I am grateful to Nick Mansfield for this reference.

15. See Huw Williams (ed.), *Public Health in Mid Victorian Wales*, 2 (Cardiff, University of Wales Press, 1983); Joseph Gross, 'Watersupply and sewerage in Merthyr Tydfil 1850–1874', *Merthyr Historian*, 2 (1978), 67–72; Raymond K. J. Grant, 'Merthyr Tydfil in the mid-nineteenth century: the struggle for public health', *Welsh History Review*, 14 No.4 (December 1989), 574–94.

16. Dowlais Iron Company Records, Glamorgan Record Office, Cardiff, D/DG Correspondence, 17 October 1853, Letter 160.

17. *Cardiff and Merthyr Guardian*, 25 November 1853.

18. Dowlais Iron Company, op. cit., 20 January 1854, Letter 155.

19. *Morning Chronicle* in Jules Ginswick (ed.), *Labour and The Poor in England and Wales 1849–1851, 3, South Wales & North Wales*, 61.

20. I. G. Jones, 'Merthyr Tydfil: the politics of survival'; *idem, Communities: Essays in the Social History of Victorian Wales* (Llandysul, Gomer Press, 1987), 239–62.

21. See Guest and John, op. cit., Ch. 8; also Elizabeth Havill, 'The respectful strike', *Morgannwg*, 24 (1980), 74.

22. Margaret Stewart Taylor, *The Crawshays of Cyfarthfa Castle* (London, Robert Hale, 1967), 85.

23. Mrs Crawshay, *Domestic Service for Gentlewomen*, 3rd thousand (n.d.).

24. *Women's Suffrage Journal*, 1 April 1872.

25. Typescript of diary of Rose Harriette Thompson Crawshay, 3 January 1868, Cyfarthfa Castle Museum, Merthyr Tydfil.

26. Stewart Taylor, op. cit., 103. For one story of the procurer see the pencil note in back of Mrs Crawshay, *Byron, Shelley, Keats* (Bwlch, n.d.), copy in National Library of Wales, where a former minister of Merthyr elaborated on this (dated 22 May 1898).

27. Rose Harriette's diary, op. cit., 25 December 1871.

28. List of members and Women's Suffrage Reports in the Blackburn Collection, Girton College, Cambridge. Despite the title, the society covered south Wales.

29. Mrs Crawshay, *Domestic Service*, op. cit.

30. Emily Davies Papers, Girton College, Cambridge. Box 1. Family Chronicle, pp.602–7a.

31. Mrs Crawshay, *Domestic Service*, op. cit.

32. A. James Hammerton, *Emigrant Gentlewomen: Genteel Poverty and Female Emigration* (London, Croom Helm), 141, 153 compares Rose Crawshay's scheme with the efforts of the Female Middle-Class Emigration Society to encourage educated women to become colonial servants. He draws attention to the critics of her scheme, Louisa Hubbard included.

33. Cyfarthfa Papers, National Library of Wales, Letter Book, 8 January 1864, Letter 1072.

34. *The Times*, 31 July 1872.
35. *The Graphic*, 10 January 1874. The feminist Emily Higginson (married to a radical Unitarian minister in Swansea) and Margaret Elizabeth Marsh of Carno (landowner) were the only other women on School Boards in Wales in the 1870s. Ryland Wallace, *'Organise! Organise! Organise!': A Study of Reform Agitations in Wales 1840–1886* (Cardiff, University of Wales Press, 1991), 168.
36. *Englishwoman's Review*, 5 (January 1871).
37. Patricia Hollis, *Ladies Elect: Women in English Local Government 1865– 1914* (Oxford, Clarendon Press, 1987). See too the work of Margaret McMillan on the Bradford School Board in the 1890s in Carolyn Steedman, *Childhood, Culture and Class in Britain: Margaret McMillan, 1860–1931* (London, Virago Press, 1990), 41–51 and Annemarie Turnbull, '"So extremely like parliament": the work of the women members of the London School Board 1870–1904', in London Feminist History Group, *The Sexual Dynamics of History* (London, Pluto Press, 1983).
38. For her work at Vaynor see the Vaynor School Board minutes, Powys Record Office, Llandrindod Wells, B/E/SB/4/M/1.
39. *Women's Suffrage Journal*, 1 April 1872.
40. *The Times*, 25 August 1871, 5 February 1872. See also *School Board Chronicle*, 5 August 1871.
41. Vaynor School Board, op. cit., 9 December 1872, 6 January 1873; *School Board Chronicle*, 5 April 1873.
42. W. Gareth Evans, *Education and Female Emancipation: The Welsh Experience 1847–1914* (Cardiff, University of Wales Press, 1990), 88–9.
43. Cyfarthfa Papers, op. cit., MS vols., 16 Cash Book, 1863–73.
44. See Michael Atkinson and Colin Baber, *The Growth and Decline of the South Wales Iron Industry, 1760–1880* (Cardiff, University of Wales Press, 1987).
45. See D. A. Reid, 'Labour, leisure and politics in Birmingham *c*.1800–75' (University of Birmingham Ph.D. thesis, 1985) for exploration of the attitudes of Keen and other paternalist employers of the Midlands.
46. For a discussion of the term 'supplement' in relation to women's history, and 'established' history, see Joan W. Scott's chapter, 'Women's history', in Peter Burke (ed.), *New Perspectives on Historical Writing* (Oxford, Polity Press, forthcoming). I am grateful to Professor Scott for allowing me to read this in draft form.

# 3

# The True 'Cymraes': Images of Women in Women's Nineteenth-Century Welsh Periodicals

## SIAN RHIANNON WILLIAMS

Hyd yn hyn, nid ydyw merched Cymru wedi derbyn y sylw a deilynga eu sefyllfa, nac wedi mwynhau cyfleustra cydradd a meibion eu gwlad. Nid oes cymaint o sylw wedi ei dalu i'w haddysg, nid oes un cyhoeddiad cofnodol wedi ei amcanu at eu gwasanaeth . . .

. . . ein cylch ni yw derchafiad y Rhyw fenywaidd ymhob ystyr, — yn gymdeithasol, moesol a chrefyddol. Ein hamcan yw cydweithredu a sefydliadau addysgiadol ein hoes er cynhyrchu morwynion ffyddlon, merched rhinweddol, gwragedd darbodus a mamau deallgar . . .

. . . ni wyddom am deilyngach gwaith na'r un sydd gennym mewn llaw.

(Up until now, the women of Wales have not received the attention that their situation warrants, nor have they enjoyed equal opportunities with the menfolk of their country. Less attention has been paid to their education, not one periodical has aimed to serve their particular needs . . .

. . . our interest is the elevation of the female sex in every respect — social, moral and religious. Our intention is to co-operate with the educational establishments of our time to produce faithful maids, virtuous women, thrifty wives and intelligent mothers . . .

. . . we know of no other task more worthy than that which we have undertaken.)[1]

Thus wrote Evan Jones ('Ieuan Gwynedd') in his introductory address as editor of the first Welsh periodical intended specifically for women, *Y Gymraes* (*The Welshwoman*). Its appearance in January 1850 followed two years of argument and debate concerning education and morality in Wales, which had become burning issues following the publication of the 1847 Education Report (the

notorious Blue Books), late that year.[2] As editor of the Nonconformist newspaper, *The Principality*, eminent Baptist minister
and Welsh littérateur Ieuan Gwynedd had been very much in the
forefront of the controversy surrounding the Report. His detailed
defence of the morality, religion and language of the Welsh people in
the face of scathing criticism by the Commissioners and their
supporters, earned him great respect as vindicator of the nation, while
his defence of the character of Welsh women made him their
champion.[3]

The publication of a Welsh monthly periodical for women was a
direct product of this debate. Not only had the Report drawn
attention to the fact that the education of girls was even more lacking
than that of boys, but the Commissioners had also portrayed Welsh
women as being unchaste and immoral, attacking in particular the
social custom of 'bundling' (courtship on beds at night) which, it was
claimed, led to widespread illegitimacy:

> There is another very painful feature of the laxity of morals . . . I refer
> to the alleged want of chastity in women. If this be so, it is sufficient to
> account for all other immoralities, for each generation will derive its
> moral tone in a great degree from the influences imparted by the
> mothers who reared them.[4]

Ieuan Gwynedd set out to disprove the allegations, attempting a
detailed comparison of illegitimacy rates in England and Wales.
Privately, however, he personally disapproved of 'bundling', and
although he defended their character to the outside world, the moral
champion of Welsh women felt that there were indeed serious
deficiencies which could be eliminated through education. To a great
extent, therefore, *Y Gymraes* of 1850 was a positive reaction to
criticism, and an attempt to right wrongs. Like the Commissioners,
Ieuan Gwynedd assumed that the education and enlightenment of the
female sex would be a powerful agent in social reform. A woman
educated for the role of wife and mother would necessarily improve
the condition of society at large, since her influence over husband and
children would have a far-reaching effect. *Y Gymraes* set out to create
a perfect Welshwoman whose high Christian morality and, in
particular, virtues of sobriety and thrift would ensure that in future
the Welsh nation would be above all criticism.

The decision to venture into the world of women's publishing had
not been taken lightly. The editor was in very poor health during the

EBRILL, 1913.

# Y Gymraes

Cyhoeddiad Misol i Ferched Cymru.

DAN OLYGIAETH

## Ceridwen Peris.

CYF. XVII.    RHIF 199.

### CYNWYSIAD.

Pris Geiniog.

Dolgellau : Argraffwyd gan E. W. Evans, Swyddfa'r " Goleuad."

An April 1913 issue of *Y Gymraes* ('The Welshwoman') edited by Ceridwen Peris. A translation of the contents is as follows:

Famous women: Helen Keller (with illustration). By Miss Ellen Hughes, Llanengan

Children's Health Essentials

What is Beautiful

Story: 'True Love is like Steel'. By Awen Mona

I love the maiden

Those who have passed away— Mrs Ellen Davies, Lasynys, Harlech (with illustration).

Miss Martha Breese, Tanllan; and Miss Elizabeth Rowlands, Cefncoch

General Titbits

Licence

'The Spring' (with illustration)

The Mad Dog

This and That

Bit by Bit

North Wales Women's Temperance Association

Price One Penny

(By permission of the National Library of Wales.)

months preceding the launch, and did not expect to live to see more than a few issues through the press. He realized how few women were able to read fluently, and regretted the lack of tradition of women's writing in Wales. In 1844, out of a total of 3,224 marriages at ten Welsh centres, only 29 per cent of the brides were able to sign their names, and various government reports of the 1830s and early 1840s had repeatedly drawn attention to the fact that women's literacy was lower than that of men.[5] Yet, Ieuan Gwynedd was motivated by a reforming zeal, and with the financial patronage of Augusta Hall, Lady Llanofer, and the wholehearted support of William Owen, the Cardiff publisher, he was determined to embark upon his project: the publication of a monthly magazine of thirty-two pages, priced at twopence a copy.

*Y Gymraes* seems to have got off to a respectable start in 1850. In the second issue it was stated that almost 3,000 copies of the first issue had been requested. The literary critic and antiquary Thomas Stephens, who, incidentally, believed it to be one of the best-quality publications in the Welsh language, claimed that the periodical had sold 3,500 copies per month in its first year, although Catherine Evans, in her study of the Welsh periodical press, put the figure at 3,000. Since newspapers and magazines were sometimes read aloud, and often borrowed by several readers, too great an emphasis should not be placed on circulation figures. Yet all available evidence suggests that *Y Gymraes* fared well in popularity and that, in spite of the difficulties anticipated at the outset, the project was not doomed to failure from the start.[6]

From its inception, the magazine created and perpetuated an ideal to which the women of Wales could aspire. This ideal was part of a more general ideal of Wales which was being created during the middle years of the century. The reaction against the unrest caused by Chartism and the Rebecca riots, and the allegations of immorality and barbarity made by the Education Commissioners of 1847, made it necessary to ensure that in future Wales would be above such criticism. 'Cymru lân, Cymru lonydd', 'Gwlad y menyg gwynion' — a still and peaceful land where violent crime did not occur — became the traditional image of Wales portrayed in the literature of the period. It was intended that women would play an important part in the achievement of this ideal.[7] And where better to convey the image of the perfect 'Cymraes' (Welshwoman) to the women of Wales than in their own magazine?

The first issue set the tone for the future. Ieuan Gwynedd's opening address outlined his vision of a Wales which was pure and uncorrupted: a Wales in which the sanctity of marriage was upheld by all, and religious observance and sobriety were a way of life. If this could be achieved, then his country would indeed become an earthly paradise. The editor's greeting was followed by an address to the women of Wales by 'Gwenllian Gwent'. If the writer was the magazine's patron, Lady Llanofer, it seems strange that she did not use her usual *nom de plume*, 'Gwenynen Gwent' ('The Bee of Gwent', so called because of her diligence in working to preserve Welsh customs). However, the content is such that it reflects exactly Lady Llanofer's views, stressing as it did the importance of the part women should play in preserving the Welsh language and native dress of Wales. (Lady Llanofer, then Augusta Hall, had received first prize for an essay on the subject at the Cardiff Eisteddfod of 1834. It had been much acclaimed, and parts of it did in fact appear in the second issue of *Y Gymraes*.)[8] The Welsh language was seen to be central to the reform of Welsh society, since it constituted the nation's main defence against immorality and irreligion. The true 'Cymraes' should make every effort to ensure that Welsh was the language of her family. She was to be proud of her Welshness, wearing at all times the native dress of Welsh flannel and a beaver hat.

Whether or not she was the author of the address referred to, Lady Llanofer was an important figure in the creation of the image of the ideal 'Cymraes'. Her drawings of local native dress formed the basis of the creation of a 'national' costume worn by the typical Welsh 'girl' (later to be caricatured in the press as 'Dame Wales'). Although far removed from the majority of Welsh women in class and religion, she nevertheless sympathized with and encouraged Nonconformity (particularly Welsh Calvinistic Methodism), and her efforts on behalf of the cause of temperance won her the respect of the leaders of Welsh society. Her belief in the social importance of a highly moral, religious and Welsh-speaking wife and mother was shared by 'Cranogwen' and 'Ceridwen Peris', editors of magazines for women later in the century (see Chapter 6).

*Y Gymraes* was therefore particularly relevant in the Welsh context of the time, yet the ideal of womanhood presented by the editor, patron and contributors was by no means restricted to Wales. The sexual division of labour where men and women had their separate spheres and the romanticization of the domestic role of the wife and mother were central to the prevalent ideology in England and Europe in general during the period following the French Revolution and the widespread impact of the industrial revolution. Like the works of the social reformers of the Evangelical movement in England, Ieuan Gwynedd's periodical portrayed women as the exalted 'Angels of the House', displaying those virtues considered particularly fitting to the female character. In February 1850, for example, it was suggested that a wife should 'keep a smile on her lips continually', and another article giving advice to married women illustrates the extent of servitude expected of them:

> Os dygwydd i'ch gŵr ddyfod adref yn lled anhwylus, peidiwch a gwneud gwynepryd brawychus a gofyn iddo, 'beth yw y mater arnoch'. Peidiwch a'i syfrdanu; os bydd eisiau i chi wybod, bydd yn sicr o ddywedyd wrthych . . . Peidiwch a gadael iddo gael allan fod coler ei grys heb fotwm bob wythnos. Y mae hyn yn mynych gynhyrfu tymhestloedd teuluaidd . . . Gwnewch y coleri mor gymhwys ag y byddo modd, ag os na byddant yn ei hollol fodloni, cofiwch fod caniatâd i ddynion rwgnach am goleri eu crysau.

> (If your husband happens to come home feeling rather miserable, do not make a frightful face and ask him, 'What is wrong with you?' Do not persist in bothering him; if he wants you to know, he will be sure to tell you in due course . . . Do not let him find that his shirt collars have buttons missing each week. This is often the cause of many a family storm. See to it that the collars are as perfect as possible, and if they do not entirely please him, remember that men are permitted to complain about the state of their shirt collars.)[9]

Much of the content of the magazine was in this vein; advice and commands which, if obeyed, would create the perfect 'Cymraes', at all times neat and tidy, modest and unassuming, thrifty, loyal, pure and religious. Many articles dealt with unchaste behaviour, their titles — 'The Unchastity of the Welsh People', or 'The Moral Condition of the Welsh People' — reflecting the crusade for the reform of the nation. In these, young, 'flighty' girls were rebuked for their shameful conduct at fairs and inns, and urged to become responsible and pure. Although much of this prescriptive writing was aimed at single women, it was the role of wife and mother which received the main attention of contributors. Most, if not all, writers assumed that their readers were married women with children, or women likely to be married. The mother was the most important agent in the process of reform and, although limited, her role would not be an entirely passive one, since it was through her influence that a new generation would be educated and trained.

Although Ieuan Gwynedd and his supporters accepted that women were equal to men in intelligence, and argued in favour of educating them, their approach was couched in terms of sexual difference. All the articles concerning education, including one written by a woman, stressed that the type of education proposed would be that most appropriate to their domestic role. In her article entitled 'Y Pwys sydd i Ferched gael Addysg' ('The Importance of Educating Women'), 'Martha' of Rhosyfedwen describes the kind of education she envisaged:

> A'r wybodaeth a'r addysg a wna y ferch yn well gwraig, a'i gwna yn well morwyn. Yr addysg a'i gwna yn well mam, a'i gwna yn well mammaeth; a'r addysg a'i gwna yn fwy cymhwys i gadw tŷ iddi ei hun, a'i gwna yn fwy cymhwys i gadw tŷ i arall.

> (The information and the education which will make the woman a better wife, and a better servant. The education which will make her a better mother, and a better nurse; and the education which will make her more fit for the task of keeping house for herself and for another.)[10]

Each month the magazine included domestic instruction, cookery and housekeeping tips. The more general instruction in History, Geography and Commerce typically took the form of a question-and-answer session between a child and its mother. The 'Cymraes' was learning, not as much for her own sake, but so as to be able to serve her husband and instruct her children. It was certainly not the editor's intention to create independent, educated women.

Yet there was a positive aspect to the magazine's support for women's education. In his work on the education of women in nineteenth-century Wales, W. Gareth Evans has shown the importance of the periodical press in making women's education an important public issue.[11] As the first magazine for women, *Y Gymraes* succeeded in drawing attention to the need to improve the condition of women in Wales. In that respect, it can be seen as a landmark on the long road to more equal recognition. However, since equality was narrowly defined within the confines of separate spheres, any improvement in their situation gave women more visibility, but not true equality.

In several other important respects, the magazine must be seen to have failed in its initial aims. *Y Gymraes* was set up in order to appeal to working-class women in particular: this did not come about. In fact, much of the material was by male writers aspiring to middle-class values. The content therefore often bore little relation to the reality of the lives of working women to whom education did not seem relevant. Certainly, most working-class women would have had very little time for learning.

Although approximately 26 per cent of the female population of Wales over ten years of age was engaged in paid employment in 1851, this important group was scarcely mentioned.[12] The dual responsibility of waged labour and caring for a home was hardly acknowledged, even though many women were in the situation of those described by a contemporary in 1856:

> Mae y gwragedd . . . dan anghenrheidrwydd o lychwino eu cyrff yn fawr bob dydd. Ond yn dod adref a molchi a golchi'r tŷ golchi'r llawr a rhoi tywod drosto a gwyngalchu.
>
> (The women . . . are obliged to get themselves very dirty every day. But they return home and wash, clean the house, scrub the floor, spread sand over it and whitewash.)[13]

The magazine's attitude towards women's work was unsympathetic. Farm servants, for example, were often portrayed as flighty, irresponsible young girls who spent much of their time courting and committing 'sinful' acts at fairs and in haylofts. One searches in vain for any reference to their physical condition — the kind of suffering described by 'Llew Llwyfo' in his novel of 1860, *Huw Huws*:

> Gwelai res o ferched o bob oedran . . . a gwaith caled wedi anffurfio eu cyrff . . . wedi crymu eu gwarau, crebachu eu dwylo . . . Cerddai dynion a gwragedd o amgylch y lluaws amryddull yma, gyda golwg beirniadol prynwyr caethion a'u holi yn y fath fodd fel ag i ddangos eu syniad nad oedd iddynt hwy . . . na rhan na chyfran ym mreintiau merched eraill, na dim i'w ddisgwyl ond llafur corff o fedydd i fedd. 'Os oes eisieu diwygiad gyda golwg ar gaethion yr America,' ebe Huw Huws rhyngddo ag ef ei hun, 'y mae eisiau diwygiad gyda golwg ar ferched gwledig Cymru'.
>
> (He could see a line of girls of all ages . . . and hard work had deformed their bodies, bent their shoulders, wrinkled their hands . . . men and

women walked around this crowd with the critical look of slave purchasers, and questioned them in such a way as to show them that they had no part in the privileges afforded to other women, and nothing to expect bar hard physical labour from cradle to grave. 'If reform is needed in the case of the slaves of America', said Huw Huws to himself, 'it is certainly needed in the case of the women of rural Wales.')[14]

Those women who worked in heavy industry were completely ignored by *Y Gymraes*, while the main occupation of Welsh women, domestic service, was romanticized and seen as the ideal opportunity for women to exhibit their natural feminine instincts of service and deference. Women's activities in benefit societies and chapels were not recorded, and other themes central to working-class women's lives, such as illness or childbirth, were not mentioned. All discussion of sex was from a male standpoint: 'fallen' women who succumbed to temptation should bear the consequences of their foolishness.

It is hardly surprising that women were preached at in *Y Gymraes* since the first publication for women was produced and supported almost entirely by men. Men were the main contributors (these included eminent ministers such as Benjamin Price ('Cymro Bach'), David Howell ('Llawdden') and William Williams ('Caledfryn')), and all evidence points to the fact that the vast majority of the magazine's readers were also men. As early as October 1850 it was claimed that *Y Gymraes* was read mainly by male readers. It was stated that while Merthyr Tydfil boasted a female population of 10,000 of reading age, only 108 copies of the magazine were sold there each month, and that less than half that number were actually read by women:

Ein barn yw fod *Y Gymraes* yn sefyll ar y parch personol a deimlir atom ni, ac nid am fod merched yn gyffredinol yn teimlo un ddyddordeb ynddi. Rhaid i ni gyfaddef nad yw ein profiad hyd yn hyn wedi dysgu yr un wers i ni, ond fod cyflwr ein merched yn uchel alw am yr ymegniadau mwyaf grymus ar ein rhan.

(It is our opinion that *Y Gymraes* rests on the personal respect felt for us, and not because women in general have the least interest in it. We must confess that our experience so far has taught us nothing but that the state of our womenfolk calls desperately for the strongest possible efforts on our part.)

The editor's final address in the last issue makes the same point in a rather bitter tone:

> Gan na chynhaliwyd *Y Gymraes* erioed gan ferched Cymru . . .
> gorfodwyd i ni i'w gwneud yn fwy llenorol a chyffredinol nag y
> dymunem . . . Pan ddechreuasom gyhoeddi *Y Gymraes*, yr oeddem yn
> awyddus am gadw ar dir newydd, gan ein bod yn annerch dosbarth
> newydd o ddarllenwyr. Ond cawsom brawf yn fuan na fynai y
> dosbarth hwnw yr hyn oedd yn briodol iddynt eu hunain . . . Nid oedd
> ein rhianod a'n gwragedd eisiau dim cynhorthwy mewn pethau fel hyn.
> Yr oedd ei ceginiaeth yn berffaith, a'u holl drefnidaeth deuluaidd
> uwchlaw gwellhâd. Ac felly y gorfu i ni eu gadael.

> (Since *Y Gymraes* was never supported by the women of Wales . . . we
> were forced to make the magazine more literary and more general in
> content than we had wished it to be . . . When we began publishing *Y
> Gymraes*, we were eager to keep on new ground since we were
> addressing a new class of reader. But we were soon to find that that
> class did not wish to accept that which was appropriate for them . . .
> Our girls and women did not need any help in these kinds of matters.
> Their cookery was perfect, their family organization above
> improvement. And so we were forced to leave them.)[15]

When these comments are considered in the light of Ieuan Gwynedd's
hopes stated in his introductory address of January 1850, one is
forced to sympathize with the disappointed editor. At that time, he
expressed the hope that it would be women's writing which would fill
the pages of *Y Gymraes*, and also resolved that he would not set
himself up as their teacher but would instead aim to encourage
women to educate each other. Given the condition of women's
education at the time, it is hardly surprising that these noble aims
were not realized. Yet the whole tone of the magazine is such that it is
difficult to believe that the working-class women for whom it was
intended were actively encouraged to feel that they had a part to play
in the venture.

By the autumn of 1851, it was clear that the publication was not
financially viable, and at the same time, the editor's health was again
deteriorating. In November it was announced that *Y Gymraes* was to
be 'united in matrimony' with *Y Tywysydd* (*The Guide*), a monthly
penny periodical for young people edited by Revd David Rees of
Llanelli. It became *Y Tywysydd a'r Gymraes* in January 1852.

The new joint periodical never really addressed itself specifically to women's issues, but much of its content was similar in tone to the original magazine in that it emphasized the importance of high moral standards, sobriety, thrift, the role of the mother and the sanctity of marriage. Again the image fostered was that of the 'sensible' and religious woman, in contrast to the 'other' type who constituted a moral threat. In the Wales of the 1850s where religious practice was much more marked than in England, this definition became extremely powerful. Several articles were aimed at young couples, and included much advice to wives. They were urged, above all, to:

> Submit, and you will conquer
> Serve, and you will command.[16]

The editor's own view of the role of women within marriage was outlined in his 'Llythyr at Wraig Ifanc' ('Letter to a Young Wife') in June 1853:

> Mae yn wir mai dyletswydd a rhagorfraint gwraig yw ufuddhau ac nid llywodraethu; ond y mae llawer, wedi'r cwbwl, wedi ei adael i'w barn hi . . . Nid creadures oddefol ydyw ond dylai fod yn weithgar a bywiog . . . Mae cylch y gŵr yn amrywio . . . ond mae cylch y fenyw yn oblygedig mewn un gair annwyl . . . CARTREF . . . Mae cynneddfau a chyfansoddiad benywaidd wedi eu cyfaddasu i'r cylch cartrefol, yr hyn ellid ystyried yn enghraifft ogoneddus o ddoethineb a daioni Duw yn y greadigaeth.

> (It is true that the duty and privilege of a wife is to obey and not rule; but many matters are, after all, left to her discretion . . . She is not a passive creature, but should be hard-working and lively . . . The husband's circle of activity is varied . . . but the woman's circle is implied by one dear word . . . HOME . . . The female nature and constitution are fitted for the home, and this can be seen as a glorious example of God's goodness and wisdom in creation.)

The overwhelming majority of the contributors to the magazine were men, yet there was a Poetry Column which provided an opportunity for women to contribute (which they often did), and the occasional article was written by a woman. These universally shared the editor's philosophy. One example is an article on womanhood by a Dorothy Rees which appeared in July 1862:

Pa le ei chylch? Cartref... Yr unig ffordd i ni gael chwaraeteg ydyw bod
ein cylch fel benywod yn ostyngedig a llafurus a glanwedd a duwiol...
Ceisiwn dduwioldeb fel y prif beth.

(Where is her place? Home ... The only way in which we can ensure
fair play is that our role as women is submissive and hard-working and
pure and godly ... Let us strive for godliness above all else.)

*Y Tywysydd a'r Gymraes* continued in much the same vein into the
1880s, but in 1879 it wished well to a new monthly periodical for
women, *Y Frythones* (*The Female Briton*).

Following the failure of Ieuan Gwynedd's *Y Gymraes* in 1851,
twenty-eight years elapsed before an attempt was made to set up
another independent magazine for women. This time, the initiative
was taken by a woman, the strong-willed Sarah Jane Rees,
('Cranogwen'), who became editor of *Y Frythones* for ten years from
1879 until 1889.[17] Born in Llangrannog, Cardiganshire, in 1839, the
daughter of a ship's captain, Cranogwen showed considerable
independence of mind as a young girl by insisting that she be allowed
to accompany her father to sea, since she hated cooking and sewing.
She had already received some instruction in navigation at the local
school (where she also learned Latin), and she later taught navigation
and mathematics at various schools in her home area and in
Liverpool and London. On returning to Llangrannog, she opened her
own school, and in 1859 became influenced by the religious and
temperance Revival which was sweeping through Wales at that time.
She became a Sunday-school and Band of Hope teacher, and later
took up lecturing and preaching, as well as writing poetry for various
eisteddfodau. Throughout her life she was dedicated to the cause of
temperance, and one of her last public contributions was the
establishment of Undeb Dirwestol Merched y De (The South Wales
Women's Temperance Union) in 1901. Tall and commanding, with a
strong husky voice, Cranogwen does not fit the image of the feminine
nineteenth-century woman. Yet from a religious and moral point of
view, here was an ideal model of virtue for Welsh women, although
her educational background and status set her aside from her sisters,
and put her in a position to advise and educate them.

Given the background of its editor, it is hardly surprising that *Y
Frythones* was firmly entrenched in the tradition of *Y Gymraes*. Like
the first magazine, its aim was also to educate women and to raise
their moral standards for the general benefit and reform of Welsh

society. The first issue paid tribute to the 'immortal' Ieuan Gwynedd, and from time to time, articles which had originally appeared in *Y Gymraes* were published in the new journal. On first perusal of *Y Frythones*, one could be forgiven for assuming that nothing had changed in the situation of women during the twenty-eight years between 1851 and 1879. Once again, womanhood was seen almost exclusively in terms of marriage and motherhood, and the majority of articles continued to expound the ideal of the domesticated 'Angel of the House'. The image of the perfect 'Brythones', like the perfect 'Cymraes', was of the pure and virtuous wife and mother who, restricted to her own sphere of activity, gave her all for the sake of the well-being of her children. A woman's power lay mainly in her silent, underlying influence within the home. The limited public role allowed her was restricted to Sunday school and chapel within the cause of promoting religion and temperance. An article entitled 'Nodweddion Cymraes' ('Characteristics of the Welshwoman') which appeared in *Y Frythones* in June 1890 could well have been written for *Y Gymraes* forty years earlier.

Notwithstanding the continuation of this ideal, the intermediate period had seen, if not positive change, at least constructive discussion in Wales of the role of women in society, and the new journal was not completely untouched by these influences. The main developments had occurred in the context of the calls for the education of women, and it was mainly in this field that the magazine gave expression to concerns over women's underprivileged status. Cranogwen herself was a staunch supporter of the education of women, and the various articles published in *Y Frythones* on this subject were particularly relevant against a background of public debate in the period following the Aberdare Report into Intermediate and Higher Education in Wales (1881) and leading up to the Welsh Intermediate Education Act of 1889.[18]

Writing on the education issue in 1884, D. Adams of Brynhaweu felt that the Welsh people were still not completely free from the misconception that women were innately inferior to men, but that the talent shown by women writers in *Y Frythones*, and the support the journal had received, proved that they were gradually changing their minds.[19] In *Y Gymraes* of 1850, Ieuan Gwynedd had used the unfortunate simile 'as ignorant as is a girl of vulgar fractions'. Such a statement was by now meaningless, according to the author. In 1887, the magazine welcomed the establishment of the Association for

Promoting the Education of Girls in Wales, and the importance of establishing secondary schools for girls was the subject of the editor's New Year address for 1888. The journal also welcomed the fact that women were gradually breaking into the field of medicine; and much joy was expressed when the new college at Cardiff decided to accept women as students.

*Y Frythones* was much more prepared to recognize the fact that women worked outside the home than the earlier magazine. In September 1880, Jenny Jones wrote of one young woman's experience of losing her job to a man who was jealous of the fact that she, being a woman, was more highly qualified than he. 'Monica', in 1881, argued that the women of Wales should be out in the world working — a situation which would be of benefit to them and to society in general (though she hastened to add that she still held the belief that women were much better suited to caring for home and family than men were). 'Olwen', in her essay 'Merched yn Enill Bywoliaeth' ('Women Earning a Living'), went further. She stressed how women were now proving that they could hold their own in a male world:

> . . . yn y dyddiau hyn, pryd y mae addysg ac addysg uwchraddol i ferched yn cael cymaint o sylw, mae sefyllfa merch, a'r amryfal ffyrdd sydd iddi enill bywoliaeth anrhydeddus ac annibynol, yn gwella ac ehangu yn raddol a sicr. Diolch i'r nefoedd mai ym Mhrydain yr ydym — y wlad lle mae . . . y rhyw fenywaidd yn nes i'w lle nag yn un wlad arall.

> ( . . . in these days, when education and secondary education for girls are receiving so much attention, a woman's situation, and the various means in which she can earn an independent and respectable living, are being improved and extended gradually and surely. Thank heaven that we are in Britain — the country where . . . the female sex is nearer its proper place than in any other country.)[20]

Yet Olwen was referring to a privileged class of women: women for whom 'the chains which held back the female sex in the race of life were beginning to be loosened'.[21] Like *Y Gymraes*, *Y Frythones* was intended to appeal to working-class women, but much of its content, for example, the attention given to the Young Women's Mutual Improvement Society (established in Aberystwyth in 1881 for that 'class of girls of whom it is generally assumed that their duty and privilege is to be completely dependent on their fathers and brothers'), was of little relevance to the majority of women in Wales.[22] The heroines of *Y Frythones* were Englishwomen of the middle class, Hannah More, Amelia Opie, Sarah Martin, Elizabeth Fry and Florence Nightingale. The philanthropic efforts of Welsh MPs' wives in London received much acclaim, while the work of female benefit societies in Wales went unmentioned. It is difficult to avoid the conclusion that *Y Frythones* had a rather condescending attitude towards working-class women. Stating the object of the monthly column 'Y Teulu' ('The Family') in the first issue, the editor specifically differentiated between middle- and working-class women. The column, it was said, was not aimed at ' . . . our intelligent sisters who are well acquainted with the world and with English Literature', but would contain 'simple, kindly, easily understood and easily managed suggestions for the common and working class of our sisters'.

Domestic service and housework apart, the magazine contains little reference (with the exception of Olwen's essay) to other types of working-class women's work. In September 1886, when public and parliamentary discussion on women's work in the coal industry was at its height, a letter was published strongly advocating that such work be banned. Considering other sources of evidence of the struggle of the Welsh tip-girls to keep their jobs (for example, a large meeting in Tredegar, where over 200 women and girls were employed by the local Iron and Coal Company), it is perhaps strange that no response to the letter appeared.[23] Was it that the editor did not wish to allow their supporters' point of view to be expressed? There is some evidence of this in the following month's editorial. Was it, on the other hand, due to the fact that *Y Frythones* was irrelevant to the lives and needs of working girls?

It was middle-class women who were affected by the developments of the 1880s, and this was reflected in the content of the journal. Among the reforms passed during this period was the right of married women to control their personal assets. D. Adams of Brynhawen supported this measure, and also proposed that women should be given the right to vote in elections, though she (or he) did temper her (or his) views by declaring the hope that it would prove possible to 'expand the minds of women without the loss of good taste', so that the advantages of culture could be brought to bear 'without injuring that unassuming purity which is the main decoration of the female sex'.[24] Rather more powerful arguments were put forward by Mair Maelor of Wrexham. Her essay, 'Merched a Gwleidyddiaeth' ('Women and Politics') was published in three parts during the spring of 1889. She was obviously familiar with the women's issues of the period. Her essay included the only reference made in the magazine to the Contagious Diseases Acts (1864–9) — opposition to which in England had been a major means of spurring women to action — and called on Welsh women to participate in election work and to take a stand on political issues.[25]

In general, however, politics, and particularly the issue of women's suffrage (which was brought before Parliament regularly between 1884 and 1887), received scant attention in the magazine. In January 1885, Cranogwen's New Year's editorial welcomed the new measure to extend the franchise, but said nothing of the attempt, which reached a second reading, to secure votes for women. It is possible that an unsigned article which appeared in August 1886 reflected her opinion on the matter. It stated:

> Y mater o ryddfreiniad y merched sydd hefyd yn ennill sylw ac yn ennill nerth yn y wlad, ac yn y Senedd yn dyfod yn fwy poblogaidd; ac er nad y'm ein hunain wedi arfer ei ddadleu nac yn dewis ceisio gwneud hyny, gwyddom nad yw ond cwestiwn o amser hyd nes iddo ddyfod yn ffaith . . . Cam yn ddiau a fydd, wedi ei gymeryd, yn dwyn y ddynoliaeth fenywaidd yn nes ymlaen ar raddfa eu dyrchafiad cyfreithlawn.

> (The matter of women's emancipation is also receiving attention and becoming stronger in the country, and more popular in Parliament; and although it has not been customary for us to advocate it, nor do we choose to do so, we realize that it is only a matter of time before it becomes a reality . . . A step which will surely bring the female section of humanity forward on the ascent to their legal rights.)

Cranogwen retired as editor in February 1889; the second article on women and politics, 'Benywod a Gwladyddiaeth', which appeared in July 1891, though unsigned, may therefore possibly have reflected the views of the new editor (or editors — the editorial control remained anonymous). It outlined the arguments for and against women's suffrage, and concluded with an appeal to the women of Wales to read a discourse by Lady Sandhurst on the subject, that they might be stirred to energetic involvement in politics.

But the new editorship did not bring the new life to the journal that Cranogwen had anticipated in her farewell address. In spite of a declaration of the intention to include the most important news of Wales in each monthly issue and to extend the usefulness and circulation of the journal, the general content did not change after 1889. Much of the news included in the editor's monthly column was news of London Society, royalty and selected foreign items, while several of the features and serializations begun under Cranogwen's editorship continued. Many of these were of a conservative or religious nature, for example, Mrs Ople's 'Domestic Scenes' translated into Welsh, 'The Life and Times of Bishop Morgan', and 'The History of the Methodist Cause at Penygarnedd, Anglesey' which continued for more than twelve editions. In general, there was less discussion of women's issues during the publication's final two years than during the 1880s. When *Y Frythones* came to an end as an independent publication in December 1891, the editor insisted that the readership was actually on the increase. It was stated that the decision to amalgamate with *Cyfaill yr Aelwyd* (*The Home Companion*), a 'family' publication under the joint editorship of Revd H. Elfed Lewis and T. C. Evans ('Cadrawd'), also published by David Williams and Son of Llanelli, was due to the fact that both publications were aimed at the same 'class of reader', though it is difficult to believe that this would have occurred had all been well with *Y Frythones*. *Cyfaill yr Aelwyd*, which emphasized the central role of the wife and mother as upholder of Christian values, continued until December 1894.

The women of Wales were not long without their own journal, however, because in 1896 *Y Gymraes* was reborn. This time the editor was a woman, Alice Gray Jones ('Ceridwen Peris'), a regular contributor to *Y Frythones* and, by 1896, the organizer of Undeb Dirwestol Merched y Gogledd (the North Wales Women's Temperance Union). She had been headteacher at Dolbadarn Girls' School until 1881 (when she relinquished the post to marry Revd William Jones of Fourcrosses), and was a well-known public speaker and a prominent member of various religious, educational and social movements.[26] The new monthly journal became closely allied to the temperance movement, and was again religious in tone and content. Although very much in the tradition of the first *Y Gymraes* and *Y Frythones*, emphasizing as it did familial duty and moral and religious observance, it paid more attention to the achievements of Welsh women (rather than to the middle-class English heroines of *Y Frythones*), and encouraged women to take an active part in public life, albeit in the 'limited' spheres of Sunday school, chapel and the temperance movement. The contributors were mainly women, and the magazine regularly reported developments such as the establishment of 'Homes for Friendless Women' and 'Shelters' for women alcoholics.

An occasional article appeared which supported the social revolution which was providing new opportunities for women in public life and employment. Each month's issues included a 'debate' on topics which often touched upon the social role of women, for example, 'Should women marry?', 'Should women become public speakers?', 'Should women read novels?', and, in December 1900, 'Should women be allowed to vote?' The latter article was in favour of women's suffrage, although the magazine made little reference to the issue generally. Undeb Dirwestol Merched y Gogledd had officially overwhelmingly rejected the inclusion of women's suffrage in their programme in 1897 (but see Chapter 6). The main thrust of the content still reflected the call for moral and religious reform, but in contrast to the earlier magazine, the readers and contributors (the large majority of whom were women) were actively involved in bringing that change about.

Although she admitted to being somewhat apprehensive regarding the feasibility of a Welsh magazine for women (due to the fact that in the past the women of Wales had never really supported their own publications), after a year the editor could report that the new magazine had received a warm welcome. By December 1900 she was able to state that the circulation was increasing annually. *Y Gymraes* continued successfully under Ceridwen Peris's editorship until the autumn of 1919 when Mair Ogwen, another prominent member of Undeb Dirwestol Merched y Gogledd, took her place. The magazine continued to follow the same format with similar regular features through the war years, and in 1922 it was still described as 'a publication which trained women in virtue, modesty and goodness'. It was advertised at the time as a 'national magazine' which would appeal to women who wished to read stories and poetry, home and cookery tips, who were interested in social issues, temperance, purity, morality and religion, and who would love to see peace reign in the world.[27] The latter point is significant given the part that women were to play in the Peace Movement in Wales during the 1930s. *Y Gymraes* finally came to an end in December 1934.

The period between 1850 and the early years of the twentieth century had seen major changes in the literacy and social situation of women, and to a certain extent the Welsh periodical press for women had reflected and influenced these changes. The 'Welshwoman' had emerged from being totally confined to the domestic sphere to being an active participant in social reform. As C. K. Evans of Cardiff, addressing her Welsh sisters in 1908, commented:

> Y mae'r hen gri mai 'cylch gwniadwaith' ydyw unig glych merch wedi llefain ei hun allan, a chadnabyddir yn awr fod eisieu ei gwasanaeth ymhob cylch. Perthyn iddi hi, nid paratoi ei phlant ar gyfer y byd yn unig, ond edrych fod y byd yn cael ei baratoi ar gyfer ei phlant.

> (The old cry that the 'sewing circle' is the only sphere open to a woman has cried itself out, and it is now recognized that her service is needed in all walks of life. It is now her duty, not only to prepare her children for the world, but to ensure that the world is prepared for her children.)[28]

The magazines of the last quarter of the nineteenth century had played a part in encouraging women to work actively in society, and this had taken place against a background of an increase in women's literacy. Daughters of the lower middle class in Wales, particularly those of ministers of the Gospel, were becoming well-educated teachers or lecturers who felt that it was their mission to share their advantages with their less privileged sisters for the benefit of the nation at large. The ideal of the enlightened 'Cymraes' had certainly become more lively.

Essentially, however, the image of the woman of Wales projected by the women's periodicals had not changed. The renewed emphasis on motherhood during the latter years of the nineteenth century ensured that women's role as mothers at home remained central. Those girls and women who did not conform to the Nonconformist way of life, centred as it was on Sunday school and chapel activities and values, were not considered to be true 'Cymruesau' (Welshwomen). Indeed, to a considerable extent the image of the ideal 'Cymraes' had become a reality. There were many women, including those of the working class, who were living up to that ideal; reading the Bible and other standard literature, educating their children in morality and religion, participating in chapel and related activities, and safeguarding the future of the Welsh language (considered to be

Wales's bulwark against moral degeneration). The continuing popularity of the chapels in Welsh Wales in particular, and the growth of the temperance movement provided a mass army of true 'Cymruesau' who were given the opportunity (though limited) to organize and take collective responsibility (see Chapter 6). Further-more, it could be argued (though this needs to be borne out by further research) that the perpetuation of the Welsh ideal of womanhood, with its emphasis on the preservation of the mother tongue and the upholding of the character of the nation, was relevant to the growth of Welsh national consciousness from the 1880s onwards, though the relationship between Welsh and British nationality, and women's dual role as mothers of the children both of Wales and of the British Empire (with all that implied) is a field as yet unexplored by historians of Wales. The fact that both the Welsh language and Nonconformity were, by the First World War, entering a period of decline in several parts of Wales also has a bearing on any further discussion of the image of the ideal 'Cymraes' and its reality.

Nineteenth-century Welsh women's periodicals, being products of the Nonconformist Wales of the period, portray only the women of that ideology. Future research into the historical inheritance of the women of Wales must lead us to search for those women who were part of the other, less documented Wales. It should also recognize that the Nonconformist ideal, while eulogizing the respectable and virtuous 'Cymraes', also confined her to her separate sphere in the home and within the chapel. In the latter she was also subordinate in that she could not become an elder or deacon, or indeed take up the ministry — Cranogwen was one of the few women lay preachers, but was refused permission to preach from the pulpit. If the nineteenth-century 'Cymraes' had, by 1900, become the kind of woman that Ieuan Gwynedd had hoped to create in 1850, the new horizons which had been opened up to her were certainly not infinite.

*Bibliographical note*

The main sources for this chapter are the women's periodicals themselves, namely *Y Gymraes* (*The Welshwoman*), 1850–1, *Y Frythones* (*The Female Briton*), 1879–91 and *Y Gymraes*, 1896–1934; together with two journals with which two of the above were amalgamated, *Y Tywysydd a'r Gymraes* (*The Guide and the Welsh-woman*), 1852–77 and *Cyfaill yr Aelwyd* (*The Home Companion*), 1891–4. For information as to their publication and circulation see Ifano Jones, *Printing and Printers in Wales and Monmouthshire* (Cardiff, William Lewis Ltd., 1925) and Catherine Evans, 'The rise and progress of the periodical press in Wales up to 1860' (University of Wales MA thesis, Bangor, 1926).

The debate on morality and education which gave rise to the first women's periodical in Wales can be found in the *Cardiff and Merthyr Guardian* for 1848 and in the works of Evan Jones ('Ieuan Gwynedd') referred to in full in note 3 below. See also Thomas Phillips, *Wales* (London, John W. Parker, 1849) and various Welsh-language denominational periodicals of the time, in particular, *Seren Gomer* and *Y Diwygiwr*. For readers of Welsh, the latter, together with other Welsh journals and newspapers, for example, *Y Traethodydd* and *Baner ac Amserau Cymru*, provide an insight into the religious and social background of the period, while other readers might consult works which illustrate the central role of Nonconformity in Victorian Wales, for example, Ieuan Gwynedd Jones, *Explorations and Explanations: Essays in the Social History of Victorian Wales* (Llandysul, Gwasg Gomer, 1981) and *Communities: Essays in the Social History of Victorian Wales* (Llandysul, Gwasg Gomer, 1987).

Welsh material on nineteenth-century ideology and the role of women remains scarce; see for example, Deirdre Beddoe, 'Towards a Welsh women's history', *Llafur* 3 No.2 (1981). The research of English and American authors has therefore been invaluable, for example, Martha Vicinus, *Suffer and Be Still: Women in the Victorian Age* (Bloomington, Indiana University Press, 1972); Deborah Gorham, *The Victorian Girl and the Feminine Ideal* (London, Croom Helm, 1982) and Sara Delamont and Lorna Duffin (eds.), *The Nineteenth-Century Woman: Her Cultural and Physical World* (London, Croom Helm, 1978). A useful volume for comparative purposes is Janet Horowitz Murray, *Strong-Minded Women* (Harmondsworth, Penguin, 1984). For an introduction to the subject in Wales see 'Gwragedd a grym yn y ganrif ddiwethaf', in *Y Traethodydd*, 1986; Ceridwen Lloyd-Morgan, 'Anturiaethau'r Gymraes', in *Y Casglwr*, 16 (March 1982); John Stevens Cabot Abbott, *Y Fam Gartref*, 2nd edition (Llanelli, Rees a Thomas, 1836); R. Tudur Jones, *Coroni'r Fam Frenhines: Y Ferch a'r Fam yn Llenyddiaeth Oes Fictoria, 1835–60* (Dinbych, Gwasg Gee, 1976);

Hywel Teifi Edwards, *Codi'r Hen Wlad yn ei Hôl, 1850–1914*
(Llandysul, Gwasg Gomer, 1989); and the work of W. Gareth Evans
listed in note 11 below.

*Notes to Chapter 3*

1.  *Y Gymraes*, January 1850. The Welsh word for Welshwoman is
    *Cymraes*. This becomes *Gymraes* when preceded by the definite article
    due to mutation rules.
2.  *Report of the Commissioners Appointed to Inquire into the State of
    Education in Wales* (870), XXVII (London, 1847).
3.  Evan Jones, *The Dissent and Morality of Wales: With Two Letters to the
    Right Honourable Lord John Russell, on the Minutes of Council in their
    bearing on Wales* (Swansea, E. Griffiths, 1847); *Facts, Figures and
    Statements in Illustration of the Dissent and Morality of Wales: An
    Appeal to the English People* (London, Miall and Cockshaw, 1849); *A
    Vindication of the Educational and Moral Condition of Wales in Reply to
    William Williams Esq. late MP for Coventry* (Llandovery, W. Rees,
    1848). See also *The Principality* and *Cardiff and Merthyr Guardian*, 1848.
4.  *Report . . . into the State of Education*, op. cit., Pt. II, 56–7.
5.  *Y Gymraes*, August 1900; *Minutes of the Committee of Council with
    Appendices: Report of Mr Seymour Tremenheere on the State of
    Elementary Education in the Mining Districts of South Wales* (182), XI
    (1839–40); *Report of the Royal Commission Appointed to Inquire into the
    Employment of Children (Mines)* (382), XVII (1842); *Report of the
    Commissioner Appointed to Inquire into the State of the Population in the
    Mining Districts* (737), XXIV (1846).
6.  Thomas Stephens, 'Agwedd bresennol llenyddiaeth Gymraeg', *Y Wawr*,
    August 1851, 38; Catherine Evans 'The rise and progress of the
    periodical press in Wales up to 1860' (University of Wales MA thesis,
    Bangor 1926); also J. Williams, 'Llenoriaeth Hirwaun', *Y Diwygiwr*,
    September 1851, 178–9.
7.  R. Tudur Jones, *Coroni'r Fam Frenhines: Y Ferch a'r Fam, yn
    Llenyddiaeth Oes Fictoria 1835–60* (Dinbych, Gwasg Gee, 1976); Hywel
    Teifi Edwards, 'Cymru lân, Cymru lonydd', in Hywel Teifi Edwards,
    *Codi'r Hen Wlad yn ei Hôl, 1850–1914* (Llandysul, Gwasg Gomer,
    1989).
8.  *Eisteddfod Gwent a Dyfed 1834: Y Traethawd Buddugol ar y Buddioldeb a
    Ddeillia oddi wrth gadwedigaeth yr Iaith Gymraeg a Dullwisgoedd Cymru
    gan Gwenynen Gwent* (Caerdydd, W. Bird, 1836).
9.  *Y Gymraes*, March 1850.
10. Ibid., January 1850.
11. William Gareth Evans, 'Secondary and higher education for girls and
    women in Wales 1847–1920 (University of Wales Ph.D. thesis,
    Aberystwyth, 1987); W. Gareth Evans, 'Addysgu mwy na hanner y
    genedl: yr ymgyrch i hyrwyddo addysg y ferch yng Nghymru Oes

Fictoria', in Geraint H. Jenkins (ed.), *Cof Cenedl IV: Ysgrifau ar Hanes Cymru* (Llandysul, Gwasg Gomer, 1989), 93–119; W. Gareth Evans, *Education and Female Emancipation: The Welsh Experience 1847–1914* (Cardiff, University of Wales Press, 1990).

12. L. J. Williams and Dot Jones, 'Women at work in nineteenth century Wales', *Llafur*, 3 No.3 (1982), 20–32.

13. David Edwards, 'Nodweddion brodorol dosbarth gweithiol Gwent a Morgannwg', *Y Traethodydd* (1856), 460.

14. Lewis William Lewis ('Llew Llwyfo'), *Huw Huws neu y Llafurwr Cymreig* . . . (Caernarfon, Cwmni'r Wasg Genedlaethol Gymreig, 1860), 22.

15. *Y Gymraes*, December 1851.

16. *Y Tywysydd a'r Gymraes*, March 1853.

17. See Chapter 6, also *Y Bywgraffiadur Cymreig hyd 1940* (Llundain, Cymdeithas Anrhydeddus y Cymmrodorion, 1953), 780; Gerallt Jones, *Cranogwen: Portread Newydd* (Llandysul, Gwasg Gomer, 1981); David Glanaman Jones, *Cofiant Cranogwen* (Caernarfon, Undeb Dirwestol Merched y De, 1932).

18. William Gareth Evans, op. cit. (1987).

19. *Y Frythones*, January 1884.

20. Ibid., February 1881.

21. Ibid., January 1884.

22. Ibid., May 1881.

23. Angela V. John, *By the Sweat of Their Brow: Women Workers at Victorian Coal Mines* (London, Croom Helm, 1980), 141.

24. *Y Frythones*, January 1884.

25. Ibid., March, April, May 1889.

26. *Y Gymraes*, October 1919, 147–9.

27. Ibid., December 1922.

28. C. K. Evans, 'At fy chwiorydd', in T. Stephens (ed.), *Cymru Heddyw ac Yforu* (Caerdydd, *Western Mail*, 1908), 151.

All spellings in the quotations from Welsh in this chapter are in their original form.

# 4

# 'Do Not Go Gentle into that Good Night'?
# Women and Suicide in Carmarthenshire,
# c.1860–1920

## RUSSELL DAVIES

> For here lies the point: if I drown myself wittingly, it argues an act, and
> an act hath three branches — it is to act, to do, and to perform. Argal,
> she drowned herself wittingly.[1]

Thus the First Clown in *Hamlet*, in his burlesque of the arguments in
the coroner's court over Ophelia's death, described the theatricality
of suicidal death.[2] This, probably the most famous example in English
literature of death by suicide, has served to colour the perception and
imagery of suicide until the present century. Ophelia's death as
performance, of suicide as 'a great work of art ... prepared within the
silence of the heart'[3] had, as we shall see in this article, its
verisimilitude.

The Victorians with their passion for statistics and their acute, if
occasionally sentimental, sensitivity to the plight of the victims of
society frequently noted with concern the increase in the incidences of
mental breakdowns and suicide.[4] Insanity and suicide were regarded
by many Victorians as the unfortunate by-products of modern
society.[5] In *Suicide: An Essay on Comparative Moral Statistics*
published in 1899, Henry Morselli claimed irrefutable proof of a
'terrible increase in suicide [in] almost all the civilized countries of
Europe, and of the New World'.[6] His views were supported by other
influential writers such as Henry Maudsley and S. A. K. Strahan. The
latter, in *Suicide and Insanity*, regarded suicide as

> due to two causes: first, because the increase of wealth has not
> beneficially affected the great mass of people; and second, because
> many of the people are deteriorating from city life, unhealthy
> occupations, and the wear and tear of modern life generally.[7]

The person most exposed to the pressures of modern life was, arguably, the male. In the Victorian world where 'separate spheres' have been perceived as operating for male and female, women were insulated from the pressures of daily life. Hers was the world of the hearth and the home whilst his was the world of work. But, although the Victorians accepted the changes and pressures of modern life as causes of insanity and suicide, nevertheless their imagery of these distressing realities was feminine.[8] In an article in the *New Review* in 1894, William Ferero warned that because of their more unstable nature and constitution women were particularly vulnerable to insanity and suicide. This identification of mental instability with feminine imagery is perhaps not so surprising if we can accept that in a male-dominated society, masculinity must be established as the dominant operational norm for the whole of society. Other expressions of sexual identity must be construed as differences, divergences or opposites to this norm. Likewise sanity has to be defined as the norm and anything discrepant from it as the non- or the in-sane.

Ferero, as did many of his contemporaries, worked on the assumption and the expectation that suicide, like madness, was a 'female malady'. Elaine Showalter has shown that because women were statistically over-represented amongst people housed in institutions for the mentally ill, they were believed to be more vulnerable to madness.[9] By the mid nineteenth century there were two strains to the argument linking women and suicide. The first argued that, because more women were confined for insanity than men, and suicide was a direct product of insanity, therefore more women committed suicide than men. In suicide, as in several other areas of domestic and social life, the Victorians believed what they chose to believe. The second strain was based on even less empirical evidence and wholly upon a crude social Darwinism. Women were lesser beings. Resisting suicidal impulses required will-power and courage. Women were not thought to possess these qualities in sufficient measure. Consequently they were more prone to suicide than were men. By the end of the nineteenth century these prejudices had transformed into beliefs. S. A. K. Strahan was convinced that women were the weaker contenders in the struggle for existence and even as enlightened a figure as Havelock Ellis offered similar arguments to explain women's predisposition to suicide.[10]

Wood engraving by George du Maurier (1834–1896) from *Once a Week*,
Vol. 7 (1862).
(By permission of University College of Wales, Aberystwyth.)

These crude arguments are reflected in the visual arts of the Victorian period. Prints, woodcuts, book illustrations and paintings of the solitary brooding female, often alongside the river-bank, abound.[11] The visual arts present a poignant tableau of each of the stages of a young girl's journey to her watery grave. The first step was her lonely melancholic contemplation of her death alongside the river-bank. Amongst the most famous in this genre was the illustration by Hablot K. Browne (Phiz) 'The River', for Charles Dickens's *David Copperfield*. In the portrait Martha Endell is shown with a toe in the water against the background of a ruined vessel, and a cloud-strewn, moonlit sky. The second stage — the leap into the waters — was rendered the more theatrical the higher the pedestal the girl had to leap from. Gustave Doré began the tradition with his *The Bridge of Sighs*. Though Doré's young lady merely ponders her fate, other artists concentrated on the girl's plunge of despair. Probably the most famous is George Cruikshank's illustration in his series *The Drunkard's Children* entitled 'The Poor Girl, Homeless, Friendless, Deserted, Destitute, and Gin Mad Commits Self-Murder'. Dramatically the girl, swooning, throws herself to the still waters below. But the moment of highest theatricality was the discovery of the girl's body in the water. This moment of frozen tragedy was most famously captured in a painting that reinforces the literary imagery of femininity and suicide, John Everett Millais' *Ophelia*. Here the corpse, decorated with flowers, mouth imploring, arms outreaching, floats silently to a flowery glade.[12]

The assertion of the masculine as the norm was reflected in Victorian popular literature. Here, apart from the metaphysical posturings of Oscar Wilde's Dorian Gray and Lord Arthur Savile, the suicide is often portrayed as a young girl, scorned by a lover, abandoned to the mercy of a cruel world; unable to cope on her own, she takes her own life.[13] Very often the girl is portrayed alongside a stream, for with the grisly theatricality of Ophelia's death, death by drowning has associations with the feminine and the irrational, since water is the organic symbol of woman's fluidity: blood, milk, tears.[14] Contemporary Welsh literature also throws up these images. The plangent song by 'Llew o'r Wern', 'Yr Eneth Gadd ei Gwrthod' ('The Girl Who Was Spurned')[15] is a mournful reflective song sung by a young girl who reveals her personal plight at the riverside:

> Mae bys gwaradwydd ar fy ôl
> Yn nodi fy ngwendidau,

A llanw 'mywyd wedi ei droi
A'i gladdu dan y tonnau;
Ar allor chwant aberthwyd fi,
Do, collais fy morwyndod,
A dyna'r achos pam yr wyf
Fi heno wedi 'ngwrthod.[16]

(The finger of shame follows me
Depicting my weaknesses,
The tide of my life has turned,
And is buried under the waves;
On the altar of lust I was martyred,
Yes, I lost my virginity,
And that's the reason why
Tonight I am spurned.)

The song not only reveals the operation of the 'double standard'[17] of Victorian morality which allowed young men the freedom of their senses — a freedom denied to young women — but also the masculine notion that women could not survive without a man. After her long river-bank reflection this young Welsh damsel in distress emulated Ophelia. The poem ends with a tragic last verse which recounts the experience of many girls who grappled with their terminal inner loneliness:

A bore drannoeth cafwyd hi
Yn nyfroedd oer yr afon,
A darn o bapur yn ei llaw
Ac arno'r ymadroddion:
'Gwnewch imi fedd mewn unig fan,
Na chodwch faen na chofnod
I nodi'r fan lle gorwedd llwch
Yr eneth gadd ei gwrthod.'[18]

(The following morning she was found
In the cold waters of the river,
With a piece of paper in her hand,
And on it the inscription:
'Make my grave in a lonely place,
Without a headstone or inscription,
To mark the place where lies the dust
Of the girl who was spurned.')

Only a crass cynic would question the longevity of the suicide note after a night immersed in the river. But these tales from the river-bank were the result of a sympathetic attempt by Victorians to understand the spiritual winter of the suicide.

Suicide, even when publicly committed, is the most private and impenetrable of human acts. The historian is presented with the insurmountable problem that the participants usually leave behind them no written records, only a rippling pool of regrets and temporary sadness, gradually wiped away by time and forgetfulness, as if they had never existed, or perhaps lingering a little more in the conscience of a friend or relative.[19] Statistics do not help the historian to penetrate these resonant silences. Throughout the nineteenth century death by suicide was recorded by the Registrar-General in the general categories of 'Violent Death' and 'Uncertified Causes'.[20] The problem is compounded, for as P. E. H. Hair has argued, 'suicide cannot be subject to statistical calculation, since all too many suicides are not reported as such'.[21] From 1911, however, suicide was identified as a cause of death by the Registrar-General, and analysis of these figures to 1919 from Carmarthenshire enables us to discern general patterns in the suicide rate.[22]

The ancient administrative county of Carmarthenshire has been chosen because it offers the historian a unique bridgehead from which the profound economic and social forces which transformed Wales at the beginning of the twentieth century can be observed.[23] Carmarthenshire, the largest administrative county in Wales, experienced not only the bitter and harrowing experiences of rural communities but also rapid industrialization and urbanization and their accompanying social dislocation. By 1911 the population of the county had risen to 160,406. But, despite the concentration of large numbers of people in the eastern parts of the county, in the area around Llanelli in particular, the county as a whole maintained a balance between rural and urban which is rarely seen in other communities. In 1911, 52.5 per cent of the population was concentrated in fifteen urban parishes where the industrial activity centred upon anthracite coal-mining and tinplate manufacture. The remaining 47.5 per cent was located in rural parishes where agriculture and its subsidiary activities gave employment. Industrialization had the effect of moving men across the county from west to east, in marked contrast with the advice of Americans as to which direction young men should go. An analysis at the parish level reveals that, while in the rural parishes there was a

ratio over the period 1888–1921 of 870 men for every 1,000 women, in
the industrial parishes of the south-east the ratio was 1,023 men to
1,000 women.[24] The difference was not as great as it was in some other
industrial communities because the industrial areas of Carmarthenshire, and particularly the manufacture of tinplate and wool,
provided employment for women. Such facts are conveniently
forgotten in the dominant mythologies of the worlds of separate
spheres. Carmarthenshire is consequently a good area in which the
interrelationships between rural and urban, male and female can be
studied.

The first conclusion to draw from the Registrar-General's statistics
is that suicide was primarily a feature of the rural areas of the county.
During the period 1911–19 rural districts of the county accounted for
66 per cent of the deaths recorded in the county. Of the suicides, 16.9
per cent occurred in Carmarthen Rural District, 15.1 per cent in
Llandovery and 13.4 per cent in Llandeilo. The lowest rates occurred
in Llandeilo Urban District, where 0.8 per cent was recorded, and in
Kidwelly Municipal Borough only 1.7 per cent. The aggregate
average for the urban districts of the county is 4.7 per cent, that of the
rural districts 9.7 per cent of deaths by suicide. The other major
conclusion which we can draw is that suicide, despite the literary
portrayal of the melancholic brooding female, was largely a male
phenomenon.[25] Between 1911 and 1919, 69.6 per cent of deaths by
suicide recorded in the rural districts and 66.7 per cent of suicides in
the urban districts of Carmarthenshire were committed by males. In
both the rural and urban districts male suicides outnumbered the
female. In Carmarthen Rural District the rate of male suicide was
63.1 per cent of all suicides; in Llanelli Rural District 81.8 per cent and
in Llanelli Urban District 71.4 per cent. Only in the Municipal
Borough of Llandovery and the Rural District of Llandeilofawr do
female suicides outnumber male.

We can also deduce that people in mid life were more apt to commit
suicide than any other age group. Suicide of people in the age group of
forty-five to sixty-four represent 48.5 per cent of the deaths by suicide
in the rural districts of the county and 47.2 per cent in the urban
districts. The next age group, aged between twenty-five and forty-
four, represent 25.7 per cent of suicide deaths in rural districts and
36.1 per cent in the urban districts. People aged under twenty-five
represent 15.1 per cent of suicide deaths in rural districts and 18.3 in
urban areas. Those aged between fifteen and twenty-five comprise

10.6 per cent of suicide deaths in rural districts and 11.1 per cent in the urban districts.

These statistics, however, can tell us little of the motives which enabled people to answer a fundamental question of theology and to go gently into that good night.[26] As the Coroners' records for the period under discussion are not available, the historian has to rely on the reports of suicide which appear in local newspapers in order to study the forces that drive an individual to desperate action. A survey of the newspapers has revealed over 260 reported cases of suicide committed in Carmarthenshire between 1900 and 1919. The survey reinforces the general conclusions which we have noted above regarding the age, sex and geographical distribution of suicide. It appears to have been primarily a middle-aged, male phenomenon most frequent in rural areas. It also reinforces P. E. H. Hair's assertion that suicide in the period was under-recorded in official statistics.

The main value of the survey, however, lies in the details which it gives of the lives of the individuals involved. The reports give details of the proceedings at the Coroner's Court. The evidence is not, of course, that of the participants but that of friends, lovers, relatives and eyewitnesses, who pieced together the detritus of the last days of a truncated life. One often feels sympathy for those who were left behind. Many were very young and for them the discovery of the dead, mutilated or hanging body of a parent must have been a profound and enduring experience. The historian can only sympathize with the five-year-old who discovered his mother hanging in a toilet, and the ten-year-old who ran to tell his grandparents that his mother was attempting to drown herself and his younger brother.[27] Stunned, witnesses frequently did not know who to turn to or what to do. The bewilderment can be seen in February 1916 when a Tregaron inquest heard that, after discovering the body of Private David Davies of the Welsh Guards hanging in an outhouse, John Williams and his master 'sat by the fire for a while before cutting it down'.[28] Was their action based on a conscious desire to rest a little before the toil of the day and restore strength to the living, or bewilderment and revulsion at Private Davies's brutal act?

Love, rebuffed or scorned, the classic suicide motive of the girl in contemporary literature, had parallels in real life. In 1917, Maggie Morgan threw herself under a GWR express train after her boyfriend 'finished with her'.[29] In the inquest into the death of Margaret Evans aged twenty-seven from Llandybïe, a servant girl at the New Inn,

Llanfihangel-ar-arth, told the court that, shortly before her death, she had heard Margaret quarrelling with a local farmer's son about the paternity of her child. Despite her brother's offers of help Margaret took her own life by hanging herself.[30] Margaret Williams, a cook, poisoned herself, and Muriel Morgan drowned herself in the Tywi following similar experiences.[31] David Davies, a farmer, found his daughter and her baby poisoned in their bedroom in November 1916. At the inquest he poignantly and painfully recalled that she normally spoke in her sleep, but that night she had been quiet and his suspicions had been aroused. She had twice attempted to take out an Affiliation Order for the child's paternity at the Llandeilo Police Court. Twice she failed. Strychnine ended her fears. At the inquest, the Coroner, Dr Thomas Walters, remarked:

> Who ever the man is who led her astray, I doubt if he will have comfortable feelings hereafter. It must have been a terrible strain on her.[32]

As in Llew o'r Wern's 'Yr Eneth Gadd ei Gwrthod', the fear of living with the stigma and shame of a love-child proved too severe a burden for her sensitive soul. But men too felt the wounds of love. James Evans, a farm servant, 'worried over a girl', hanged himself at Cae'r-bryn, Pen-y-groes, in January 1905.[33] Henry Thomas, a collier, drowned himself in Pwlldu in the River Morlais when a Paternity Order was awarded against him.[34]

Those who survived the trials and tribulations of courtship found life no easier when married. Mary Lewis took carbolic poison when her husband left her.[35] Mary Davies, a farmer's wife, committed suicide when she and her husband separated in March 1905.[36] Thomas Rees Richards committed suicide rather than appear in court for arrears of £30 on a Separation Order awarded to his wife.[37]

Some women in the nineteenth century appear to have taken quite literally the instructions in the marriage vows to obey. Catherine Harris informed a court that she had attempted suicide because Dai (her husband) 'told me to'.[38] Having just lost a child, Mary Ellen Davies of Pen-clawdd murdered her three daughters, aged between four and two, and then committed suicide in an upstairs bedroom.[39]

The inability to cope with adverse economic fortunes also features prominently in the reasons witnesses gave to inquests for the suicide of a friend or acquaintance. Charles Griffiths cut his throat with a razor because of his worries about his unemployment.[40] Arthur

Williams, a bookmaker, committed suicide in July 1907 because of his financial problems.[41] George Blake, agent to the Stradey Estate, cut his throat in a greenhouse when his employer told him that his services were no longer required as the son would manage the estate.[42] David Bowen, a publican and timber merchant, a man, according to witnesses, with few problems, hanged himself with a horse's harness after he had failed to sell the animal.[43] John Jones of Llangynnwr, a coachman, committed suicide when he was sacked by his employer as the result of the purchase of a car.[44]

The First World War had a profound psychological impact on the home front as well as on the soldiers and this is reflected in Carmarthenshire suicide cases. Soldiers suffering from 'shell-shock'[45] and hysteria — which had previously been considered peculiar to women — committed suicide with distressing regularity between August 1914 and November 1918.[46] Receipt of a letter confirming that the King required a person's service in the trenches was a frequent trigger to suicide. Henry Ridgen, having volunteered, reconsidered his willingness to serve and attempted to commit suicide at Llanarthne on receipt of such an invitation in August 1915.[47] Ernest Lloyd Morgan, a court registrar and nephew of the poet and lawyer, Sir Lewis Morris, was more successful. He 'shot his face off' after being passed fit to serve his King and country.[48] But it was not only those directly involved in the fighting who found the pressures of the war too great to bear. Ruth Williams, worried about her sons in the colours, hanged herself in an outhouse, and Ann Williams, who had two sons on the Western Front, cut her throat.[49] When her husband Frank returned to the war in August 1917, Elizabeth Mundy drowned her youngest son and attempted to drown herself.[50]

Religion, one of the dominant forces in Welsh society in the nineteenth century, often intensified mental instability. The evidence of suicide cases confirms this. In the millenarian excitement of that remarkable year 1905 when the Welsh people underwent one of their periodic religious awakenings, the Medical Superintendent at the Joint Counties Lunatic Asylum in Carmarthen reported on the high incidence of suicide amongst the patients and noted:

> sixteen cases were admitted as a result of the emotional influences of, in this instance, a religious kind of which their hereditary unstable natures were unable to withstand. Religious emotion being more massive and more intense, and having so to say a wider striking area

than other causes of emotion, is more apt to cause mental breakdowns, and more apt to tinge mental disorder than other factors.[51]

Religious factors also had longevity. Seven years later, in 1912, in Glanmôr Terrace in Llanelli, Anthony Thomas, one of the 'religious maniacs' sent to the asylum in 1906, hanged himself.[52] In 1919, Revd John Crwys Evans committed suicide after prolonged depression following the death of his son.[53] Revd John Thomas of Capel Isaac, suffering from indigestion but apparently no other problems, hanged himself in the garden shed.[54] But religion itself not only coloured the problems of an individual, it created new fears. Fears of God's revenge, of the fallen nature of man, of Hell, of the Day of Judgement, were real anxieties for a large number of individuals. William Morgan, a forty-year-old collier from Llanarthne, advised to take a change of air by his doctor, walked to Dryslwyn Castle where he jumped into the Tywi. Dragged out five hundred yards downstream, he insisted that his sins were unpardonable. He was admitted to the asylum.[55] David Davies, a master tailor from Llanarthne, attempted suicide the week before he successfully drowned himself in the Gwendraeth. On the first occasion he was prevented by his wife's persuasion that it was the Devil who was persuading him to go to the pool near his home to drown himself.[56]

In the majority of suicide cases the evidence which the historian has to consider is the recollections of witnesses. Only infrequently do we encounter the words of an individual who had wrestled with the 'Savage God' and resigned herself or himself to death.[57] Despite the plots of melodramatic Victorian novels, suicide notes were infrequent. The note left by Thomas Hambury Powell tells us much about the motives that drove him to his death in Llanelli Dock and the forces which operated in his society:

> I did this rash thing because of drink. It forced me to do it, and I must make an end to myself in this way. The snares of death compressed me round about, and the pains of hell got hold upon me. O Thou Great and Merciful God, wilt thou forgive and pardon my sins that I have sinned against Thee, and for this wicked thing that I have done — Dear Father, Mother and Sister, will you forgive me for this wicked thing I have done. Do not let it trouble you for I shall have forgiveness in the Lord. I hope all the young men of Llanelli will give up the evil drinking, and take a warning from me, dear friends.[58]

The motives that we have considered are but a few of the reasons which compelled individuals to end their lives. One factor from which there could be no escape was one's genetic inheritance. In studying suicide, as in the study of mental disorder in general, one notices the predisposition of certain families to suicide. In April 1913, the *South Wales Press* reported the third death by suicide of three brothers.[59] In 1893 Jane Davies of Tyllwyd Farm, Llanegwad, followed her sister's example and committed suicide by hanging.[60] The plethora of motives is mirrored in the enormous variety of methods chosen — hanging from trees, bacon hooks, in toilets, outhouses and bedrooms, drowning in rivers, streams, docks, baths and ponds, and, surprisingly frequently, the death of women in fresh-water casks, taking strychnine, liquid ammonia, acid and other poisons, swallowing broken glass, shooting, cutting one's throat with a razor or a blunt table knife, even decapitation underneath an express train.[61] Suicide is a random phenomenon that corresponds to the infinite variety of motives which drive human actions. Each individual's death had its own idiosyncrasy, its own peculiarities. In Wilkie Collins's *No Name* (1862), the main character, Magdalen Vanstone, sits before a window looking out onto the river. She decides to count the ships which pass and makes her decision to commit suicide or not depend upon whether an odd or an even number of ships has passed in a set time. In her version of Russian roulette she allows her will to yield to chance in deciding her fatal action. Other people were more determined in ending their disenchanted worlds in south-west Wales.

*Bibliographical note*

The major sources used in this chapter are the newspapers circulating in south Wales at the turn of the twentieth century. They provide detailed reports of inquests and the proceedings at the Coroner's Court. The reports flesh out the details of the human experience of suicide in a way which is unavailable in the transcripts of the proceedings of the Coroner's Court kept in the Record Office. The statistics on causes of death contained within the annual reports of the Registrar-General of Births, Marriages and Deaths provide guides as to the incidence and geographical distribution of suicide. Useful contemporary works are Charles Williams, *Religion and Insanity* (London, Kegan Paul, 1908) and *Insanity: Its Causes and*

*Prevention* (London, Kegan Paul, 1908); Henry Morselli, *Suicide: An Essay on Comparative Moral Statistics* (London, Kegan Paul, 1899) and S. A. D. Strahan, *Suicide and Insanity: A Physiological and Sociological Study* (London, Swan Sonnenschein, 1893). Modern historians have begun to unravel the complexities of suicide. Pre-eminent are Olive Anderson's superlative *Suicide in Victorian and Edwardian England* (Oxford, Oxford University Press, 1987) and Barbara T. Gates, *Victorian Suicide: Mad Crimes and Sad Stories* (Princeton, Princeton University Press, 1988), both of which contain a substantial bibliography.

## Notes for Chapter 4

1. William Shakespeare, *Hamlet*, V.i. 9–13.
2. On the influence of Ophelia see Bridget G. Lyn, 'The iconography of Ophelia', *English Literary History*, 44 (1977), 65, 70–2, and Carroll Camden, 'On Opehlia's madness', *Shakespeare Quarterly*, 15 (1965), 254.
3. Albert Camus quoted in A. Alvarez, *The Savage God: A Study of Suicide*, 3rd edn. (Harmondsworth, Penguin Books, 1979), 121.
4. For a brief discussion see Tom Davies, 'Bedlam yng Nghymru — datblygiad seiciatreg yn y bedwaredd ganrif ar bymtheg', *Transactions of the Honourable Society of Cymmrodorion* (1980), 105–22.
5. See for example D. H. Tuke, *Chapters in the History of the Insane in the British Isles* (London, Dawson's, 1882) and Videa Skultaus, *Madness and Morals: Ideas on Insanity in the Nineteenth Century* (London, Routledge and Kegan Paul, 1975).
6. Henry Morselli, *Suicide: An Essay on Comparative Moral Statistics* (London, Kegan Paul, 1899), 15.
7. S. A. K. Strahan, *Suicide and Insanity* (London, Swan Sonnenschein, 1893), 123.
8. On the sexual segregation of Victorian and Edwardian life see Jane Lewis (ed.), *Labour and Love: Women's Experience of Home and Family, 1850–1940* (Oxford, Basil Blackwell, 1986) and Judith L. Newton *et al.*, *Sex and Class in Women's History* (London, Routledge and Kegan Paul, 1983).
9. Elaine Showalter, *The Female Malady: Women, Madness and English Culture, 1830–1980* (London, Virago Press, 1987), 167–94.
10. S. A. K. Strahan, op. cit., 179.
11. I am grateful to Mr Robert Meyrick of the Art Department at the University College of Wales, Aberystwyth, for access to the College's extensive collection of visual images of the nineteenth century.

12. For a wider discussion of the importance of Victorian art see Christopher Wood, *Victorian Panorama: Paintings of Victorian Life* (London, Faber and Faber, 1976).

13. For a useful discussion of suicide in Victorian literature see John Stokes, *In the Nineties* (Hemel Hempstead, Harvester Wheatsheaf, 1989).

14. For these associations see J. G. Frazer, *The Golden Bough: A Study in Magic and Religion* (special abridged edn., London, Macmillan, 1983).

15. I am grateful to Mr E. G. Millward of the Welsh Department at the University College of Wales, Aberystwyth, for advice and sources on suicide in Welsh popular literature of the nineteenth century.

16. Llew o'r Wern, 'Yr Eneth Gadd ei Gwrthod'; the text of the song is given in full in E. G. Millward, *Ceinion y Gân: Detholiad o Ganeuon Poblogaidd Oes Victoria* (Llandysul, Gomer, 1983), 30–1.

17. For the double standard see Keith Thomas, 'The double standard', *Journal of the History of Ideas*, 20, No.2 (1959), 195–216.

18. Llew o'r Wern in Millward, op. cit.

19. Olive Anderson, *Suicide in Victorian and Edwardian England* (Oxford, Oxford University Press, 1987), 166–73; Michael MacDonald, 'The secularisation of suicide in England 1660–1800', *Past and Present* (Spring 1986), 50–100; Richard Cobb, *Death in Paris* (Oxford, Oxford University Press, 1978).

20. Annual Reports of the Registrar for Births, Marriages and Deaths, *passim*, 1884–1911.

21. P. E. H. Hair, 'Deaths from violence in Britain: a tentative secular survey', *Population Studies*, 25 (1971), 15.

22. Russell Davies, 'A social history of Carmarthenshire, 1870–1920', unpublished University of Wales Ph.D. thesis (1989), p.141, fn.80.

23. Ibid.

24. Ibid., 161.

25. For a discussion of female suicide in literature, see Margaret Higgonet, 'Speaking silences, women's suicide', in Susan Rubin Suleiman (ed.), *The Female Body in Western Culture* (Cambridge, Mass., Harvard University Press, 1986), 68–83.

26. Albert Camus, *The Myth of Sisyphus* (Harmondsworth, Penguin, 1977).

27. *Cambrian Daily Leader*, 11 January 1917.

28. *Carmarthen Weekly Reporter*, 27 November 1909. Their reason was that they were unsure of the legal position and deemed it best to await the arrival of the police. It is interesting to note the following incident which occurs in the opening of Caradoc Evans's short story, 'The Blast of God':

Owen Tygwyn . . . was ploughing when his wife Shan came to the break in the hedge crying: 'For what you think, little man? Dai is hanging in the cowhouse. Come you now and see to him'. Owen ended the furrow and unharnessed the horse, which he led into the stable and fed with hay. Then he unravelled the knot in the rope which had choked the breath of his son Dai. (Caradoc Evans, *My People* (London, Andrew Melrose, 1915), 265. The needs of the living, especially a horse's needs, took precedence over those of the dead.)

29. *Cambrian Daily Leader*, 11 January 1917.
30. *Carmarthen Journal*, 25 March 1904.
31. *Llanelli Mercury*, 27 April 1899; *Carmarthen Weekly Reporter*, 5 November 1915; *Carmarthen Journal*, 25 March 1904; *South Wales Daily News*, 25 November 1897; *South Wales Press*, 1 December 1887.
32. *Carmarthen Weekly Reporter*, 3 November 1916.
33. *Carmarthen Journal*, 19 January 1905.
34. *South Wales Press*, 24 August 1910.
35. Ibid., 8 February 1900; *Carmarthen Journal*, 8 February 1900.
36. *South Wales Press*, 5 April 1905.
37. Ibid., 25 November 1918.
38. Ibid., 3 June 1908.
39. For other suicides linked with marital problems see ibid., 28 April 1904 and 29 May 1902; *Carmarthen Journal*, 24 October 1902.
40. *South Wales Press*, 17 December 1917.
41. Ibid., 11 July 1907.
42. Ibid., 17 January 1907.
43. Ibid., 14 June 1900.
44. *Carmarthen Weekly Reporter*, 4 June 1909.
45. For a discussion of the treatment of shell-shock and hysteria brought on by the First World War, see Elaine Showalter, *The Female Malady*, 167–94.
46. *Carmarthen Weekly Reporter*, 9 October 1914, and 1 December 1916; *South Wales Press*, 17 October 1917.
47. *Carmarthen Weekly Reporter*, 15 September 1915.
48. *South Wales Press*, 3 July 1918; *Cambrian Daily Leader*, 3 July 1918.
49. *South Wales Press*, 9 August and 18 October 1916.
50. *Carmarthen Weekly Reporter*, 17 August 1917.
51. Agenda and Minutes, Vol. 5, Joint Counties Lunatic Asylum Forty-first Annual Report, 8 January 1906. Dyfed Record Office.
52. *South Wales Press*, 10 April 1912.
53. *Carmarthen Weekly Reporter*, 4 April 1919.
54. Ibid., 6 November 1903; *South Wales Press*, 5 November 1903.
55. Ibid., 24 May 1906.
56. Ibid., 31 May 1900.
57. A. Alvarez, op. cit.
58. *South Wales Press*, 24 June 1880.
59. Ibid., 9 April 1913.
60. *Carmarthen Journal*, 13 October 1893.

61. For some of the more unusual methods of death, see ibid., 14 February 1914 (broken glass); ibid., 18 January 1906 (liquid ammonia); ibid., 7 March 1900 (hanging off a bacon hook); *Cambrian Daily Leader*, 2 November 1916 and *Carmarthen Reporter*, 24 January 1908 (strychnine).

# 5

# *Counting the Cost of Coal: Women's Lives in the Rhondda, 1881–1911*

DOT JONES

This chapter focuses on the women who were wives and mothers of south Wales coal-miners in the period before 1914. In the traditional view of the mining community, miners occupy the foreground as men engaged in dirty and dangerous work while women figure in the background as those who wait and support.[1] The aim is to correct this stereotype in two key respects. Firstly, by examining working conditions in the home, the chapter emphasizes the importance of women's unwaged service contributions to the mining industry. Secondly, by examining mortality records, the cost of domestic labour in coal-mining households is measured in terms of shortened lives. The mortality rates of women who worked in the home were higher than those of their menfolk who worked in the pit, in direct contrast to national mortality trends.

A detailed analysis of census returns and mortality figures has been undertaken for the two valleys of the Rhondda Fawr and Rhondda Fach since this central region of the coalfield experienced the most vigorous growth of population during this period. In the thirty-mile length of two narrow valleys a string of colliery communities were crammed together: Treherbert, Treorchy, Pentre, Ystrad, Llwynypia, Tonypandy, Clydach Vale, Pen-y-graig, Porth, Hafod, Ynyshir, Wattstown, Pont-y-gwaith, Tylorstown, Ferndale, Blaenllechau and Maerdy. By 1901, they were all part of an urban district with a population of 113,735, comparable to that of Preston or Halifax. More than any other region in the UK, these communities were dependent upon coal and the export of coal. In a male-dominated industry this had important implications for female employment opportunities.

'The Rhondda' has become synonymous with Welsh coal-mining in popular imagination yet the opening up of these central valleys was a comparatively late and short-lived period in the development of the south Wales coalfield and should be viewed within this wider context.

An elongated basin of coal deposits lies beneath nearly 1,000 square miles of south Wales, from Pontypool in the east to Llanelli in the west, from Ammanford and Aberdare in the north to Bridgend in the south. A narrow band of anthracite coal is separated by the Bristol Channel and reappears across south Pembrokeshire near Haverfordwest. A variety of coal types have been mined; anthracite in the more open western half of the coalfield, bituminous coal in the east, and steam coal in the central valleys of the Cynon, Rhondda, and Taff. Different types of coal are also found at different levels in the same area.

The development of the south Wales coalfield in the nineteenth century can be divided into two main phases. Before 1840, the greater proportion of output went to supply the great and small ironworks situated along the rim of the coalfield where the coal seams outcropped.[2] Then, as demand for south Wales iron declined, activity shifted towards the central valleys where steam coal was discovered at a higher level than previously realized. In response to a growing world market from the 1870s, millions of tons of coal from these central valleys were raised to fuel the reign of steam power at sea throughout the world. Steam power generated by Rhondda steam coal won the blue ribbon of the Atlantic for the *Mauretania* in 1909. It is interesting to note that, in a male-dominated industry, a woman — Lucy Thomas, the 'Mother of the Welsh Steam Coal Trade' — takes credit for the first shipment of Welsh steam coal to London.[3] By 1894 almost half UK coal exports came from south Wales and at that time south Wales steam coal played a vital role in the context of UK foreign trade because coal was Britain's only bulk export commodity.

The second phase of development after 1840 was rapid: 366,000 men and women poured into south Wales between 1851 and 1911.[4] At first the migrants came mainly from Cardiganshire, Carmarthenshire and nearby rural counties of England, as well as from the Aberdare valley where the ironworks and supplying collieries were suffering depression. Then, natural increase added to in-migration when second- and third-generation coal-miners followed their fathers and brothers into an industry which was expanding as new shafts were sunk and new seams exploited. The migration involved so many

Mrs George, the washerwoman.
(W. E. Jones Collection, National Museum of Wales.)

Welsh-speakers who might otherwise have followed the Irish to America that it gave the language a new industrial base.[5] And the values of a shared Nonconformist background provided firm social foundations for the new colliery communities.

Communities in the Rhondda and elsewhere in the south Wales coalfield shared a pattern of life and work common to all coal-mining communities. As John Benson has observed, 'perhaps in no other industry did the way in which a man earned his living have a more profound effect on the way in which he and his family lived at home'.[6] For the four out of five men who worked underground the most fundamental distinction in his day was the segregation of home/ above ground and work/below ground. Men's work below ground was hard, dirty and dangerous. Each man who worked underground depended upon his own skill and care as well as on that of others for his life as well as his livelihood. His workplace excluded all except fellow workers. The various work processes required skill and strength. Each worker had a large measure of control over his work practice. As a result miners became proud, independent men yet still strongly bonded together by mutual dependency. These values were articulated above ground as well as below. Mining communities were fiercely cohesive and neighbourly with help always at hand in times of trouble.

The mutual dependency of the workplace helped create leisure patterns segregated by gender which reinforced women's primary identification with the home. For miners' wives and mothers, there was total integration of home and work. The woman was always 'at work', and miners' wives faced difficult working conditions. Income was uncertain, families were large and the occupation of husbands, sons and lodgers created a heavy burden of domestic work.

Fear of the death or injury of a family bread-winner was ever present. The south Wales coalfield had the worst safety record in Britain. Strata here were subject to lateral 'squeeze' so that sudden roof falls continually picked off men and boys in ones and twos. In the more gassy, 'fiery' eastern half, occasional calamitous explosion was a more publicized cause of death. Twenty-three colliery accidents claimed over one hundred lives each in England and Wales between 1850 and 1914; no less than eleven of these occurred in south Wales, four of them in the Rhondda valleys.[7]

Difficult geological conditions also had an economic effect. Coal seams in the south Wales coalfield were not as continuous as in other

Table 1. Proportion of men to women and of married women in the population

| 1891 | Males/100 females age 15–34 | % married or widowed women aged 20–24 |
|---|---|---|
| England and Wales | 93 | 29.9 |
| Durham | 105 | 43.3 |
| Monmouth | 116 | 40.2 |
| Glamorgan | 120 | 42.4 |
| Rhondda | 167 | 59.1 |

Source: Census 1891

coalfields. Faults and folding made ease of working unpredictable and deeper shafts were needed to reach the better-quality steam coal. As a result of geological difficulties, output per man in the south Wales coalfield was below that in other coalfields and, indeed, declined over time. In an industry where labour costs accounted for a large part of final production costs, this in turn meant additional and increasing pressure to keep wages down and an increasing source of friction in industrial relations.[8]

Although wage rates were high, earnings were uncertain. Quite apart from the daily lottery of injury, piece-rate payment meant continuous uncertainty. Fluctuating coal demand resulted in periodic lay-offs or short-time working. Geological difficulties could restrict output and therefore earnings. Industrial disputes, strikes and lock-outs added to uncertainty about earnings. A miner's wife did not know from one pay-day to the next what the household income might be.[9]

Demographic characteristics also set mining communities apart. The typical pattern was a high proportion of males to females, early marriage and large families. Earning capacity was greatest when a man was young and strong in a male-dominated industry where any opportunity for women's employment was negligible.[10] In all the mining regions the demand for a young male work-force and high early earning potential led to a high proportion of males in the population and early marriage. Glamorgan, Monmouth and Durham consistently appear at the top of the county tables of male/female ratios in the census (see Table 1). The imbalance is particularly marked for the age group 15–34 years.

An 1884 study gives 24 years as the average age at marriage for a miner, 22 years 6 months for his wife. Though marriage came early, that fact is not sufficient to account for the miners' reputation as 'a notoriously prolific section of the population'.[11] A variety of other factors were at work. Expectations of early high earnings went along with expectation of later incapacity. Children were needed to provide for old age. Boys at least were assured of early employment in mining. Girls could always be sent away into service. High fertility was also linked to high infant mortality. All these factors combined to produce a customary life-style which itself became a causal factor. As Table 2 shows, fertility amongst mining communities remained high and was slow to follow the national trend when the birth-rate fell for other occupation groups towards the end of the nineteenth century.[12] This indicates the insularity of coal-mining communities and the strength of the customary life-style.

If we turn now to look at the Rhondda valleys in more detail we see that, despite a late development and a short-lived prosperity, the Rhondda deserves its special place in coal-mining history.[13] The steam-coal seams there were among the deepest measures worked in the south Wales coalfield. Colliery communities there were the most dependent upon coal, and upon export markets, for their livelihood. Part of the uniqueness of the Rhondda can also be attributed to the topography of the two valleys themselves. Gwyn Thomas, the novelist, describes the Rhondda as:

> one of Britain's darker marvels. It is made of two deep gulches in the North Glamorgan hills. Between 1870 and 1920 it poured out enough coal to have coked the globe if ignited at one stroke. Pit shafts opened like the holes in a mature cheese. Never was a small stretch of earth so majestically ransacked . . . created by a world mad for steam, warmth and money.[14]

Table 2. England and Wales. Fertility by marriage cohort, 1911

| Date of marriage | Children born/100 couples | | Col.(ii) as % of Col.(i) |
| --- | --- | --- | --- |
| | (i) All occupations | (ii) Miners | |
| 1852–61 | 690 | 759 | 110 |
| 1862–71 | 662 | 760 | 115 |
| 1872–81 | 602 | 717 | 119 |
| 1882–86 | 551 | 684 | 124 |

Source: 1911 Census Fertility Tables

It was observed of the Fife miners in 1904 that 'the man is the keystone to the house arch, Woman's place is to support and buttress him from every side'.[15] This was true also for the Rhondda where the valleys were physically isolated, other industries were absent, and there was not even a substantial agricultural background in which women could play a part outside the home. Thus for the women of the Rhondda, even more than in coal-mining communities elsewhere, their role was defined in relation to their husband's occupation. Her sacrifice was taken for granted. Yet her domestic labour in the home was, like the miner's labour at the coal-face, also hard, dirty and dangerous. Like the man, she needed mental fortitude as well as physical strength to cope with the demands of home and family, and hers was the responsibility for the management of the household budget with a fluctuating income.[16]

Her working environment, like her husband's, gave little comfort. Until the turn of the century housing conditions, water supply and waste disposal were not only inadequate but deteriorating under pressure of population growth. These conditions were a continual burden on the woman as she struggled to perform her daily tasks of household service — washing, cleaning, cooking and child care. The main problems arose from the rapid rate of development along the valleys and from the failure of the local authority to respond effectively to a worsening situation.[17] In the forty years up till 1911, the Rhondda valleys absorbed a fourfold increase in population. At that time almost half the population of Wales lived in Glamorgan; the Rhondda Urban District contained a population larger than Swansea and not much smaller than Cardiff, crowded along two narrow valley floors.

The rate of house-building failed to match increasing demand. Initial construction of huts and blocks of houses by colliery companies was followed mainly by private, speculative building of the familiar rows of tiny, two-up, two-down, terraced houses — 'endless chains of tiny houses so small even the mice had to join in the singing'.[18] Under these conditions the overcrowding in the Rhondda was worse than in England's largest industrial cities. The 1891 census evidence summarized in Table 3 gives 6.5 as the number of inhabitants per house in the Rhondda compared with 5.0 in Manchester or 5.6 in Liverpool. Twenty years later, in 1911, the Rhondda household size was little lower while the number of houses had more or less doubled.

Table 3. Housing in the Rhondda

|      | Rhondda Urban District | | |
|------|------------|-------------------|-------------------|
|      | Population | Inhabited houses | Inhabitants per house |
| 1871 | 23950 | 2710 | 6.2 |
| 1881 | 55632 | 9193 | 6.0 |
| 1891 | 88351 | 13551 | 6.5 |
| 1901 | 113735 | 19201 | 5.9 |
| 1911 | 152781 | 26250 | 5.8 |

Source: Census 1911

The houses were small and lacked amenities. Few, if any, had bathrooms. In 1903, when Mrs Smith was nineteen years old and newly married to a Rhondda miner after being brought up in the metropolitan environment of Cardiff, she

> was very shocked that we had no convenience for our husbands to bath in. We had to bring a tub or tin bath, whichever we had, into the same room that we lived in, and heat the water over our living-room fire in a bucket or iron boiler, whichever we possessed.[19]

As late as 1920 only 2.4 per cent of the 26,822 working-class homes in the Rhondda had baths.[20]

The lack of an adequate water supply was an even more fundamental difficulty. Three different companies were responsible for water supplies in the Rhondda. According to the Medical Officer of Health the water in 1889 was 'all of very bad quality'[21] and many households drew their supply from taps in the street. For washing clothes the heated water was poured into large, wooden, 'dolly' tubs and pounded with poss sticks (see illustration on p. 111). Bert Coombes moved from his native Herefordshire to work underground before the First World War. In his autobiography, though he speaks from the point of view of a lodger on night shift trying to sleep during the day, he gives a realistic picture of the difficulties which women faced when washing and drying clothes under these conditions:

> There were no roaring loud-speakers in those days, but there were children playing in the street and hawkers with voices that sounded to be shaking the bed I tossed about on. The wind was the right way that

morning, so that the dust of the colliery screens blew away from the village. Tubs were bumped and washing-boards banged right underneath my window. All the water had to be carried from taps which were set at various spots throughout the village and a crowd of women were usually near these taps waiting for their water-vessels to be filled. These taps were great places for gossip, and every now and then I would hear a sharp voice calling 'Our Lizzie Ann! D'you know I'm waiting for that water?' or 'Gwennie! Gwennie! You've been up at that tap all the morning'.[22]

The Rhondda Urban District Council eventually took over the ineffectual Ystrad Gas and Water Company in 1895 after a legal case but it was not until 1910 and 1912 that two new necessary reservoirs were completed.

Neglect of refuse and sewage disposal was another problem which persisted even after it was recognized as a major cause of the Rhondda's appalling rate of infant mortality. An otherwise complacent sanitary survey of the Rhondda in 1885 reported the facilities as: 'Some WCs with or without water, Ash-closets and pails. In some places full and stinking privy pits'.[23] Until 1894 there were no main sewers for an urban population of almost 100,000. Waste of every description found its way to the river at the bottom of the valley. The Medical Officer of Health reported in 1893:

The river contains a large proportion of human excrement, stable and pigsty manure, congealed blood, offal and entrails from the slaughterhouses, the rotten carcases of animals, cats and dogs in various stages of decomposition, old cast-off articles of clothing and bedding, old boots, bottles, ashes, street refuse and a host of other articles. The water is perfectly black from small coal in suspension . . . In dry weather the stench becomes unbearable.[24]

Rhondda women undoubtedly laboured under poor working conditions. They were also faced with extreme demands for their domestic labour for demographic and industrial reasons. The sex imbalance and high fertility meant a high proportion of men and children per household; the demands of servicing the coal-mining industry were relentless. Tradition too was a hard taskmaster.

The measurable aspect of the demand for domestic labour relates to household structure. To quantify this, census enumerators' returns

Rhondda 1881; Age groups, males and females

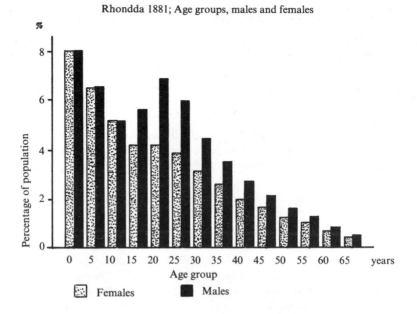

Age group

Females          Males

for 1881 were analysed. Details of age, sex, marital status, relation to head of household, and occupation were obtained for a 50 per cent sample (20,647 individuals in 3,822 households) from Ystradyfodwg (Rhondda) Registration Sub-district. The sub-district comprises the Rhondda valleys down to their meeting-place at Porth.

The aggregate census figures for mining counties and the Rhondda (Table 1) have already indicated the extent of a population imbalance towards youth and maleness in 1891. The chart above summarizing enumerators' returns for the Rhondda sample in 1881 duplicates these findings; 40 per cent of the population were under fifteen years of age and males in the 15–34 years age group outnumbered females by seventeen to ten.

The position is similar if we look at the size of households and the proportion of the population in large households. The Rhondda sample results tabulated in Table 4 show that most people lived in households of six or more. The sample also shows that a quarter of households shared houses because it was usual for young couples with one or even two children to share a house. In effect, therefore, three-quarters of Rhondda's inhabitants either shared with another

Table 4. Household size and house sharing, Rhondda, 1881

| Number in household | % of households | | % of population | | % of household size sharing |
|---|---|---|---|---|---|
| | (Figures for England and Wales in brackets) | | | | |
| 1 | 0.7 | (0.3) | 0.1 | (1.2) | 55.0 |
| 2 | 8.4 | (3.6) | 3.1 | (7.4) | 46.2 |
| 3 | 13.2 | (9.1) | 7.2 | (13.3) | 41.8 |
| 4 | 15.1 | (13.7) | 11.1 | (16.6) | 27.6 |
| 5 | 16.6 | (15.7) | 15.2 | (16.6) | 22.0 |
| 6 | 15.4 | (15.7) | 16.9 | (14.3) | 17.2 |
| 7 | 11.4 | (13.8) | 14.6 | (11.1) | 11.0 |
| 8 | 8.3 | (10.7) | 12.2 | (8.0) | 16.3 |
| 9 | 5.1 | (8.1) | 8.3 | (5.2) | 7.4 |
| 10 | 3.2 | (4.8) | 5.9 | (3.1) | 8.4 |
| 11 | 1.5 | (2.5) | 3.1 | (1.6) | 6.7 |
| 12 or more | 1.0 | (1.9) | 2.4 | (2.2) | 6.7 |
| Total households sharing | | | | | 24.4 |

household or else were part of a household of six or more. In the cramped conditions of the tiny terraced houses, sharing created problems for the housewife. Thirty years later conditions were much the same. Bert Coombes recalled his early married days:

> The front room, our living room, was about ten feet square, and the bedroom above about the same size . . . The scrape of a chair or even the creak of a bed, could be heard by the other family. Certainly they had only one child, and we none at that time, so we were not so crowded or noisy as those other houses — and they were many — where a considerable family was living in the front and back of each house.[25]

The other family in Bert Coombes's house 'claimed the strip of garden, and it had only room for one line, so our washing was done in the room and the drying on lines under the ceiling'.[26] The heavy tub for Bert's bath had to be carried through the kitchen to the back.

Lodgers also contributed to the crowding and added to the domestic workload. As Table 5 shows, one-third of all households in the sample took in lodgers, mostly in ones and twos. Twelve per cent of the total population were enumerated as lodgers or boarders (see Table 6). Taking in lodgers, like house-sharing, was an accepted

Table 5. Households by number of lodgers, Rhondda, 1881

| Household size | Number of households | | | | | | |
| | Number of lodgers | | | | | Total with lodgers | All households |
| | 0 | 1 | 2 | 3 | 4+ | | |
|---|---|---|---|---|---|---|---|
| 1 | 23 | 1 | | | | 1 | 24 |
| 2 | 333 | 6 | 1 | | | 7 | 340 |
| 3 | 450 | 56 | 6 | 1 | | 63 | 513 |
| 4 | 427 | 110 | 50 | 4 | 0 | 164 | 591 |
| 5 | 419 | 109 | 74 | 19 | 1 | 203 | 622 |
| 6 | 338 | 109 | 73 | 32 | 17 | 231 | 569 |
| 7 | 235 | 87 | 67 | 47 | 21 | 222 | 457 |
| 8 | 172 | 55 | 41 | 19 | 23 | 138 | 310 |
| 9 | 83 | 33 | 33 | 18 | 24 | 108 | 191 |
| 10+ | 81 | 32 | 32 | 25 | 35 | 124 | 205 |
| Total | 2561 | 598 | 377 | 165 | 121 | 1261 | 3822 |
| % total households | 67.0 | 15.6 | 9.9 | 4.3 | 3.2 | 33.0 | 100.0 |

means of cutting down living costs.[27] In the 1880s the weekly charge varied between 2*s*.6*d*. [12.5p] and 3*s*.6*d*. [17.5p] per lodger. The service provided included washing and, at the higher price, 'potatoes or tea' (evening meal).[28] Lodgers were not always complete strangers; those who were not relatives often came from the same home village. A number of households in the Rhondda sample lodged married men who came from the same Cardiganshire district as the head of household. These men probably returned home in the summer for the harvest.[29] Where conditions were very cramped, men on different shifts shared beds. How else could life have been managed at 111 Ystrad Road in 1881 where the census enumerator's returns show 42-year-old Elizabeth Morgan was providing board and lodging for four miners as well as looking after her five children and a husband? The eldest boys, aged thirteen and fifteen, like their father, worked underground. The youngest child was under one year old. With such a work-load, one wonders how Elizabeth Morgan would fare with another pregnancy.

Whether coal-miners in the household were husband, sons or lodgers, they necessarily created a great deal of work for the women. Daughters, as well as wives and mothers, became domestic labourers. When interviewed, one Rhondda woman recalled her working day at home in the inter-war period when her father and seven brothers worked underground on different shifts. Baths and hot meals had to be prepared for seven in the morning after the 11 p.m.–7 a.m. night

Table 6. Household composition, Rhondda, Ogmore and Garw Valleys, 1881

|  | Rhondda | | Ogmore and Garw[1] | |
|---|---|---|---|---|
|  | Number | % | Number | % |
| Heads of households | 3765 | 18.4 | 1020 | 17.1 |
| Relation to head: |  |  |  |  |
| Wives | 3299 | 16.1 | 875 | 14.7 |
| Children | 9775 | 47.7 | 2867 | 48.1 |
| Other kin | 826 | 4.0 | 213 | 3.6 |
| Lodgers | 2393 | 11.7 | 859 | 14.4 |
| Servants[+] | 445 | 2.2 | 127 | 2.1 |
| Total resident population | 20503 | 100.0 | 5961 | 100.0 |
| Visitors | 196 |  | 69 |  |
| Others | 25 |  |  |  |

1. Philip N. Jones, *Mines, Migrants and Residence in the South Wales Steamcoal Valleys: The Ogmore and Garw Valleys in 1881* (Hull, Hull University Press, 1987), 17.
+ This group were mostly living-in shop assistants.

shift; at three in the afternoon after the 7 a.m.–3 p.m. shift; and at eleven at night after the 3–11 p.m. afternoon shift.[30] In 1881 Hannah Rutley of Pentre might have given a similar response if interviewed. She was the eldest of nine children, the youngest under one year old. The occupation of her father and three oldest brothers was listed as 'coalminer'; hers as 'assisting in household duties'. In the aggregate occupation tables she was counted with her mother among the 'unoccupied'.

The needs of the men of the household claimed priority over all other demands and dictated the daily household routine. Childcare came second. Yet children were everywhere and comprised 40 per cent of the population. Table 7 shows that 30 per cent of households in the Rhondda sample contained four or more children; there were very few houses indeed that did not contain at least one child under fifteen years of age. The overcrowding of large families into tiny houses, poor sanitary conditions and poverty contributed to one of the highest infant mortality rates in England and Wales and a high incidence of infectious diseases amongst young children. As Table 8 shows, each year through the 1890s, pneumonia, diarrhoea, measles, whooping cough, diphtheria, scarlet fever, convulsions, and other causes were killing one out of every twelve children under five years of age. Fifty-five per cent of all deaths were of children under five years old. It is not surprising that playing funerals was a popular childhood

Table 7. Households by number of children, Rhondda, 1881

| Household size | Number of children in household | | | | | | |
| --- | --- | --- | --- | --- | --- | --- | --- |
| | 0 | 1 | 2 | 3 | 4 or more | 1 or more | Total |
| | Number of households | | | | | | |
| 1 | 24 | 0 | | | | 0 | 24 |
| 2 | 298 | 42 | 0 | | | 42 | 340 |
| 3 | 111 | 363 | 39 | 0 | | 402 | 513 |
| 4 | 91 | 143 | 325 | 32 | 0 | 500 | 591 |
| 5 | 35 | 99 | 157 | 296 | 35 | 587 | 622 |
| 6 | 36 | 54 | 99 | 129 | 251 | 533 | 569 |
| 7 | 14 | 24 | 60 | 80 | 279 | 443 | 457 |
| 8 | 6 | 13 | 16 | 31 | 244 | 304 | 310 |
| 9 | 4 | 5 | 8 | 25 | 149 | 187 | 191 |
| 10+ | 3 | 2 | 13 | 13 | 174 | 202 | 205 |
| Total | 622 | 745 | 717 | 606 | 1132 | 3200 | 3822 |
| % total | 16.3 | 19.5 | 18.8 | 15.9 | 29.6 | 83.7 | 100.0 |

game. Yet there were many children who suffered illness and were nursed to survival. For example, in the Rhondda in 1899, which was a bad year for diphtheria, of 1,804 cases notified, 1,618 survived. Or again in 1900 and 1901, which were bad years for scarlet fever, of 3,221 cases notified, 2,443 survived. To their other functions as washerwomen, charladies, and cooks, the women of the Rhonddas could add child-nurse.

In 1915, the Co-operative Women's Guild published a collection of letters in which members had written about their experience of motherhood. Letter 87 is entitled 'Struggles of a Miner's Wife'. The writer's eight pregnancies had produced seven live births of which only four children now survived. She wrote:

> I dare say I could write a book on my early struggles with my seven children, and a miner's home to contend with; and many a week my husband has not had a penny of wage to bring home, besides the experience of three big strikes and many small ones.
>
> I may say we were married nineteen years before we lost one, and then I lost my baby first, a grand little girl of two. Then, a year and a half after, I lost a fine lad of fourteen in the fever hospital, of scarlet fever and diphtheria. Two years after that we lost a girl of twelve from

Table 8. Cause of death of children under five years of age in the ten years 1891–1900, Pontypridd Registration District

| Cause of death | Total deaths under 5 years |
| --- | --- |
| Measles | 1136 |
| Scarlet fever | 332 |
| Diphtheria | 694 |
| Whooping cough | 826 |
| Enteric fever (typhoid) | 50 |
| Diarrhoea and dysentery | 1560 |
| Cholera | 28 |
| Tabes mesenterica (wasting) | 243 |
| Phthisis (Pulm. TB) | 88 |
| Other TB and Scrof. Dis | 270 |
| Diseases of: | |
|   Nervous system (fits) | 3907 |
|   Respiratory system (pneumonia) | 4501 |
| Violence | 325 |
| Other causes | 3653 |
| Total | 19724 |
| Annual death rate per 1000 | 80.91 |
| Total deaths all ages | 35745 |

Source: Registrar-General's Decennial Supplement for 1891–1900

tubercular disease of the kidneys from cow's milk. The doctor was treating her for eight years for Bright's disease of the kidneys. I brought them up breast-fed, so she must have contracted it after she was weaned. Such a clever child she was. So you will see we have had our troubles.

I may say I had very good times at confinements, except the first and the last. The youngest was born feet first, which was an awful experience, and her heart was nearly stopped beating; so I think that left her heart weak, and she cut her teeth with bronchitis I used to get up always by the ninth day until the last. I was between forty-one and forty-two when she was born, so had to rest a bit longer, but had to see to household duties as soon as possible.[31]

The writer speaks with typical lack of self-pity, passing lightly over her experiences of childbirth. Probably the only help available at childbirth would have been a midwife to attend the birth and a neighbour's daughter to do the washing and care for the younger children for a week or two after confinement. Neighbours rallied round at times of birth, death, illness and misfortune but independence was a matter of pride and many aimed to take up control of household duties as soon as possible.

Bearing and raising large families, like servicing the male labour force, required much domestic labour. The effort was increased because tradition demanded that these jobs should be performed to a high standard. The Rhondda miner took great pride in his work and the place of Rhondda coal in world trade. His wife took a corresponding pride in the results of her domestic labour. Looking at the domestic work-load of Rhondda women between the wars, Rosemary Crook concluded that 'the women spent time and energy on cleaning far beyond that needed to keep the house habitable'. It was one aspect of demonstrating the 'ability to service one's man, and to find satisfaction in doing so [which] was the criterion by which women judged each other'.[32] It can also be interpreted as a way of demonstrating control over the home as workplace in the same way as men at the coal-face felt in control of their workplace.

Exacting standards for domestic labour go back a long way. In 1846 H. Seymour Tremenheere, reporting on 'The State of the Population in Mining Districts', contrasted the habit of south Wales miners with those of miners in other regions of Britain who did not take the daily bath that was customary in Wales.[33] Sons of these men joined others from rural Wales in the first wave of immigrants to the Rhondda valleys. They were Welsh-speaking and strongly Non-conformist in culture and religion. Eisteddfodau and preaching festivals were an important part of social life. Many of the early miners' leaders were also chapel deacons. Religious revivals periodically swept through the Rhondda valleys, most notably in 1859, 1879 and 1904–5, with reports of services held underground in some pits.[34] The Nonconformist code of life and work was strict and its implications for household labour were straightforward. 'Cleanliness is next to Godliness' was a Nonconformist maxim which Rhondda women made their own.

Women paid a high price for their committed response to the demands of domestic labour; their own welfare was undoubtedly sacrificed for the welfare of others. The unremitting toil of childbirth and domestic labour killed and debilitated Rhondda women as much as accident and conditions in the mining industry killed and maimed

Table 9. Mortality rates (deaths per 1000 population), male and female, by age group
(a) 1901–1910

| | Pontypridd Registration District | | England and Wales | |
|---|---|---|---|---|
| | Female | Male | Female | Male |
| under 5 | 54.3 | 66.3 | 41.9 | 50.0 |
| 5– | 3.8 | 3.5 | 3.6 | 3.5 |
| 10– | 2.2 | 2.1 | 3.7 | 5.0 |
| 15– | 3.2 | 3.7 | 2.2 | 2.1 |
| 20– | 5.0* | 3.8 | 2.9 | 3.1 |
| 25– | 6.2* | 4.7 | 3.5 | 4.2 |
| 35– | 9.5* | 8.0 | 4.7 | 5.6 |
| 45– | 14.2 | 14.9 | 7.5 | 9.2 |
| 55– | 15.5 | 16.2 | 24.9 | 31.8 |
| 65– | 64.9 | 78.8 | 53.9 | 64.9 |
| 75– | 127.3 | 137.6 | 136.2 | 152.5 |

Source: Supplement Part III to 75th Annual Report of Registrar-General
(b) 1891–1900

| | Pontypridd Registration District | | England and Wales | |
|---|---|---|---|---|
| | Female | Male | Female | Male |
| under 5 | 73.3 | 88.5 | 52.8 | 62.7 |
| 5– | 5.6* | 5.0 | 4.4 | 4.3 |
| 10– | 4.6* | 3.8 | 3.7 | 5.0 |
| 15– | 7.0* | 5.3 | 4.5 | 5.1 |
| 25– | 8.6* | 6.5 | 6.1 | 6.8 |
| 35– | 10.6* | 9.9 | 9.6 | 11.5 |
| 45– | 15.6 | 18.6 | 14.7 | 19.0 |
| 55– | 33.1 | 40.4 | 28.4 | 35.0 |
| 65– | 66.4 | 79.0 | 60.7 | 70.4 |
| 75– | 129.0 | 143.4 | 146.5 | 160.1 |

Source: Supplement to 65th Annual Report of Registrar-General
(c) 1878–80

| | Pontypridd Registration District | | England and Wales | |
|---|---|---|---|---|
| | Female | Male | Female | Male |
| under 5 | 63.9 | 69.7 | 56.4 | 66.4 |
| 5– | 5.0 | 6.3 | 4.7 | 4.9 |
| 15– | 7.9* | 6.8 | 5.8* | 5.4 |
| 25– | 9.0* | 8.1 | 7.7 | 8.2 |
| 35– | 11.5* | 10.1 | 10.9 | 12.8 |
| 45– | 16.2* | 15.8 | 15.1 | 19.6 |
| 55– | 27.2 | 31.5 | 28.4 | 35.0 |
| 65– | 52.3 | 57.4 | 60.9 | 69.5 |
| 75– | 120.1 | 161.9 | 158.2 | 173.3 |

Source: Calculated from Annual Reports of Registrar-General
*indicates female mortality rate significantly higher than male.

Rhondda men. What is startling is the extent of women's sacrifice and the way it was accepted without being noticed or questioned.

Tables 9(a) and 9(b) show official mortality rates for the decennial periods 1901–1910 and 1891–1900 for Pontypridd Registration District. The district includes the town of Pontypridd as well as the Rhondda Valleys but overall the vast majority of households are still mining households. For the earlier decennial period the Registrar-General's annual reports do not include a male/female breakdown by age but it is possible to calculate on the same basis up to 1880. Table 9(c) shows average mortality during the three years 1878–1880, per 1,000 population in 1881. With such a fast-growing population during this period, the figures for Pontypridd District are likely to underestimate, so care must be taken in making comparisons with both the figures for England and Wales and those for Pontypridd in the later periods.

Nevertheless, the message is quite clear. For age group 20–44 years, in the Pontypridd Registration District, the death rates for women are significantly higher than for men for the whole period. This is in marked contrast with the experience of England and Wales as a whole where mortality rates for women are lower than for men in every age group over fifteen years of age for every sub-period (except for 1878–80 when the mortality rate for women 15–25 years of age is marginally higher than for men). Such a 'traditional' mortality pattern is characteristic of pre-industrial communities.[35] Like living in an undeveloped economy, early marriage to miners was not good for women's health.

Later investigation of mortality figures more directly linked to occupation groups confirms the earlier findings. Miners' wives fared badly in relation to wives of men in other occupation groups. The wives of face-workers were particularly at risk; the Registrar-General commented that 'young wives of hewers and getters were in the highest risk category of any women with occupied husbands . . . their mortality being considerably above those for all married women for almost every cause'.[36]

One cause of the high mortality rates for women in mining households was their exposure to the dangers of pregnancy and childbirth. As Table 10 shows, maternal deaths per 1,000 live births in the Pontypridd District were well above the England and Wales average, indeed they were amongst the highest in England and Wales.

Table 10. Maternal mortality 1881–1910 (maternal deaths/1000 live births)

|  | Pontypridd Registration District | England and Wales |
| --- | --- | --- |
| 1881–1890 | 8.0 | 4.7 |
| 1891–1900 | 8.1 | 5.1 |
| 1901–1910 | 6.1 | 4.0 |

Source: Decennial Supplements of Registrar-General

The connection with domestic labour was not recognized in contemporary discussion of these facts before 1914. The problem of maternal mortality, like infant mortality, was seen largely as a medical and educational problem to be solved by the medical profession and local authorities. Women themselves were blamed for high rates of infant and maternal mortality: as mothers and midwives, they were ignorant and/or careless.[37] This was the position adopted by Dr E. J. Maclean, Senior Gynaecologist at the Cardiff Infirmary, when he gave evidence before the Royal Commission on the Poor Laws and Relief of Distress in 1909. Maclean observed: 'It is in the densely populated mining districts of Glamorgan and Monmouth that the high [infant and maternal] mortality rates . . . are chiefly evident, and in my opinion such mortality rates are referable to the large number of confinements which are attended by midwives only.' He claimed that 80 to 90 per cent of confinements in Glamorgan were attended only by 'untrained and uneducated' midwives. In response to persistent questioning by Charles Booth he was reluctant to agree that poor housing and insanitary conditions might also play a part.[38] The subject of women's domestic work-load was not raised by Maclean or by Booth.

Some local campaigners did, however, recognize the wider 'feminist' issues. Elizabeth Andrews, a Rhondda miner's wife, helped to form the Co-operative Women's Guild there in 1910. She worked tirelessly to improve conditions for women through campaigns for pit-head baths and maternity and child welfare. She also played an active role in the suffragette movement (see Chapter 7) and was a woman organizer for the Labour Party in Wales from 1919 to 1948.[39]

In one initiative to improve welfare provision Elizabeth Andrews followed up a recommendation of the 1918 Maternity Act and wrote to the (all-male) county and borough councils in Wales suggesting that they co-opt two representatives of women's organizations onto the Maternity and Child Welfare Committees which the councils were then obliged to establish. The hostile and negative response of many county medical officers surprised her:

> Our letters were quite courteous and businesslike, but one County M.O.H. referred to them as 'wild hysterical effusion' and falling back on a scriptural phraseology, said the Council must be charitable to such people 'as they know not what they are talking about'. In another county we were called a 'lot of interfering busybodies'.[40]

The implications were clear; the matter was a medical and educational one in which women's proper role was to be the passive patient and pupil.

It was the issue of pit-head baths which at last highlighted the damage done to women in their own homes in a way that convinced a wider public. In their 1920 introduction to *Pithead and Factory Baths*, Robert Smillie and Frank Hodges saw 'no reason why his [the miner's] wife or mother should be the life-long slaves of the pit'.[41] Elizabeth Andrews was in the forefront of the campaign. As one of three miners' wives giving evidence before the Commission on the Coal Industry in 1919, she argued:

> Pithead baths would reduce the physical strain on the mother caused through lifting heavy tubs and boilers. A midwife of twenty-three years' experience in the same district in Rhondda stated to me that the majority of cases she has had of premature births and extreme female ailments are due to the physical strain of lifting tubs and boilers in their homes.[42]

She, too, described the drudgery of women's work in the Rhondda as 'nothing but slavery'.[43] The debilitating effects that 'the double burden of work cast upon the women folk'[44] were at last being recognized. Responsibility for that double burden lay firmly with the unrewarded service demands of the coal-mining industry.

But these battles were fought at a later period. Although the mortality tables of the Registrar-General provided clear evidence for the Rhondda and in other areas of the south Wales coalfield before the First World War, the spotlight played upon the man's labour and the dangers of the miner's occupation. It was accepted or unnoticed that his wife's working day was longer and her life at greater risk.

*Bibliographical note*

One of the most exciting recent books which fully places women's labour in a wider context is R. E. Pahl (ed.), *On Work: Historical, Comparative and Theoretical Approaches* (Oxford, Basil Blackwell, 1988). For women in employment and in the home in England in the nineteenth and early twentieth centuries, Angela V. John (ed.), *Unequal Opportunities*, and the companion volume, Jane Lewis (ed.), *Labour and Love* (both Oxford, Basil Blackwell, 1986) have up-to-date introductions and bibliographies.

Little has yet been written about women's employment in Wales. L. J. Williams and D. Jones rework the census occupation tables in 'Women at work in nineteenth century Wales', *Llafur*, 3 No.3 (1983), 20–9. For the coal industry, Wales is included in Angela V. John, *By the Sweat of Their Brow: Women Workers at Victorian Coalmines* (London, Routledge and Kegan Paul, 1980) and north Wales in Val Lloyd, 'Attitudes to women workers at North Wales' coalmines, 1840–1901', *Llafur*, 5 No.2 (1989), 5–16. The more important role of women in tinplate is described in Sheila Owen-Jones, 'Women in the tinplate industry in Llanelli, 1930 1950', *Oral History*, 15 No.1 (Spring 1987), 42–9. The largest gaps are in the service sector and in agriculture although David Jenkins, *The Agricultural Community in South West Wales at the Turn of the Twentieth Century* (Cardiff, University of Wales Press, 1971) contains fascinating detail about women's contribution to the complicated networks of interdependence in rural Wales.

For women's household labour in the south Wales coalfield, David Egan, *Coalfield Society* (Llandysul, Gomer, 1987) and E. D. Lewis, *The Rhondda Valleys* (London, Phoenix House, 1959) present the general background. Rosemary Crook, '"Tidy Women": women in the Rhondda between the wars', *Oral History*, 10 No.2 (Autumn 1982), 40–6, records first-hand experience of household labour. Autobiographies can also be revealing: Elizabeth Andrews, *A Woman's Work is Never Done* (Ystrad Rhondda, Cymric Democrat Publishing Society, [1956]); Wil Jon Edwards, *From the Valley I Came* (London, Angus and Robertson, 1956); Bert Coombes, *These Poor Hands* (London, Victor Gollancz, 1939); Will Paynter, *My Generation* (London, Allen and Unwin, 1972); Walter Haydn Davies, *The Right Place, The Right Time* (Swansea, Christopher Davies, 1972). Anyone using a home microcomputer as a tool in historical analysis will find the *Amateur Historian* frequently contains articles of interest. And *History and Computing*, the journal of the Association for History and Computing, reviews suitable software for micro- and mainframe computers as well as containing articles based on machine-readable historical data. No one should plunge into computer analysis of census material without first reading a guide such as Edward Higgs, *Making Sense of the Census* (London, HMSO, 1989). A detailed illustration of what can be extracted from census enumerators' returns is Philip N. Jones, *Mines, Migrants and Residence in the South-Wales Steamcoal Valleys: The Ogmore and Garw Valleys in 1881* (Hull, Hull University Press, 1987).

## Notes to Chapter 5

This chapter expands part of a paper 'Serfs and slaves; women's work in Wales, 1890–1930', published in D. R. Hopkin and G. S. Kealey (eds.), *Class, Community and the Labour Movement:Wales and Canada 1850–1939* (Aberystwyth, Llafur/Labour–Le Travail, 1989). The paper also examined the contribution of women's unpaid labour to agriculture in Cardiganshire.
My thanks to Karel Williams for helpful comments on the final draft.

1. N. Dennis, F. Henriques, C. Slaughter, *Coal is My Life: An Analysis of a Yorkshire Mining Community* (London, Eyre and Spottiswoode, 1956) is a classic account of daily life in a Yorkshire colliery community in the 1950s which has been criticized for its unquestioned acceptance of the miners' view of women solely in a supportive role. See Ronald Frankenberg, 'In the production of their lives, men(?) . . . Sex and gender in British community studies', in D. L. Barker and S. Allen (eds.), *Sexual Division and Society: Process and Change* (London, Tavistock, 1976), 25–51. As for the future, Angela John discusses possible new approaches to issues of gender in mining history in 'A miner struggle? Women's protests in Welsh mining history', *Llafur*, 4 No.1 (1984), 72–90.
2. For the development of the south Wales coalfield up to 1874 see J. H. Morris and L. J. Williams, *The South Wales Coal Industry 1841–1875* (Cardiff, University of Wales Press, 1958).
3. C. Wilkins, *The South Wales Coal Trade* (Cardiff, D. Owen and Co., 1888), 72–3. However, there is some doubt about Mrs Thomas's direct responsibility. See J. H. Morris and L. J. Williams, op. cit., 19–20 and Revel Guest and Angela V. John, *Lady Charlotte* (London, Weidenfeld and Nicolson, 1989), 289 fn.2.
4. David Egan, *Coal Society: A History of the South Wales Mining Valleys 1840–1980* (Llandysul, Gomer, 1987).

5. See Brinley Thomas, 'The Industrial Revolution and the Welsh language', in L. J. Williams and C. Baber (eds.), *Modern South Wales: Essays in Economic History* (Cardiff, University of Wales Press, 1986), 6–21. Also his earlier papers: 'The migration of labour into the Glamorganshire coalfield, 1861–1911', *Economica*, 10 (1930), and 'Wales and the Atlantic economy', *Scottish Journal of Political Economy*, 6 (1959), reprinted in B. Thomas (ed.), *The Welsh Economy* (Cardiff, University of Wales Press, 1962).
   See also L. J. Williams, 'The move from the land', in T. Herbert and G. Elwyn Jones (eds.), *Wales 1880–1914* (Cardiff, University of Wales Press, 1988), 11–47.
6. John Benson, *British Coalminers in the Nineteenth Century* (London, Longman, 1980), 113.
7. Benson, op. cit., 219.
8. For the history of later unionism see R. Page Arnot, *South Wales Miners, Vol. I, 1889–1914* (London, George Allen and Unwin, 1967), *Vol. II, 1914–1926* (Cardiff, Cymric Federation Press, 1975); Hywel Francis and Dai Smith, *'The Fed': A History of the South Wales Miners in the Twentieth Century* (London, Lawrence and Wishart, 1980).
9. See Chapter 3, 'The miners' earnings', in Benson, op. cit.
10. A very few women worked in coal-mining in the Rhondda, an area which was developed after the outcry against women's employment below ground. In the 50 per cent Rhondda household sample of 1881, fifteen girls and women were returned as working at the pit top. Of this number nine were from three households. Angela V. John gives a detailed account of the work of pit-top women in *By the Sweat of Their Brow: Women Workers at Victorian Coal Mines* (London, Croom Helm, 1980).
11. Poor Law Commission Report 1834, Appendix A, Part I, No. 5, as quoted in n.12 below.
12. See M. R. Haines, 'Fertility, nuptiality and occupation: a study of coalmining populations and regions in England and Wales in the mid nineteenth century', *Journal of Interdisciplinary History*, 8, 2 (Autumn 1977), 245–80.
13. The best and most detailed history of the Rhondda is still E. D. Lewis, *The Rhondda Valleys* (London, Phoenix House, 1959).
14. Foreword by Gwyn Thomas in Cyril Batstone, *Old Rhondda in Photographs* (Barry, Stewart Williams, 1974).
15. K. Durland, *Among the Fife Miners* (London, S. Sonnenschein and Co. Ltd., 1904), as quoted in Benson, op. cit., 128.
16. For discussion of women's unpaid labour in the home see Maureen Mackintosh, 'Domestic labour in the household', in R. E. Pahl, *On Work: Historical, Comparative and Theoretical Approaches* (Oxford, Basil Blackwell, 1988), 392–406, previously published in S. Burman

(ed.), *Fit Work for Women* (Croom Helm, London, 1979), 173–91. For a historical view see Catherine Hall, 'The history of the housewife', in Ellen Malos (ed.), *The Politics of Housework* (London, Allison and Busby, 1980), 44–71, and for interesting theoretical issues see Leonore Davidoff, 'The rationalization of housework', in Sheila Allen and Diana Barker (eds.), *Dependence and Exploitation in Work and Marriage* (London, Longman, 1976), 121–51.

17. See E. D. Lewis, op. cit., 202–46, and Hamish Richards, 'Investment in public health provision in the mining valleys of South Wales 1860–1914', in Williams and Baber (eds.), op. cit., 128–39.

18. Gwyn Thomas, *A Welsh Eye* (London, Hutchinson, 1964), 35.

19. Mrs F. H. Smith, 'In a mining village', in Margaret Llewelyn Davies (ed.), *Life As We Have Known It* (London, Co-operative Women's Guild, 1931, reprinted Virago, 1977), 67–72.

20. E. L. Chappell and J. A. Lovatt-Fraser, *Pithead and Factory Baths* (Cardiff, Welsh Development Agency, 1920).

21. Report of M.O.H. for Rhondda Urban District Council, 1889.

22. B. L. Coombes, *These Poor Hands: The Autobiography of a Miner Working in South Wales* (London, Victor Gollancz, 1939), 41.

23. Report (dated 1885) by Dr. D. S. Davies, Sanitary District Inspector, in William Williams, *A Sanitary Survey of Glamorganshire* (Cardiff, Daniel Owen and Company Limited, 1895).

24. Report of M.O.H. for Rhondda U.D. Council, 1893. Also quoted in E. D. Lewis, op. cit., 210 and David Egan, op. cit., 88.

25. B. L. Coombes, op. cit., 90.

26. Ibid., 91.

27. Enumerators were inconsistent in distinguishing lodgers from boarders. Leonore Davidoff considers the general issue of keeping lodgers in 'The separation of home and work? Landladies and lodgers in nineteenth and twentieth century England', in Sandra Burman (ed.), *Fit Work for Women* (London, Croom Helm, 1979), 64–97.

   Two studies based on census enumerators' returns which include discussion about lodgers are Michael Anderson, *Family Structure in Nineteenth Century Lancashire* (Cambridge, Cambridge University Press, 1971), and Philip N. Jones, *Mines, Migrants and Residence in the South Wales Steamcoal Valleys: The Ogmore and Garw Valleys in 1881* (Hull, Hull University Press, 1987).

28. Daniel Davies, 'The Rhonddas in the eighties', *Quarterly Review*, 558 (April 1951), 217–30.

29. See David Jenkins, *The Agricultural Community in South-West Wales at the Turn of the Twentieth Century* (Cardiff, University of Wales Press, 1971), 66.

30. Mrs Jenkins interviewed by Rosemary Crook, 'Women of the Rhondda Valley between the wars', MA thesis, University of Leeds, 1980.

31. Margaret Llewelyn Davies (ed.), *Maternity: Letters from Working Women* (Women's Co-operative Guild, London, 1915, reprinted Virago, 1978), 111–12.

32. See Rosemary Crook, op. cit., chapter 8.

33. *Report on the State of the Population in Mining Districts, 1846*, 38. See E. D. Lewis, op. cit., 183.

34. A contemporary report is given in Elvet Lewis, *With Christ among the Miners: Incidents and Impressions of the Welsh Revival* (London, Hodder and Stoughton, 1906).

35. See Sheila Ryan Johansson, 'Sex and death in Victorian England: an example of age- and sex-specific death rates 1840–1910', in Martha Vicinus (ed.), *A Widening Sphere* (Bloomington, Indiana University Press, 1977), 163–81.

36. *Registrar-General. Decennial Supplement 1931, Part IIa: Occupational Mortality, 85.*

37. An interesting account of the change in attitude to the problem of infant mortality in this period is given in Carol Dyhouse, 'Working-class mothers and infant mortality in England 1895–1914', *Journal of Social History*, 12 (1978), 248–67, reprinted in Charles Webster (ed.), *Biology, Medicine and Society 1840–1940* (Cambridge, Cambridge University Press, 1981).

   For an inter-war investigation into maternal mortality in the Rhondda which was surprised by its conclusion that maternal malnutrition could be an important factor, see Lady Williams, 'Malnutrition as a cause of maternal mortality', *Public Health* (October 1936), 11–19.

38. *Report of the Royal Commission on the Poor Laws and Relief of Distress, 1909, Appendix Vol. V, Minutes of Evidence from Dr E. J. Maclean*, q 47495, q 49524–31 (P.P. 1909 Cd 4888 XLI).

39. See Elizabeth Andrews's autobiography, *A Woman's Work is Never Done* (Ystrad Rhondda, Cymric Democrat Publishing Society [1956]).

40. Elizabeth Andrews, op. cit., 30.

41. Chappell and Lovatt-Fraser, op. cit., vii.

42. *Report of the Royal Commission on the Coal Industry, 1919, Minutes of evidence from Elizabeth Andrews*, q 24393.

43. Ibid., q 24396.

44. Chappell and Lovatt-Fraser, op. cit., xi.

# 6

## *From Temperance to Suffrage?*

CERIDWEN LLOYD-MORGAN

'From the 1890s the temperance movement in Wales, as in Britain generally, declined.' Such is the conclusion of W. R. Lambert in his study of *Drink and Sobriety in Victorian Wales*,[1] echoing the similar views of Brian Harrison, historian of the English temperance movement.[2] Yet nothing could be further from the truth as far as women were concerned, for it is precisely in the 1890s that women began to take a more active role in temperance activity and to set up major organizations of their own, separate from the men. If the masculine or mixed societies were on the wane, this period saw a rapid, widespread expansion of women's work for total abstinence from alcohol, an expansion which continued into the first decade of the twentieth century.

The temperance movement itself, from its beginnings in America, had spread through the British Isles during the first half of the nineteenth century. It had attracted the support of women from the start, but while societies remained mixed, women's influence, and opportunity for active participation, remained limited. In Wales, women became members of the earliest, mixed, abstinence societies. The Aberystwyth Auxiliary Temperance Society, founded in 1835, lists a number of women amongst its members,[3] and a roll of those who signed the pledge in Aberystwyth between 1836 and 1855 similarly includes a large number of women, ranging in social class from servants to ministers' wives.[4] A few societies exclusively for women had been set up from the 1830s onwards. In 1837, for example, women members of the Nonconformist Welsh-speaking chapels in Liverpool organized their own temperance group,[5] and in January 1850 a Ladies' Temperance Association was founded in Merthyr Tydfil,[6] but these were rare exceptions, with their activities being short-lived and very limited geographically. From the 1870s, however, the Order of Good Templars began to allow women greater opportunities for participation in committees, and indeed it was out of this association that a women's temperance organization on a national scale first developed in England: it was women delegates to the convention of the British Independent Order of Good Templars in April 1876 who founded the British Women's Temperance Association (BWTA).[7]

As one of the leading figures in the women's temperance movement in north Wales, 'Ceridwen Peris' (Alice Gray Jones, 1852–1943), noted in 1931, within the mixed societies women were regarded as helpers, while the men were firmly in charge.[8] None the less, she acknowledged that the experience gained by women in those organizations such as the Good Templars, albeit as handmaids, was crucial to their developing the necessary confidence to organize independently of men later on.

By 1892 the BWTA claimed 570 branches with a total membership of some 50,000[9] but it remained weak in Wales. According to D. D. Williams, tracing the history of temperance in Gwynedd in 1921, and to Annie C. Prichard writing in 1910,[10] the first impetus for setting up a women's temperance union in north Wales came from a group of men. Revd John Eiddon Jones, Samuel Owen and William Jones MP had thought that a women's organization might be a useful way of spreading the temperance message, especially in view of the success of the BWTA in England. It seems, however, that a small group of women had been thinking on the same lines, and the men's role may have been more that of a catalyst. Ceridwen Peris stresses that Mrs Sarah Matthews of Amlwch had been corresponding with prominent men and women in the temperance movement about the possibility of setting up a separate women's organization in north Wales, and she suggests that the women's conference called by Mrs Matthews, her sister Miss Gee, and Miss Parry of Bala, in Blaenau Ffestiniog in 1892 was a direct outcome of Mrs Matthews's activity.[11] It is true, however, that Cymanfa Ddirwestol Gwynedd (the association of temperance groups in Gwynedd) provided the framework for this meeting, since it was through that organization that women delegates were invited to the conference, to represent the six north Wales counties of Anglesey, Caernarfon, Denbigh, Flint, Merioneth and Montgomery, and the English towns with Welsh communities in contact with Cymanfa Gwynedd. At this conference it was resolved to set up Undeb

Sarah Jane Rees ('Cranogwen'), photographed by John Thomas.
(By permission of the National Library of Wales.)

Dirwestol Merched Gogledd Cymru (UDMGC, the North Wales Women's Temperance Union) to unite, direct and expand the hitherto scattered activities of Welsh women involved in temperance work.[12] UDMGC developed rapidly: by 1893 there were 25 branches, 52 by 1894, and 65 by 1895.[13] In 1896 there were 11,821 members belonging to 106 branches, including 16 branches in Liverpool and 8 in Manchester, with a total of 461 women serving as branch officers.[14] The existence of large Welsh communities east of Offa's Dyke still in close contact with their home districts is demonstrated by the strength of the North Wales Union's branches in London and Birmingham as well as Liverpool and Manchester, and, of course, in towns such as Oswestry with a large native population of Welsh-speakers. In Wales itself, the largest branch was Blaenau Ffestiniog, which had 1,497 members by 1903, although most branches had between 50 and 150 members, and some, in small villages such as Y Groeslon, Caernarfonshire, had as few as 7.[15]

By the turn of the century, the success of the North Wales Union inevitably gave rise to the idea of starting a similar union in the south. The obvious candidate to set the ball rolling was 'Cranogwen' (Sarah Jane Rees, 1839–1916),[16] already a veteran champion of the temperance cause, and a highly influential figure as a lecturer, writer and above all as the first woman editor of a Welsh women's magazine. After the failure of *Y Gymraes*, which had been founded by 'Ieuan Gwynedd' (Evan Jones) in 1850, Cranogwen had launched her own magazine, *Y Frythones*, in 1879 (see Chapter 3).[17] From the very first volume she had included articles on the dangers of alcohol. Although she was already over sixty, Cranogwen took up the new challenge and formed a women's union for temperance work following a religious meeting at Jerusalem Calvinistic Methodist chapel, Tonpentre, Rhondda. Enlisting the support of women of other denominations, and having formally founded Undeb Dirwestol i Ferched y Ddwy Rhondda (temperance union for women of the two Rhonddas) in March 1901, a month later, at a further meeting in Porth on 10 April, the name Undeb Dirwestol Merched y De (UDMD, the South Wales Women's Temperance Union) was adopted. By the end of 1901 ten branches had been set up, all in Glamorgan, and in 1902 further expansion included their first branch in Cardiganshire, when the New Quay branch of the North Wales Union transferred to UDMD, in view of its isolation from the northern branches. By the time of

Cranogwen's death in 1916, there were some 140 branches through-out south Wales, through the counties of Cardigan, Pembroke, Carmarthen, Glamorgan, Brecon and Monmouth.[18]

A glance at the names of those most prominent in the two women's unions reveals a preponderance of middle-class, chapel-going women. In north Wales Miss Gee and Mrs Sarah Matthews were daughters of the influential publisher, Thomas Gee of Denbigh, himself a temperance activist since the 1830s, and Mrs Matthews's bank-manager husband was also active in the cause. Wives of MPs such as David Lloyd George, J. Herbert Lewis and Ellis Jones Griffiths, were leading members of UDMGC. Although this element was not quite so obvious in south Wales, the officers still tended to be drawn from a particular social class, whose status reflected that of their husbands. The founders of UDMD included Mrs Evans, wife of Pentre's librarian, ministers' wives, and Mrs E. H. Davies, wife of the president of Cymdeithas Cymreigyddion y Ton. The dominance of middle-class women was perhaps inevitable, as they alone had the leisure, confidence and family support to organize meetings and speak in public. Cranogwen was an exception in this respect, for although by 1901 she was a respected public figure, her home background was humbler and she had always worked for her living.

The control of the movement in north and south Wales by a small group of women from comparatively privileged backgrounds does not necessarily reflect a wish on their part to dominate the cause. On the contrary, more than one president of UDMGC regretted the difficulties of persuading more women to take part in public speaking. In 1896, for example, Sarah Matthews expressed her disappointment that

> we do not find that readiness to speak, either in branch or public meetings, that we expected 4 years of holding women's meetings would have produced! We are perfectly aware that it involves a considerable effort to address a mixed audience, and it is a new and untried field of influence to us, as Welshwomen . . . Let me appeal to each one of you . . . to determine that henceforward, cost what it may, *your* voice will not be silent at the women's meetings, and, if necessary, that you will conquer the nervousness and reserve which has hitherto overcome you when the call to battle in a more public manner reaches you.[19]

Two years later Mrs James Hughes reported similar difficulties, although expressing cautious optimism:

This want is being remedied by degrees, and the coming generation will be better equipped for public work, having been trained while young to take their part in debates etc. We who are older were brought into the work without any special training, but were constrained to do our utmost because the evil was so great.[20]

None the less, on a social level it is clear that the crossing of class boundaries was one of the achievements of which the officers were most proud: UDMGC, its President declared in 1902, 'has done away with social distinctions, and drawn us as women nearer together, making us in the true sense of the word SISTERS and COMRADES',[21] her words embodying a rhetoric of sisterhood nowadays usually associated with the women's movement of the 1970s.

The over-representation of one particular religious denomination as well as social class among the officers also caused concern within UDMGC. Whereas the founding members of the South Wales Union included Congregationalists and Wesleyans as well as Calvinistic Methodists such as Cranogwen, in the north the Calvinistic Methodists provided the majority of committee members. In 1904 Mrs Griffith Davies raised the question of better representation of other denominations in her presidential address:

> One denomination preponderates as is evident to all, but it may not be as well-known that this is in spite of the continuous efforts of the members of that denomination to change this, and have it otherwise. Probably it will never be known how great an effort has been made. Year after year members of all denominations are nominated for the various offices, but the nominations are declined, and that very much to our regret.[22]

That this problem arose at all reflects the close link between the Nonconformist sects in Wales and the temperance movement in general. W. R. Lambert has stressed the politico-religious alignment that created a polarity between, on the one hand, Anglicans, Conservatives and the drink interest and, on the other, Nonconformists, Liberals and temperance workers.[23] Certainly it was out of the chapels that the temperance movement grew and flourished. Long before UDMD was founded, the children's Bands of Hope had formed an important strand of chapel activity in the south. In Cardiganshire Cranogwen herself was leader and teacher of Banc-y-felin Band of Hope, whose rules laid emphasis on rejecting alcohol in favour of living a quiet, pure and god-fearing life. In the Dyffryn

Ogwen district of Caernarfonshire the Band of Hope was still a regular feature of children's lives into the 1960s.

It was, of course, inevitable that the culture and outlook of Nonconformity should leave its mark on the Welsh women's temperance movement. Meetings were held in vestries, chapel schoolrooms or in the chapel itself, and minute books and printed reports testify repeatedly to the centrality of Christian belief and worship in their activity and thought. Prayer and hymn-singing formed a major part in meetings, and the reminder to the North Wales Union in 1896 that 'we are relying upon prayer as the source of our strength' is typical.[24] UDMGC's motto, '*Er mwyn Crist, Cartref a Chymydog*' ('for Christ, home and neighbour') again stressed that it is a *Christian* duty to fight against the evils of alcohol. Presidents of UDMGC repeatedly stressed that temperance work was done for God, and was allied to the winning of souls; the question of major social reforms to alleviate the working and social conditions that might lead to alcohol abuse is barely mentioned. The aim was above all to educate others in the Christian way of life, especially through teaching by example, and making temperance, like other Christian virtues, a personal responsibility. The women's temperance movement placed almost equal stress on what was referred to as social purity, for sexual morality and abstinence from alcohol were seen as walking hand in hand. A close connection was perceived between prostitution and alcoholism, and UDMGC campaigned against the employment of barmaids, for fear that young women would fall in both senses. Prostitution tended to be associated with public houses and prostitutes might depend on drink as a means of coping with their way of life — as the French socialist and feminist, Flora Tristan, had observed in her London journal of 1842.[25] Contemporary temperance literature is full of dire warnings to young girls to avoid the first fateful drink that will let men take advantage of them, thus leading them on the road to ruin. This emphasis on the link between alcohol and extra-marital sex is also a common element of temperance literature in England, but it takes on a further dimension in the Welsh context, where it can be traced back to the reaction to the publication of the report of the English commissioners on education in Wales, the infamous Blue Books of 1847. Ieuan Gwynedd's *Y Gymraes*, the first Welsh-language magazine for women, had been a direct response to the report, and the following years saw tremendous efforts by religious and social leaders to prove that the Welsh were not as immoral and degraded a race as might appear from the Blue Books. The role of drink in the traditional social life of Wales — at fairs, weddings, funerals, harvest-time and virtually any social gathering — created particular problems for temperance activists. In his eisteddfod prize essay of 1860, *Sefyllfa Bresennol Merched Cymru* ('the present situation of Welsh women'), 'Ioan Arfon' (J. O. Griffiths) relates how young men looked out for girls in the markets and fairs, and lured them into taverns to get drunk, before walking them home in the dark with the expected consequences.[26] The concern to prove that, in terms of sexual morality and rate of illegitimacy, Wales was no worse at least than England, became a national obsession, and continued throughout the second half of the nineteenth century. The increasing influence of English Victorian values towards the close of the century simply reinforced a tendency that had begun as a reaction to the Blue Books. 'With shame and sorrow', the President of UDMGC reported as late as 1901, 'we have to confess that Wales needs to be purged of impurity and immorality.'[27]

The literature published by the Welsh women's temperance movement reflects this concern. Many of its booklets were aimed at young girls and bore titles such as 'Purdeb i ferched' ('purity for girls'), 'Urddas Merch' ('a girl's dignity' — a euphemism for virginity) and 'Rhybudd i ferch yn amser rhyfel' ('a warning to a girl in wartime'), though the information they contain is usually very vague about the precise nature of the 'dangers' threatening their 'purity', But mothers were the main target, as they had been throughout the post-Blue Books period. Mrs Sarah Matthews, as one of the leaders of UDMGC, would regularly urge mothers to maintain the sanctity of the Welsh home.[28] Woman's chief role was seen as that of wife and mother, and hers was the responsibility for keeping the home free of alcohol, and making it a comfortable place so that husbands should not be tempted to leave it for the rival attractions of the public house. Hers too was the duty of raising sons and daughters as pious, totally abstaining, moral Christians. 'If we could only teach and help one another', said Sarah Matthews in 1896, 'to keep our houses clean and comfortable, our language and habits pure and proper, and instil right ideas and principles into our children and members of our household we should . . . have done a grand work for Temperance and Purity.'[29]

Temperance literature was an important medium for communicating the message, and many of the cautionary tales published as short stories, or playlets for performance at local meetings, were written by members of UDMGC and UDMD. Cranogwen and Ceridwen Peris were the best known and most prolific of women temperance writers in Welsh, and indeed the best-known women writers of their day. Cranogwen had been editing *Y Frythones* for ten years before she became organizer of UDMD, and was herself responsible for much poetry and prose on temperance themes published in that magazine, with titles such as 'Hawddamor Faner Dirwest' ('hail, the flag of temperance').[30] In 1896 Ceridwen Peris, whose 1895 booklet *Mor Bur a Deigryn* ('as pure as a tear') was one of the earliest and most successful publications of UDMGC, set up a magazine similar to *Y Frythones*, but named *Y Gymraes* after Ieuan Gwynedd's earlier attempt. The new *Y Gymraes* was to serve the women of north Wales, and here again the commitment to the temperance cause was absolute, to the extent that from the beginning *Y Gymraes* regularly included news of UDMGC and its branches, and was praised by the union's President, Mrs James Hughes, in 1897 for voicing 'the thoughts and feelings of this Association and plead[ing] so powerfully for purity and righteousness'.[31] At their committee meeting in Liverpool on 30 January 1901, it was agreed that *Y Gymraes* should be 'formally accepted as the official organ of the North Wales Union, and the General Secretary instructed how to utilise the 200 copies taken monthly by the Union'.[32] By 1902 the secretary was sending out 2,400 copies of *Y Gymraes* for distribution by the branches.[33]

Less prominent members were also encouraged to compose temperance literature, particularly by the competitions organized by UDMGC, inspired, no doubt, by the tradition of the Welsh institutions such as the eisteddfod and *cwrdd cystadleuol*. In 1903 UDMGC printed 3,000 copies of *Dylanwad Esiampl Merched* ('the influence of women's example') by 'Megan', the winning entry in a competition for a short novel, whilst in 1907 a member of the Mold branch, Miss Rebecca Rich, saw her story, *Teulu Bron Awel* ('the Bron Awel family'), added to the list of the North Wales Union's publications.[34] Winners also gained a small money prize. Most of the leaflets and booklets distributed in north Wales were in Welsh, reflecting the high percentage of Welsh speakers, but in order to cater for the needs of branches in more anglicized areas such as Flintshire and parts of Denbighshire, English tracts were brought in from outside, presumably from the BWTA.[35]

One effect of the increasing activity of women in the temperance movement, and the need for suitable literature, was the vast increase in the number of women writing and publishing both poetry and prose in Welsh in the late nineteenth century, an index, perhaps, of increasing self-confidence. Not until 1850 do we find the publication of a book by a woman author: the first was Elen Egryn's collection of poetry, *Telyn Egryn*.[36] But as Iorwen Myfanwy Jones's pioneering survey (1935) of Welsh women's writing from 1850 to 1914 reveals,[37] the majority of women writers in the last decades of the century were active in the temperance movement, even if they did not always write on temperance themes. Ellen Hughes of Llanengan, for example, was involved with UDMD from at least 1902 and was a member of its literature committee, along with Cranogwen.[38] Ellen Hughes's second published volume, *Murmur y Gragen*, a selection of her poetry and prose, appeared in 1907.

Although much of the material published by women during the heyday of the temperance movement is now of purely historical rather than literary interest, there can be no doubt that the movement itself provided a major incentive for women to write and publish, as well as boosting their self-confidence as writers, and it created a respectable context in which to write. And those women writers who did emerge, such as Ellen Hughes or Gwyneth Vaughan (the latter a BWTA stalwart in north-west Wales), certainly paved the way for later major literary figures in Welsh such as Winnie Parry and Kate Roberts.

Literature was not, however, the only means of spreading the word, and not the only new area of activity which the temperance movement opened up for Welsh women, bringing them further into the public sphere than hitherto. It is true that in some branches the meetings seem to have been somewhat limited in scope and repetitive in format. The minute book of one of the Cardiganshire branches of UDMD gives a dismal catalogue of prayers, hymns, Bible readings, recitations and solos, from October 1902 until March 1909, when entries cease.[39] Small wonder that the minutes of a meeting held on 13 January 1904 record: 'Buwyd yn treio dyfalu sut i wneyd y cyfarfod yn fwy dyddorol' ('it was attempted to work out how to make the meeting more interesting'). But annual reports from northern branches bear witness to a considerable variety of work, with the UDMGC executive committee, as well as the branches themselves, making suggestions for both social and more directly evangelical meetings. Marches, temperance teas, choirs, concerts, outings, all helped to provide social outlets, while propagandizing could take the form of home visiting, lectures, public meetings, arranging petitions to ban alcohol from, for example, the field of the National Eisteddfod (a ban still in force today). Some branches, such as Oswestry, ensured that stocks of temperance literature were always available at the local library and railway station, and, as time went on, importance was attached to lobbying councillors in the new and expanding area of local government. Emphasis was placed on providing attractive alternatives to public houses or activities associated with the consumption of alcohol: temperance cafés were set up by women in Bodedern, Llannerch-y-medd and Rhos-goch in Anglesey, and the Machynlleth branch provided a temperance refreshment tent each year at the local agricultural show. Temperance and general moral teaching could be combined with traditional 'good works' such as sewing for the poor — the temperance branches often overlapped with chapel Dorcas societies — and what might be described at a later date as 'moral welfare' work. The Wrexham branch of UDMGC co-operated with the local English-medium branch of the BWTA in running a girls' home, which was dealing with thirty girls a year in 1903. And if Cranogwen herself did not live to see the realization of her dream of a home for women who had ended up in court on charges of drunkenness and the 'drygau sydd ynglŷn â hynny' ('the associated evils'), a fund was raised for this purpose after her death and 'Llety Cranogwen' was finally opened by the Rhondda branch in 1922.

In short, although the vast majority of women active in the temperance movement in Wales were presumably also regular attenders at chapel and perhaps involved with ancillary activities such as Sunday school, their membership of a temperance union must have introduced them to a far wider range of activities outside the home. And as in the chapel, Welsh-speaking women who could speak little or no English had the chance to participate fully in a variety of activities in their own language, to a far greater extent than they could have in the BWTA, whose official language was English.

The existence of the Welsh language, and the perception that Wales had its own culture and traditions had, indeed, been one of the reasons for organizing a separate women's temperance association in Wales, rather than simply supporting the England-based BWTA. This is not to say that a number of prominent Welsh women were not active with the BWTA, even in Welsh-speaking areas: Gwyneth Vaughan, the novelist,[40] and Catherine Anwyl, sister of Professor Edward Anwyl and of the lexicographer John Bodfan Anwyl,[41] were both cases in point. When the founding conference of the UDMGC was held in September 1892, Lady Henry Somerset was invited as President of the BWTA, though, unable to attend, she sent two representatives. Again, in Wrexham a year later, at the conference where the constitution of UDMGC was drawn up, a BWTA representative was present. The BWTA was anxious that the new North Wales Union should simply operate as part of the English association, with each branch being a direct member of the BWTA, but after considerable discussion the Welsh women unanimously decided to keep their union entirely separate and independent. According to Ceridwen Peris, this was partly due to the influence of Sarah Matthews.[42] Echoing the arguments put forward in 1881 for passing a separate Sunday Closing Bill for Wales, the distinct identity of Wales as a nation was stressed: 'Gan ein bod yn genedl ar wahan o ran iaith, arferion a diwylliant, teimlent mai fel Undeb Cymreig y llwyddid orau' ('since we are a separate nation as far as language, traditions and culture are concerned, they felt that it was as a Welsh Union they would best succeed'). In 1895, however, it was resolved that UDMGC should federate to the BWTA, in order to become 'rhan o Undeb mawr a gymerai i mewn Ferched y Byd' ('part of a large Union that would take in the World's Women').[43] From then on an affiliation fee was sent annually to the BWTA, and representatives sent to the BWTA's executive committee, but UDMGC remained entirely autonomous. By the time the South Wales Union was founded, the principle had thus been established, and it was able to form itself on the lines of the northern union. The consciousness of women in both north and south Wales of a specifically Welsh, national dimension to their work, and the Welsh identity of members, even those working in English towns, was enhanced by membership of the two unions, especially by the regular appeals to members as Welsh women to consider the specific needs of Wales. Contact between north and south was maintained by sending representatives to each other's meetings — Cranogwen participated in the north Wales annual meetings in 1903 and 1906, for instance.

Commitment to the Welsh language was enshrined in the constitution of UDMGC. The President and Secretary were required to be fully bilingual in Welsh and English, and 'the preparation and circulation of Welsh literature on temperance and moral purity' was one of the aims listed there. The North Wales Union must have been one of the first associations in Wales to have an official bilingual policy, and to publish its constitution and annual reports in both languages, with Welsh taking precedence; the South Wales Union's reports follow a similar pattern. None the less, the language did pose problems, especially since many members came from anglicized districts. In some towns, such as Wrexham and Colwyn Bay, the problem was resolved by having two groups working in parallel, a Welsh one belonging to UDMGC, and an English-speaking BWTA branch which was nevertheless affiliated to the Welsh Union. Many branches must have been mixed linguistically, however, and this led to complaints about the excessive use of one language or the other. In 1902, for example, one branch reporting to the Secretary of UDMGC proposed that more English should be spoken in the union's council, whilst another asked that all discussion be in Welsh. The President, Mrs Jacob Jones, admitted that 'this question of language is a growing difficulty' but urged 'sympathy and forebearance on both sides'. 'Our Union', she continued, 'from the commencement has recognised this fact, and we have made use of both languages for the furtherance of our cause.' To confine meetings to one language alone, she argued, was 'a mistaken policy', contrary to their aim of 'unity and cooperation' between Welsh women.[44] But in 1903 the 'desirability of having more Welsh spoken in the Annual Meetings' was again raised as a discussion topic at the conference.[45]

In 1904 the language question was once more perceived as a sensitive issue when the possibility was mooted of inviting the British society's new president, the Countess of Carlisle, to come to address UDMGC:

> Of course she would have to address us in English, and we should have to appeal — as we have indeed to do already to the generosity of those of our members who feel that our Union is too much tinged with English. We sympathise with our ardent Welsh sisters, but we have to bear in mind all of us that we have . . . many English members whose co-operation we desire and value so much. This question of language is one of the difficulties of our Union . . . '[46]

The use of *Y Gymraes* as the official magazine of UDMGC, and the close link between the well-established *Y Frythones* and temperance ideals, especially later, when its former editor, Cranogwen, became organizer of the emerging South Wales Union, again reinforced the connection made between temperance, womanhood, the Welsh language and the sense of belonging to a Welsh nation. But if involvement in the temperance movement enhanced a feeling of Welshness and of separateness from English culture (which reached back — ironically, perhaps — to the Blue Books scandal), it also clearly raised women's consciousness in the modern, feminist sense. It is all too easy to underestimate the radical change in women's lives which was brought about by participation in what may appear to us today as an essentially conservative organization, reinforcing the view of women as wives and mothers above all. The emphasis in Welsh temperance literature and, indeed in the annual reports, on this aspect, setting standards of moral purity in the home and in society, may obscure the dramatic nature of the step the founders took, and it is a useful corrective to study the extremely negative reactions of many Welsh men to the emergence of women into public life through the movement.

One of Mrs Sarah Matthews's aims in setting up UDMGC was to enable women to develop skills which found no other outlet in domestic life: 'Teimlai . . . ers tro fod gan y merched alluoedd ac adnoddau oeddynt yn segur — heb sianel i droi allan yn wasanaeth er lles eraill' ('She had felt for some time that women had abilities and resources that were lying idle — without a channel for turning them to serve for the benefit of others').[47] But the prejudice against women was strong, especially among chapel elders. The prejudice facing this first generation of women temperance workers, such as Sarah Matthews, is graphically described by Ceridwen Peris, looking back from emancipated 1931:

> Peth anodd yw gwrthweithio rhagfarn gwlad. Cafodd y chwiorydd a fu yn cychwyn yr Undeb deimlo hynny. Yr oedd gwaith merch yn esgyn i lwyfan i siarad yn gyhoeddus yn taro yn erbyn y syniad cyffredinol am safle merch mewn cymdeithas. Yr aelwyd oedd lle merch, a distawrwydd oedd ei rhinwedd — dyna farn y cyhoedd y pryd hynny. Wynebu y rhagfarn yna a fu raid i'r merched oeddynt yn ceisio argyhoeddi y wlad fod gan ferch ei chenadwri a'i chenhadaeth yn y byd, a bod cylch ei gwasanaeth yn helaethach na phedwar mur ei chartref.
>
> Ofnai y blaenoriaid mewn llawer lle dynnu gwg aelodau'r eglwys wrth gyhoeddi fod *chwiorydd* yn dod yno i siarad ar Ddirwest.[48]

(It is not easy to work against a people's prejudice. Those sisters who started the Union were made to feel that. A woman's action in climbing onto the stage to speak in public struck against the general idea of a woman's place in society. The hearth and home was a woman's place, and silence her virtue — that was the public's opinion at the time. That prejudice had to be faced by those women who wished to convince the nation that women had their own message and mission in the world, and that their sphere of service extended beyond the four walls of their homes.

In many places chapel elders feared the scowls of other members when announcing that *sisters* were coming there to talk about Temperance.)

Often they were not allowed to use the pulpit, and would be warned in advance: 'Ofnir y bydd amlhau cyfarfodydd yn peri iddynt [*sc.* y merched] esgeuluso eu haelwydydd, a phrif waith gwraig yw gofalu am ei chartref' ('It is feared that increasing the number of meetings will make [the women] neglect their homes, and a woman's chief work is to look after her home'). Sometimes they were not allowed to use the chapel but forced to make do with the schoolroom, and in 1894 the annual meeting held at Llangefni discussed an 'Apêl at Flaenoriaid ac Arweinwyr Crefydd i roddi pob cefnogaeth i'r Chwiorydd i hyrwyddo Dirwest yn y gwahanol eglwysi' ('Appeal to chapel elders and religious leaders to give every support to the sisters in promoting temperance in the various denominations').[49]

The same prejudice faced women in south Wales, and in the case of Cranogwen, who had gone on a lecture tour in America as early as 1869, an unpleasantly personal dimension was added. Cranogwen's biographer, Revd D. G. Jones of Pontardawe, recalls how some men still believed:

mai rhyw bethau i'w cau i fyny mewn tai i weini ar 'wyr a gweision' oedd ac yw merched a gwragedd; rhyw bethau i fod at wasanaeth eu harglwyddi ym mhob dim; golchi eu dillad pan fo eisiau, gwneuthur bwyd blasus iddynt, glanhau eu hesgidiau ac edrych ar eu perchnogion fel bodau hollwybodol a hollalluog. Pan welsant Cranogwen yn y pulpud yn annerch torf o ddynion, credasant fod diwedd y byd wedi dod. Bu'n wych ganddynt awgrymu mai gwryw ar wedd benyw, neu fenyw ar wedd gwryw, ydoedd; a chlywsom rai yn awgrymu nad oedd yn perthyn i'r naill ryw neu'r llall.[50]

(that women and wives were things to be kept shut up in houses to wait upon the menfolk, things to be at their lords' service in every respect:

washing their clothes when need be, preparing tasty meals for them, cleaning their shoes and looking after their owners as if they were omniscient and almighty beings. When they saw Cranogwen in the pulpit addressing a crowd of men, they thought that the end of the world had come. They thought it excellent to suggest that she was a man in female form, or woman in masculine form, and we heard some suggest that she belonged neither to the one sex nor the other.)

It is hardly surprising that Cranogwen suffered bouts of depression and lack of self-confidence in face of such reactions, but the important Nonconformist leader Thomas Levi rushed to her support in an article on Cranogwen in *Trysorfa y Plant* (a denominational magazine which he edited), where he addressed the whole question of women preaching in very positive terms.[51]

It is possible that the very difficulties encountered by women temperance activists in the later nineteenth century made them more aware of the injustice of their position as women. As the increasing provision of basic education led to increased female literacy — and the temperance literature distributed by the two Welsh women's unions presupposes that the women they wished to reach could read — it became possible for women to glimpse a world beyond the home. And although the temperance movement was basically conservative in its emphasis on morality, there can be no doubt of its importance in broadening the horizons of Welsh women and in helping them move into new spheres of activity, outside the home.

Membership of a Welsh-speaking temperance organization rather than the BWTA did not mean that a woman would look no further than Wales, even if it might enhance her consciousness of belonging to a Welsh nation. From their inception both UDMGC and UDMD, partly, admittedly, through their federation with the BWTA but also through their affiliation to the World's Women's Christian Temperance Union, stressed that as Welsh women they were only one branch of a sisterhood extending through the British Isles and beyond. The two unions became involved in lobbying and petitioning Parliament in London whenever relevant bills were being debated, and, on an international level, in 1898 a representative from UDMGC was sent to both the Dominion of Canada convention and the World's Women's Christian Temperance Union meeting in Toronto.[52] A year earlier, UDMGC had sent money and clothing to help Christian refugees in Armenia, having already sent a resolution to the government about the atrocities there;[53] financial aid was also sent that year to quarrymen in dispute at Bethesda.[54] They sent messages of condemnation of state control of prostitution in India when new legislation was passed in 1895.[55]

Apart from thus encouraging women to see an international dimension to their work, and a sense of solidarity with women in other countries, the women's temperance unions gave women a chance — for the first time in many cases — to learn new skills of organization, public speaking and the like. The procedure and administrative structure of the two unions, modelled on male-run societies, with their formal meetings and constitution, election of officers and keeping minute books, gave women a chance to take part in committee work, to cut their teeth at public speaking and to take on responsibility in a supportive, all-female environment, a useful preparation for work in a wider sphere later. UDMGC could, therefore, boast by 1902 that it had 'done much to develop talent lying dormant, and given an opening to exercise latent powers for good', as well as broadening women's outlook.[56] Mrs Jacob Jones, in her 1900 presidential address, rejoiced in the 'revolution in the position, responsibilities, and opportunities of women', and reminded members that women had 'by sheer force of intellect and ability, pushed their way into the professions; education, taking University Degrees; School Boards and Poor Law Boards; Government appointments . . . and many others'.[57] Looking back in 1931, Ceridwen Peris stressed that women's involvement in the temperance movement had helped them achieve a stronger, more public role in the chapels.[58] As with the women's movement of the 1970s, the temperance leaders recognized the importance of increasing women's self-confidence, for year after year the presidential address of UDMGC would urge that 'we women *can* do the work' and 'do not be persuaded that you have *no power, no ability*'.

Gradually, too, they introduced women to the possibility of political action — lobbying local government officers, voting for temperance supporters at local elections. As early as 1897 Mrs James Hughes, then president of UDMGC, exhorted members to take 'a more active interest in municipal matters . . . The elections take place on the 1st of November; see to it, dear sisters, that both vote and work is given to the candidate who represents the great cause for which we are striving'[59] — thus bringing home to women their own duties and responsibilities as *citizens*, not just as wives, mothers or daughters.

Citizenship, in its fullest sense, implied the vote, and the extent to which temperance activity provided a rehearsal for the suffrage campaigns is a controversial question. Certainly, the renamed National British Women's Temperance Association supported suffrage from 1893 onwards, and succeeded in drawing many women into political action in this way, whilst the President of the BWTA until 1903, Lady Henry Somerset, was anxious to link temperance with the suffrage cause; her successor, Rosalind Howard, Countess of Carlisle, was committed to votes for women.[60] In North America too, the leaders of the temperance cause, such as Frances Willard, became leaders in the struggle for women's suffrage, with Miss Willard's Women's Christian Temperance Union coming to terms with the idea of votes for women as early as the 1880s.[61] It is worth noting that Frances Willard was regarded as a heroine in Wales and UDMGC even published a little book about her.[62]

None the less, the situation in Wales was less clear-cut than in England or North America, and the fact that in 1896, for example, after postponing discussion for a year, UDMGC voted over-whelmingly against including in its programme 'the question of women's suffrage', has been seen as evidence that the movement was opposed to it.[63] But this does not necessarily mean total opposition to the idea of votes for women; the evidence of the minute books and reports of this period suggests rather that the issue was simply felt to be separate, or parallel, and not the main interest or priority of the members as a whole. The commitment of Lady Somerset to women's suffrage, and indeed to other radical ideas, did not preclude her being invited to the founding conference in Blaenau Ffestiniog in 1892, and, as we have seen, the chief obstacle to inviting Lady Carlisle to address the Welsh women was not her views on suffrage, but her inability to speak Welsh! The question of votes for women was in fact raised at the foundation of UDMGC, and the minutes reveal no hostility to the idea. The question arose during discussion in 1893 about the relationship of UDMGC to the BWTA, with one delegate asking whether affiliation would mean that the North Wales Union would be 'expected to take up the suffrage *or any other political questions* except simply those that bear on temperance' (my italics). They were assured that they need only take up temperance issues, but Mrs Lloyd Jones of Rhyl argued strongly that 'woman's suffrage was intimately connected with the advancement of the Temperance question', and it was resolved that any individual member who supported suffrage was free to speak in public 'on her own responsibility'.[64] In view of the fact that the temperance unions were attempting to reach all women, regardless of political hue as of religious denomination, this seems a practical response, especially in the crucial early years of the movement, for a strong stand on the suffrage issue too soon could have hampered recruitment. Objection to the BWTA was not because of its support for votes for women but was based largely on the English character of that organization, and an unwillingness to be told what to do, in Wales, by the English. 'Welshwomen', one speaker at the UDMGC executive committee meeting in September 1894 remarked crisply, 'know better what the necessities of their countrywomen and of their country are than any Englishwoman could possibly do.'[65]

It is, perhaps, natural that support for suffrage within the temperance movement in Wales came from those women living in English towns or more Anglicized areas, since women's suffrage societies in both north and south Wales tended to operate in English and to be dominated by middle-class immigrant women.[66] It was the Rhyl branch of UDMGC which proposed the suffrage resolution in 1895 and 1896, with the support of Miss Evans of Newtown and Mrs D. R. Jones of Manchester.[67] It should not be overlooked either that one leading member, Mrs James Hughes of Manchester, was not only in favour of suffrage but also chose to take advantage of her position to spread the message, devoting much of her 1899 presidential address to arguments in favour of votes for women:

> When we ask ourselves why our progress is slow . . . and our legitimate wishes for the good of our country frustrated, there is but one answer. It is all largely owing to the fact that we have not the compelling power of the vote . . . I trust that in the struggle on this question which we shall surely see in the near future, our Union will not be behindhand . . . It is for the Union by its Members, and its Committee to decide what course to pursue. I am speaking my own opinion, but it seems to me that it is our duty to seek the vote in order to help our fellow-men by securing the passing of good laws . . . We may speak and work as we will, but . . . until we can follow up our work with our votes, until then we shall constantly be set aside, and the work which as women we have laboured long and earnestly to accomplish, may at any moment be overturned . . . There is no way of securing the rights we already possess to serve God and Humanity, but by striving incessantly until the full rights of citizenship are accorded to us.[68]

In south Wales, too, there were temperance workers who publicly expressed their support for women's suffrage. Ellen Hughes, Llanengan, a member of the literature committee of UDMD, published in 1907 an essay, 'Angylion yr Aelwyd' ('angels in the home'), composed in 1899, mocking men's arguments for keeping women out of Parliament.[69] Nor were the Welsh women's magazines entirely silent nor opposed to the idea. Even in 1883, Mary Jones writing in *Y Frythones* on 'Hawliau a dyledswyddau y rhyw fenyw' ('rights and duties of the female sex') referred to 'galwedigaeth ddiamheuol ar ferched hefyd i gyflawnu dyledswyddau cyhoeddus' ('the undoubted calling of women to perform public duties as well'), whilst in 1913, for example, Miss M. M. Lloyd of Bedlinog argued in *Y Gymraes* that simple justice demanded the vote for women.[70] And both magazines published articles on prominent women who had succeeded in fields formerly closed to women, thus gradually preparing readers for the idea of full rights of citizenship and extensive opportunities outside the home.

We should, perhaps, be careful not to make support or otherwise of the single question of suffrage an index of the degree of emancipation among Welsh women at this period. Important strides could be made even without the vote: for many women the new work and social opportunities provided by the First World War seemed equally liberating. Moreover, many Welsh women, especially those of working-class or rural, Welsh-speaking backgrounds, must have found some aspects of the suffrage campaign profoundly alienating, and felt suspicious of the fact that it was English-speaking women who were most anxious to introduce the idea to them; the reaction of many Welsh-speaking women in rural north and mid Wales to feminist activity in the 1970s and 1980s — that it was brought in by the English, who did not understand their ways, and that it was irrelevant to them and their experience — provides a comparable model. And in view of the negative reactions that the pioneering women temperance workers received from men, open support of so emotive a question as that of the vote for women could have been counter-productive, if not suicidal, as far as the main aim of the movement was concerned.

Although in Welsh-speaking Wales, therefore, the temperance movement and the struggle for women's suffrage did not overlap to the same degree as they did in North America or even in England, there is plentiful evidence to demonstrate that many individual women involved in the former — including some of the most prominent members — were vocal supporters of votes for women. And despite the essentially conservative and Christian aims, the Welsh women's temperance unions undoubtedly played an important part in helping women in Wales, including those in rural areas, to emerge from the home and to step out more confidently into the world with a broader outlook. The role of UDMD and UDMGC could perhaps be compared to that of the Women's Institute later on, and, more recently, the Welsh-medium Merched y Wawr ('women/ daughters of the dawn'); it is worth noting that in some cases membership has overlapped. On the surface, all three movements have provided a comfortably domestic and supportive atmosphere in which women can socialize with each other whilst at the same time learning new skills, but all three, in their different ways, have involved women in campaigning for what are in fact political issues. For many women, this could be the first step leading them on the road to more radical action. In this respect, the importance of the Welsh women's temperance unions in the late nineteenth and early twentieth century should not be underestimated.

*Bibliographical note*

There is no general history of the women's temperance movement in Wales: W. R. Lambert's *Drink and Sobriety in Victorian Wales c.1820–c.1895* (Cardiff, University of Wales Press, 1983) covers only male and mixed societies, though it is useful for background. The best starting points are D. D. Williams, *Hanes Dirwest yng Ngwynedd* (Liverpool, Hugh Evans a'i feibion, 1921), covering the temperance movement generally, including UDMGC, in the north-west, and Annie C. Prichard's account of UDMGC's early history, *Boreu Oes* (Dinbych, Gee a'i fab, [1910]). These have no parallel in south Wales, except for D. G. Jones, *Cofiant Cranogwen* (Caernarfon, Argraffdy'r M.C., [1932]). Ceridwen Peris's memorial of one of the northern leaders, *Er Cof a Gwerthfawrogiad o Lafur Mrs Mathews* (Liverpool, Hugh Evans a'i feibion, [1931]), likewise sets biographical detail in the context of the movement's development. Otherwise the main sources are the published annual reports of UDMGC and UDMD, and of the BWTA/NBWTA; and periodicals such as *Y Frythones*, *Trysorfa y Plant* and especially *Y Gymraes*. The National Library of

Wales has important manuscript sources such as minute books and correspondence. A thorough reading knowledge of Welsh is *essential* for research on this topic.

*Notes to Chapter 6*

1. W. R. Lambert, *Drink and Sobriety in Victorian Wales, c.1820–c.1895* (Cardiff, University of Wales Press, 1983), 247.
2. Brian Harrison, *Drink and the Victorians: The Temperance Question in England and Wales, 1815–1872* (London, Faber, 1971), 20, 387. See also Lilian Lewis Shiman, *Crusade against Drink in Victorian England* (London, Macmillan, 1988), 240.
3. National Library of Wales (NLW) MS 8322B.
4. NLW MS 8342D.
5. 'Ceridwen Peris' (Alice Gray Jones), *Er Cof a Gwerthfawrogiad o Lafur Mrs Mathews [sic]* (Liverpool, Hugh Evans a'i feibion ar ran UDMGC, [1931]), 6. Massive Welsh migration to Liverpool throughout the nineteenth century and beyond led to close ties between the city and the north Wales counties, and to the existence of a Welsh-speaking social life in Liverpool centred on the chapels.
6. Lambert, op. cit., 78.
7. Lilian Lewis Shiman, 'Changes are dangerous: women and temperance in Victorian England', in Gail Malmgreen (ed.), *Religion in the Lives of English Women, 1760–1930* (London, Croom Helm, 1986), 193–215 (204), and idem, *Crusade Against Drink*, 183.
8. Ceridwen Peris, op. cit., 6.
9. Lilian Lewis Shiman, 'Changes are dangerous', 204; *Crusade Against Drink*, 185.
10. Parch. D. D. Williams, *Hanes Dirwest yng Ngwynedd* (Liverpool, Hugh Evans a'i feibion ar ran Cymanfa Ddirwestol Gwynedd, 1921), 90; Annie C. Prichard, *Boreu Oes* (Dinbych, Gee a'i fab, [1910]), 3.
11. Ceridwen Peris, op. cit., 7.
12. D. D. Williams, op. cit., 90–1; Annie Prichard, op. cit., 3–6; Minute Book of UDMGC, 1892–5, NLW Minor Deposit 637A.
13. Ceridwen Peris, op. cit., 8–9.
14. *Adroddiad a Gweithrediadau Pedwerydd Cynghor Blynyddol UDMGC 1896*, 12–13, 25.
15. *Adroddiad . . . UDMGC 1903*, 36–8.
16. See Parch. D. G. Jones, *Cofiant Cranogwen* (Caernarfon, Argraffdy'r M.C. ar ran UDMD, [1932]). The more recent biography, Gerallt Jones, *Cranogwen: Portread Newydd* (Llandysul, Gwasg Gomer, 1981), is little more than a summary of D. G. Jones's work.
17. See, for example, Sian Rhiannon Williams, '*Y Frythones*: portread cofnodolion merched y bedwaredd ganrif ar bymtheg o Gymraes yr oes', *Llafur*, 4 No. 1 (1984), 43–54.
18. D. G. Jones, op. cit., 132–45; dates of foundations of all branches from

1901 are given at the beginning of the printed annual reports (*Adroddiad o Weithrediadau a Chyfrifon Arianol UDMD*).

19. *Adroddiad . . . UDMGC 1896*, 9.
20. *Adroddiad . . . UDMGC 1898*, 9.
21. *Adroddiad . . . UDMGC 1902*, 13.
22. *Adroddiad . . . UDMGC 1904*, 9.
23. Lambert, op. cit., 241. See also D. G. Lloyd Hughes, *Hanes Tref Pwllheli* (Llandysul, Gwasg Gomer, 1986), 189, for close links between the temperance movement and the chapels: compare Huw Walters, 'Chwifio baner dirwest: cenhadaeth Dafydd Daniel Amos', *Cof Cenedl*, 5 (1990), 85–115.
24. *Adroddiad . . . UDMGC 1896*, 15.
25. Jean Hawkes (tr. & ed.), *The London Journal of Flora Tristan* (London, Virago, 1982), 105; see also Brian Harrison, *Drink and the Victorians*, 175. For connections between the temperance activists and the social purity movement, see Judith R. Walkowitz, *Prostitution and Victorian Society* (Cambridge, Cambridge University Press, 1980); Edward J. Bristow, *Vice and Vigilance: Purity Movements in Britain since 1700* (Dublin, Gill and Macmillan, 1977), 76–174; Sheila Jeffreys, *The Spinster and Her Enemies: Feminism and Sexuality, 1880–1930* (London, Pandora, 1985), 6–26.
26. J. O. Griffiths ('Ioan Arfon'), *Sefyllfa Bresennol Merched Cymru. Buddugol yn Eisteddfod Beddgelert* (Tremadog, Robert Isaac Jones, 1860), 23.
27. *Adroddiad . . . UDMGC 1901*, 11.
28. Ceridwen Peris, op. cit., 8.
29. *Adroddiad . . . UDMGC 1896*, 9.
30. *Y Frythones*, March 1882, 69.
31. *Adroddiad . . . UDMGC 1897*, 7.
32. *Adroddiad . . . UDMGC 1901*, 17.
33. *Adroddiad . . . UDMGC 1902*, 25.
34. *Adroddiad . . . UDMGC 1903*, 26; *1907*, 23.
35. *Adroddiad . . . UDMGC 1905*, 20.
36. Ceridwen Lloyd-Morgan, 'Elin a'i thelyn: carreg filltir yn hanes llenyddiaeth y ferch', *Barn*, 314 (March 1989), 17–19.
37. Iorwen Myfanwy Jones, 'Merched llên Cymru, 1850–1914' (University of Wales MA thesis, 1935).
38. D. G. Jones, op. cit., 139.
39. NLW, C.M. Archives MS 13233. Although the name is not given, internal evidence shows that it belonged to the Rhydyfelin branch near Aberystwyth.
40. Iorwen Myfanwy Jones, op. cit., 151.
41. See NLW Anwyl Family Papers, especially bundles 11, 42, 60.
42. Ceridwen Peris, op. cit., 12.
43. Ibid.
44. *Adroddiad . . . UDMGC 1902*, 17.
45. *Adroddiad . . . UDMGC 1903*, 15.
46. *Adroddiad . . . UDMGC 1904*, 9.

47. Ceridwen Peris, op cit., 6.
48. Ibid., 14.
49. Ibid., 15.
50. D. G. Jones, op. cit., 88–9.
51. *Trysorfa y Plant*, 5 (1866), 204–6; see also D. G. Jones, op cit., 89.
52. *Adroddiad... UDMGC 1898*, 11–13.
53. *Adroddiad... UDMGC 1896*, 23; *1897*, 9, 13–15.
54. *Adorddiad... UDMGC 1897*, 9.
55. Ibid., 31.
56. *Adroddiad... UDMGC 1902*, 11.
57. *Adroddiad... UDMGC 1900*, 9.
58. Ceridwen Peris, op. cit., 16.
59. *Adroddiad... UDMGC 1897*, 19.
60. Lilian Lewis Shiman, 'Changes are dangerous', 207; *Crusade Against Drink*, 185–7.
61. Ruth Bordin, *Woman and Temperance: The Quest for Power and Liberty, 1873–1900* (Philadelphia, Temple University Press, 1981), 156–8.
62. *Hanes Miss Willard*: see *Adroddiad... UDMGC 1899*, 35.
63. Sian Rhiannon Williams, op. cit., 52.
64. NLW Minor Deposit 637A, 27–8.
65. Ibid., 54.
66. This emerges clearly from minute books of northern groups, e.g. NLW MS 22636B (Llangollen branch); see also 'The Swansea suffragettes', in Luana Dee and Katell Keineg (ed.), *Women in Wales: A Documentary of Our Recent History* (Cardiff, Womenwrite Press, 1987), 67–76.
67. *Adroddiad... UDMGC 1895*, 17; *1896*, 23.
68. *Adroddiad... UDMGC 1899*, 13–15.
69. Ellen Hughes, *Murmur y Gragen* (Dolgellau, E. W. Evans, 1907), 37–40.
70. Compare Sian Rhiannon Williams, op. cit., 50–1.

# 7

# 'The Petty Antics of the Bell-Ringing Boisterous Band'? The Women's Suffrage Movement in Wales, 1890–1918[1]

KAY COOK and NEIL EVANS[2]

Traditionally the women's suffrage movement has been the one part of women's history that has not been hidden from historians. Yet in Wales women have not even been given this consolation prize. The participation of Welsh women in the movement has been overlooked and disregarded, though recently attempts have been made to redress the balance. We need a thorough study of the impact of women's suffrage activity in Wales. This chapter is not that, but is simply a preliminary exploration based on evidence gathered more widely than has been done hitherto.

Women's suffrage was predominantly a movement of middle-class women. Recent research has made us aware of the working-class dimension in Lancashire, and there has been a welcome and necessary shift away from the Pankhursts and the Women's Social and Political Union (WSPU) towards the more widespread and significant non-militant movement, especially the National Union of Women's Suffrage Societies (NUWSS), led by Millicent Garrett Fawcett.[3] In Wales there was little possibility of the working-class movement which existed in Lancashire; the proportion of women engaged in waged work outside the home was unusually low, especially in the burgeoning coal-mining communities which were the dynamo of its economy.[4] If women did not enter waged work in large numbers they did not join trade unions and achieve the organizational coherence necessary to support a working-class suffrage movement.

Concentrated in the coastal belts of north and south Wales, the Welsh middle class was a relatively late and weak arrival on the scene. In south Wales geography was associated with class in a stark manner. The working class was disproportionately concentrated in the valleys and the middle classes in the coastal towns — in Cardiff,

Newport, Swansea and Barry.[5] Beyond the suburbs of these towns
was a network of country houses to which the most successful
beneficiaries of Welsh industrialization withdrew. The Vale of
Glamorgan and the more salubrious areas of Gwent were an upper
middle-class carriage society (and subsequently a motor-car society)
linked to the ports which were the prime locations of the Welsh
bourgeoisie. In north Wales the geographical distribution of classes
was also uneven. The focus of the middle class was amongst the
100,000 Welsh-born people living in Lancashire in 1891 and from
these trailed a tail which curled along the north Wales coast,
thickening in the major resorts and ending in Aberystwyth.[6]

Both Welsh magazines and the expanding English-language press
aimed at women as a distinct category. By 1880 the *Cardiff Times*
carried a women's column. It was metropolitan in tone and probably
syndicated from London. It represented a world of aspiration far
removed from the homely pieties in *Y Frythones*, and connected an
aspiring bourgeoisie to London Society. Its columns were full of
fashion, the 'servant problem' ('The position of a mistress in an
ordinary English household in the present day is far from an enviable
one') and the difficulties posed for mothers by long school holidays.
Much of it was frippery. Subsequent columns were entitled 'Girl's
Gossip' and 'Tea Table Talk'. The *Western Mail* had a column from
the same period and from 1893 a special Saturday supplement. Titles
for the latter were equally frivolous and it was edited by 'a lady'. The
intention was to attract suitable advertisers and a permanent group of
readers.[7] Yet such columns also broached questions of female
emancipation, with consideration of the schemes for female
emigration of the 1880s, made necessary because 'popular prejudice as absurd as it is deeply rooted, declares it to be out of place
for women to enter any of the more lucrative professions'. In 1881,
there was a meeting in favour of votes for women in the Town Hall in
Cardiff.[8]

Charity was one possible way out of the home for women.
According to the Victorian precept it began there and could be seen as
a suitable area for the female touch. As a vehicle for female
emancipation it created a bridgehead. In some ways it confirmed
Victorian stereotypes; the distaff side was the one to which soothing
functions — the heart in a heartless world — could readily be
devolved. Women were rarely the equals of men in charities. Cardiff
Infirmary had a Women's Visiting Committee which inspected the

A Liberal view of the suffrage campaign.
(*South Wales Daily News*, 11 July 1908, by permission of the National Library of Wales.)

wards and ensured that discipline was maintained. Yet women did not become officials in the period before the First World War. Mrs Cory visited the wards while her husband made the decisions and wrote the cheques.[9] The Cardiff Dorcas Society was unusual in that it was run by a female committee. The money involved was minimal compared with a vast enterprise like the Infirmary. The taste of power was for three days a year when the town hall — normally a male preserve — was taken over for the distribution of the clothes which the women had sewn in their regular meetings. Women were also prominent in the Queen Victoria Institute for Nursing, which also provided jobs for women and undertook maternity work.[10] Visiting societies were similar in their organization; women were allowed to intrude upon the homes of the poor. Such activity exposed them to what would have been seen as the danger of contamination. Women who ran soup kitchens were running the gauntlet of being insulted by male working-class recipients. The confrontation of class privilege with that of gender could be an animated one.[11] Similar risks were involved in the efforts to reclaim prostitutes for 'respectable' society. This activity was linked to the women's suffrage movement. In 1912 the Cardiff and District Women's Suffrage Society (CDWSS) explained 'that it is the existence of such problems as the White Slave Traffic which makes some of us Suffragists'.[12]

Expanding educational opportunities also influenced developments. The network of intermediate schools created by the 1889 act absorbed socially mobile children from the working class. A woman celebrated their creation in 1896; 'The educational ladder is complete, and he who wills may climb it.' In the 1870s women had been admitted to the college at Aberystwyth nominally to study music, but really because of the need for female voices in Joseph Parry's choir. This was temporary and partial but the situation changed in the 1880s with equal admission being granted at Cardiff and Bangor from their inception; Aberystwyth also conceded in 1884.[13] For one woman equal admission was an expression of the Christian and democratic ideals of Wales, and she contrasted it with the attitudes of the ancient, and Continental universities.[14]

If the experience of women in philanthropic bodies was ambiguous there was one charitable organization where the relationship between activity and emancipation was clear. This was the University of Wales Settlement established on the East Moors in Cardiff in 1900 with the aim of reconciling classes. Here there were debates on women's suffrage which ended in victories for the principle of equality. The leading woman in the settlement was Lilian Howell who later went to London to train as a social worker. Her sister Mabel became secretary of the CDWSS. They were nieces and beneficiaries of the founder of one of the city's leading department stores. University graduates sometimes introduced ideas to their working-class sisters. By 1914 the Men's Club had also been converted.[15] But East Moors with its settlement workers was an unusual location in turn-of-the-century Wales.

By the Edwardian period the rigid Victorian boundaries of gender roles were being probed. The coming of mass party organization in the wake of the Reform Acts of 1867 and 1884 gave women a clear political role. The Primrose League (attached to the Conservative Party), developed this most extensively, and even in Liberal Wales it achieved widespread coverage though it lacked depth in membership. It did better in the more Anglicized areas; in 1913 about 300 people were attracted to its summer fête in Colwyn Bay.[16] Liberal women also had their own organizations and they refused an entirely subsidiary role. Women's organizations were seen as an integral part of the structure of the Liberal Party; for one event an invitation was offered to 'every Liberal Association, every branch of "Cymru Fydd", to every branch of the Welsh Women's Liberal Union, to members of every chapel, and to all the representative authorities of the several Nonconformist bodies in North Wales . . .'[17]

The organization of women in the Liberal Party in Wales began around 1890. Prominent parts were played by Gwyneth Vaughan (a doctor and successful Welsh writer), Nora Phillips (wife of the MP Sir Wynford Phillips) and Sybil Thomas (wife of the MP and coalowner D. A. Thomas). Nora Phillips benefited from having a broad circle of correspondents in British political and charitable movements, including Mrs Fawcett and the Liberal activist the Countess of Carlisle. A branch of the Women's Liberal Foundation was established in Aberdare in November 1891, and quickly built up a following throughout the constituency. Within three months it was advocating votes for women on the same terms as men. It gained permission from its Warwick and Leamington counterpart to translate leaflets into Welsh. By March 1893 there were said to be 7,000 women in the Welsh Union of Women's Liberal Associations, and 9,000 by 1895.[18]

In 1895 at a meeting of the North Wales Liberal Federation and the cultural and political pressure group for home rule, Cymru Fydd (lit. Wales To Be = Young Wales), the Women's Liberal Associations merged with them to create a new Welsh Liberal Federation. Ominously the South Wales Liberal Federation stood aloof from this process, but equal rights for women were written into the objects of the new body. Women's suffrage had already become established as one of the aims of Cymru Fydd. The journal *Young Wales* gave the social and political claims of women a special section. Women's Liberal organization became widespread and branches were established in relatively small places like Barmouth and Caernarfon. By 1897 women Liberals in the Rhondda were active in School Board elections. Nora Phillips was a frequent speaker and her oratorical gifts were seen as evidence for the equal capabilities of the sexes.[19]

In March 1896 delegates from all parts of Wales gathered at Newtown for the meeting of the Welsh Women's Liberal Union. Above the stage was inscribed: 'We *will* have the vote.' They discussed issues like disestablishment, temperance, Welsh home rule, the Armenian massacres, the suffrage and the economic position of women. A number of them were Poor Law guardians; they included almost a quarter of the eighty-eight female guardians elected in Wales and Monmouthshire in 1894, following the legal changes of the previous year — changes which they had advocated. Women could utilize their real skills as domestic managers of large establishments to claim an expertise in such work. Mrs Rawlins of Rhyl argued that the 'work of women Guardians is mother's work, i.e. the management of the workhouse . . . ' The work took women beyond domesticity into an appreciation of a wide range of social problems; health, mental illness, unemployment and illegitimacy. Opponents of women's suffrage would argue that this kind of work marked the limits of advance for women. Parliament was an exclusion zone because its sphere was political and imperial and women's experience and aptitudes did not suit them for it. However, women could use domesticity to gain purchase on the wider world; as one woman argued, they might start with these domestic concerns, but that meant that they could gain time to acquire the 'masculine' skills: ' . . . for after all the duty of a Guardian, man or woman, is to do the work of a Guardian to the best of their ability, and not merely fractions of it as may be convenient or agreeable'. The more that social issues became an integral part of high politics in the Edwardian period, the harder it became to deny women a role in political institutions. Politically alert women saw clearly the advantages of working out from domesticity to a place in the outside world.[20]

Despite these early successes, women's Liberal organization seems to have lost some of its impetus. *Young Wales* found it difficult to secure a regular editor for its women's section, which appeared only intermittently. Women's issues were never as prominent in journals like *The Welsh Leader* or *Wales*. The defeat of Cymru Fydd in the famous joint meetings of the North and South Wales Liberal Federations at Newport in 1896 probably cost it dear. By 1900 the Aberdare branch was foundering, and efforts to organize the Welsh Union meeting in the town in 1900–2 were a fiasco. By 1900 there were apparently only fifteen branches in Wales, a fact which may have had damaging consequences for the Liberals. The Aberdare branch tried to revive itself from a long period of torpor in 1907, but its minute book ends in that year. In Cardiff in 1905 the efforts of a few women were said to be keeping the branch going, though it had achieved some successes. In 1908 it held a well-attended meeting in favour of women's suffrage and in 1911 it was discussing disestablishment. Swansea women Liberals also promoted the suffrage cause in the Edwardian period. Holyhead had 120 members in 1913.[21]

Yet the heritage was not dissipated. In 1908, Edward Thomas ('Cochfarf') used his stentorian voice to try to gain a hearing for advocates of women's suffrage in an unruly public meeting in Cardiff; he had also advocated this at the Aberystwyth meeting of 1895. So had Lloyd George. When Tom Ellis died in 1899, Aberdare women remembered him as someone 'who in addition to his loyalty to the Liberal cause proved himself an ardent advocate of women's claims to Political rights'. Liberals like Nora Phillips tried to associate Welshness and religion with the rights of women. Mrs D. M. Richards who gave lectures (in Welsh) around Aberdare on 'The Position of Women in All Ages' associated women's emancipation with the Christian era. Gwyneth Vaughan made the most sweeping claims for the Welshness of the issue:

> I may be wrong, but I fancy the Saxon has not the courtesy of the Celt to women. At any rate it is a matter of history that British women enjoyed more liberty than Saxon women, and the Saxon than the Norman. All our great men believe in the equality of the sexes, and we would very soon have equal political rights if it depended upon Wales.

Women's Liberal groups also provided political apprenticeships for many and discussed a variety of causes, such as equal divorce laws and protective legislation for women workers.[22]

The most prominent organizations promoting women's suffrage were non-party pressure groups. Although such suffrage societies existed in England in the 1860s it was in 1897 that the National Union of Women's Suffrage Societies was formed when seventeen of the strongest societies came together under the leadership of Mrs Fawcett. The Women's Social and Political Union followed in 1903, adopting its militant tactics two years later. A break away from this in 1907, when it was felt by some members that the Pankhursts' methods were too autocratic, resulted in the creation of the Women's Freedom League (WFL). This also stayed closer to the socialist movement from which the Pankhursts increasingly distanced themselves. The militancy of the WSPU escalated during the period, but until 1912 it was usually possible for the constitutional and militant societies to work together. Much had been hoped for from the Liberal Government elected with a huge majority in 1906, but it found the conflicts over women's suffrage to be a morass into which it nearly sank. The Cabinet was divided, with Liberal imperialists like the Prime Minister from 1908, Asquith, against women's suffrage as they wanted women to be held to their domestic roles in order to raise a healthy race of little Britons. Others like Lloyd George, Chancellor of the Exchequer from 1908, favoured enfranchisement.

Women's suffrage was far from a straightforward demand. The simplest cause was for votes for women on the same terms as men, but given the limited enfranchisement of men this might have provided an electoral advantage for the Tories. Lloyd George wanted a broad extension for men and women as a counter, but this risked alienating Tory support for a measure on which both parties were divided. As the issue became increasingly intractable, so the WSPU escalated its militancy to force politicians to face the dilemma which many would have preferred to avoid. From 1912 there was a series of complex manoeuvres in favour of Conciliation Bills which sought the widest measure of agreement based on a compromise between universal suffrage and equal voting. None of the three bills reached the statute book, and by 1912 suffragist disillusionment with the government was at a peak. Complex political games increased the scope for accusations of duplicity. The NUWSS then formed an alliance with the Labour Party, and by 1914 the issue seemed to have found its place in the queue of Liberal reform measures. The war reduced opposition to the issue, and ensured that the opinion mobilized before 1914 had its due reward. Frequently in the last decade of the struggle Wales had a ring-side seat, and sometimes got drawn into the ring.[23]

The first organization for women's suffrage in Wales that we have traced was established at Llandudno in January 1907. Branches throughout Wales followed hard on its heels.[24] There had been straws in the wind for some time before this. Lady Amberley addressed a 'crowd' of nine women and a man on the subject at Trelleck (near Monmouth) in 1871; a committee was established, but only the village schoolmistress turned up to the following meeting! There were also some meetings in Monmouth in 1873, addressed by members of the Bristol branch of the National Women's Suffrage Society. Bristol was an early centre of the movement and possessed a large middle class.[25] In 1874 the American suffragist Miss Beedy along with Mrs Lucas (sister of John Bright) and the journalist 'Gohebydd' campaigned in north and mid Wales in favour of the vote for single and widowed women who possessed the necessary qualifications. Mrs Lucas observed that 'the rich cannot legislate for the poor, neither could men legislate for women'. Meetings were held at Holyhead, Aberystwyth, Bangor, Rhuthun, Denbigh, Caernarfon and Porthmadog and were often well attended and 'influential'. The tour was organized by the Manchester National Society for Women's Suffrage.[26] Richard Pankhurst — husband and father of the WSPU's Pankhursts — shared a platform with Gladstone at Rhyl in 1878 and urged him to adopt universal suffrage.[27]

Early activity originated outside Wales. Even the formation of the Llandudno society in 1907 was related to the presence of a large English middle class in the town. Militant activity was also apparent, and it soon came into conflict with expressions of Welsh national identity. In 1909 the WSPU disrupted the Welsh National Eisteddfod which was being held at the Albert Hall in London. Soon after this Dr Helena Jones tried to hold a WSPU meeting in her native Conwy, and she and her speaker received a very hostile reception.[28] In the previous year the socialist feminist Charlotte Despard of the WFL and Mrs Fawcett had gone on a short speaking tour of south-east Wales, with meetings at Cardiff, Caldicot and Pontypridd. The meeting at Cory Hall in Cardiff proved impossible because of the riotous behaviour of the crowd, many of whom were students. The meeting was described as 'one of the most disgraceful scenes ever witnessed at a public meeting at Cardiff'. The speakers had to be shepherded to the Independent Labour Party's (ILP) Ruskin Institute where a closed gathering was held.[29] The sense of isolation and a hostile environment became overwhelming at Pontypridd. Sitting in her hosts' garden Charlotte Despard contemplated the coming meeting:

> Never shall I forget that quiet afternoon in the beautiful old garden, with the throbbing anticipation of the evening's tumult before us — the messages, the rumours, the consultations, the calm resolution of our host and hostess . . . When an hour before the meeting opened we drove to the hall, we found it surrounded by a great crowd . . . The tumult was tremendous — shouting, cat-calls, ringing of bells, bursts of laughter, with occasionally, in mellow voices, snatches of some Welsh song, the music coming as a welcome relief from the hideous clamour.[30]

All that was possible was a small and virtually silent meeting held furtively. The journal of the WFL, *Women's Franchise*, concluded that 'little Wales' was 'ungallant'.[31]

Not long after this, in July 1908, the Cardiff and District Women's Suffrage Society was formed. One of its objects — like its parent National Union of Women's Suffrage Societies — was votes for women on the same terms as men. It was non-party and open to men and women equally. It aimed to hold meetings in all parts of the constituency within weeks of its foundation. The *Western Mail* was patronizing and remarked that the women were generally held in 'good-humoured tolerance'. At the beginning there were about seventy members and amongst the most prominent was Millicent Mackenzie (Vice-President), wife of the University's Professor of Philosophy. In 1918 she would be the only female parliamentary candidate in Wales. The President was Mrs Henry Lewis of Tongwynlais; she was a Tory active in many areas of life, including archaeology, voluntary work and fox-hunting. In September 1908 she held a garden party in aid of the movement. Cardiff was reputed to be a centre of anti-suffrage activity and Ivor Guest, the Liberal MP for Cardiff, was prominent in the organization. Interestingly he was the grandson of the staunchly Whig Lady Charlotte Guest, though he was not prominent enough in the anti-suffrage cause to rate a mention in Brian Harrison's standard work on the subject.[32]

The WSPU had also begun to send speakers into the area. Emmeline Pankhurst and Mary Gawthorpe held meetings throughout Wales in 1906; Mrs Pankhurst and Annie Kenney contributed to Keir Hardie's safe return at Merthyr. One of the prominent women drawn into the WSPU was Margaret Haigh, daughter of Sybil and D. A. Thomas, whose cousin Florence recruited her shortly after her own release from prison in 1908. In July she went on the WSPU's march in London, accompanied by her mother, who felt that her daughter needed a chaperone on such a venture. This was well supported from south Wales, with special trains being run from Cardiff and Newport. Also the WFL held women-only meetings in Cardiff, where there was a branch. It was accused of admitting only women who would give their names at the door, but this it strenuously denied.[33]

In 1908 both the WSPU and the NUWSS were active in south-west Wales. Mrs Pankhurst, Annie Kenney, Mrs Pethick-Lawrence and Mrs Massey held a number of meetings in Pembrokeshire in July, during a by-election. The WSPU's slogan of 'Keep the Liberals Out' was hardly calculated to resonate in a Wales which had not elected a single Tory in 1906. The WSPU felt that the Tories — for reasons of electoral advantage — were more likely to enfranchise women on the same terms as men and thus establish the principle of votes for women. Voters were urged to press candidates to adopt their cause.[34] Some indication of the difficulties which could arise over the tactics of the WSPU is given by an incident in Margaret Haigh's early involvement in the movement. She was invited to address the Merthyr Liberal Club, enlisting the help of Annie Kenney for the occasion, but they could not gain a hearing. Before this Winston Churchill had been threatened by members of the WSPU at Bristol and dogwhipped. Widespread anger had resulted in the Liberal ranks; it had also affected Despard's reception at Cardiff in 1908. In Merthyr the speakers' voices were drowned out by gongs, tin trumpets and other musical instruments. Tomatoes and herrings were thrown at them. Despite persisting for an hour they were refused a hearing, and the chairman closed the meeting.[35]

The spread of the movement in north Wales continued this pattern of external stimulus. In 1909 women from the Liverpool branch of the WFL took the cause into Anglesey, holding the first meeting on the island at Newborough. A local activist, Miss Bessie Jones, made the necessary arrangements. Other WFL meetings followed at Holyhead,

Bangor and Caernarfon. The NUWSS followed up its activity by establishing further branches at Rhyl in 1908, at Bangor the following year, with Caernarfon bringing up the rear in 1910.[36] Militants played a part in the 1910 elections by harassing candidates known to be hostile to votes for women. Lloyd George was a favourite target for contemptuous comments, and this drew a hostile response from local crowds. Against the advice of the police two suffragettes from London addressed an open-air meeting in Castle Square in Caernarfon. As soon as they started the hostile crowd rushed them and tried to push the wagon which was serving as their platform towards the fountain in the square; it was meant to become a ducking-stool. The police had difficulty in rescuing the women and while they did so the crowd turned its attention towards the suffragette headquarters in High Street. Several members of the crowd breached the police cordon and got into the building. Flags and papers were thrown from the windows and furniture damaged. At about midnight a crowd of several hundred gathered around the women's lodgings, and the police used force to restrain them.[37] There was also hostility to the attempts to prevent Lloyd George's re-election in Llandudno. A WFL meeting suffered a violent response and the women had to be escorted back to their hotels by police. At Pwllheli the women's car was rushed, flags and placards torn and a tyre punctured. Refuge was taken in the Conservative Club and the women remained there for some time to escape the wrath of a large crowd.[38]

Militancy continued to encounter violence, but the non-militant NUWSS developed steadily along the north Wales coast. Between 1910 and 1912 new branches opened at Penmaen-mawr, Cricieth, Llanfairfechan, Pwllheli and Porthmadog. These were tourist centres with large numbers of visitors from England. Some of these were of Welsh extraction from Merseyside, coming back to their roots, and there was also a locally rooted middle class to draw upon. At Llandudno 700 people signed a suffrage petition; the total electorate numbered only just over twice that. Bangor assumed leadership because of the presence of the University; the support of professors and their wives gave it prestige and influence. A key figure was Mrs Charlotte Price White, a former student of the University and a teacher. She was secretary of the Bangor Branch at its foundation, served on the regional executive and was nominated for the national executive. Though not a native of Wales, she realized the importance of translating suffrage literature into Welsh so that it could capture the imagination of local people. The Bangor Branch assumed the role of translator for the whole of Wales and helped disseminate literature after 1910. It may have had an impact in the immediate area, for the movement spread beyond the Anglicized, middle-class coastal belt to the Welsh, working-class interior — the slate-quarrying districts of Bethesda, Tal-y-sarn and Pen-y-groes.[39]

The chance survival of records for Bangor allows a glimpse of branch life in north Wales. By the end of 1912, work was increasing, and membership growing. It had raised £90 in a year, plus another £166 to send members to conferences. Like all voluntary organizations it exhorted its members to greater efforts; around seven members were usually present for an executive committee meeting. A hostile source suggests it had 200 members, a respectable total in a town with a population of just over 11,000 in 1911 — though there were another 26,000 people in its hinterland. It was part of a regional and national network of effort, and organized canvasses of voters in municipal elections as well as educational and agitational activity. Municipal voters were seen as potential supporters of the suffrage question. It was pleased when 32 out of 42 women voters in the south ward voted for a Poor Law guardian. Outside activists were brought in to raise membership and morale. A fund-raising fête was organized in the Belmont Grounds, by courtesy of Lady Lewis; several ladies lent their maids for the occasion. The branch also invited trade unions to meetings that seemed to be of mutual interest, and in 1914 were prepared to co-operate with the Labour Party in the run-up to the expected general election. They offered to work with the leading ILP man, David Thomas, in the organization of meetings. The general impression is of a small but active group working hard to cover the town with personal effort, facing some discouragements, but not feeling that its work was in vain.[40]

In south Wales too there was steady growth for the non-militant movement after 1908. The Cardiff and District Women's Suffrage Society reached out over much of south-east Wales. During 1912–13 it was the largest society in Britain outside London, reflecting the wide area it covered as much as anything. In that year it raised over £355 and organized — or its members addressed — forty-six meetings. As the earliest, largest and wealthiest branch of the NUWSS in south Wales it tended to take the leading role.[41]

The movement spread beyond Cardiff with branches appearing at Bargoed, Farmers, Kidwelly, Pontypool, Rhondda Fach and Upper

Rhondda. The Ferndale branch was established after an address by Miss W. L. Waring in the Workmen's Hall in November 1911. A year later another was operating at Tonpentre. The Penarth branch was active during elections, generally mobilized opinion, and exerted pressure on its MP, William Brace, to vote in the appropriate way in Parliament. It also ran a tea shop. By 1913–14 there were 1,200 members in the Cardiff and District Society and a wide range of activities was arranged including open-air meetings in Cathays Park and Llandaff Fields. Expanded work had led to the taking of larger office premises in Queen Street. Campaigns continued until war intervened in 1914. Membership suffered because of a lack of the propaganda work which was always necessary to make up for losses occasioned by removals. It still stood at 1,100, however, at the outbreak of war. It was also getting sympathetic hearings from trade union branches — something at first sight, perhaps, a little surprising for a movement which organized garden parties and was well sprinkled with degrees — but it reflected a growing bond between the labour movement and women's suffrage following the Labour Party's espousal of votes for women on the same terms as men in 1912. Socialists in the Rhondda stressed that it was only the labour movement which backed women's claims for equal suffrage, and found it easy to convict the Liberal Party of hypocrisy and ingratitude for women's contribution to the Liberal cause in its handling of the suffrage issue. Some newspapers were becoming more responsive; the *Glamorgan Free Press* requested weekly accounts of the Cardiff society's activities. In the Rhondda the issue was even used in advertising, though not in an enlightened way: 'Every Woman Allowed to Vote in favour of dealing with Bevan & Co. Ltd, Taff Street, Pontypridd, Wales' largest House Furnishers'.[42]

Militant activity also continued in south Wales. Inaugurating a vigorous campaign in Cardiff in May 1909 the WSPU held a meeting addressed by Annie Kenney at the Park Hall Hotel. The aim was for weekly meetings and the opening of a shop on Newport Road. At one meeting Sybil Thomas said that two years before she had not been an advocate of militant action, but now she saw the necessity for it. Only her husband's status as an MP had kept her aloof. 'I hold this cause very much at heart. I believe it is necessary that women should be able to vote, especially working women.'[43] Eventually she was arrested for her part in demonstrations in London. The WSPU under Christabel Pankhurst's direction organized these like military exercises with precise instructions given to participants about their conduct. It was also good at using sympathetic and prominent Welsh women such as the singer Eira Gwyn who was recruited to sell *Votes For Women* on Westminster Bridge and sang Ethel Smyth's 'March of the Women' at its première hearing, a meeting in Cory Hall, Cardiff. Catherine Griffiths, a Glamorgan miner's daughter who became a nurse in London, was recruited to put tin tacks on Lloyd George's seat in the Commons.[44]

In November 1909 there were violent scenes when three women tried to speak on women's suffrage in Mountstuart Square, the heart of Cardiff's business district. A crowd some 1,000 strong shouted them down, and bags of flour and fireworks were thrown. D. A. Thomas and the police had to come to their rescue.[45] His daughter, Margaret Haigh, continued militant action at nearby Newport. Her branch of the WSPU booked the Temperance Hall for a meeting to be addressed by Emmeline Pankhurst. The power of her oratory was sufficient to hold in check an unruly group of youngsters in the audience. Activity was spread from here to a nearby (but unnamed) mining village. Against the advice of a member who lived there it was decided to hold an open-air meeting, but it attracted unwelcome attention from the time that members began chalking notices on the pavements. The members from Newport were pelted with rotten eggs and similar material when they eventually tried to speak. The women were forced to take refuge in the women's waiting room of the railway station, but the crowd did not respect even that sanctuary. Only the arrival of Mrs Thomas in her car, accompanied by a posse of police, saved them from the wrath of the village.[46]

The vigour of 1910 was inspired by the frenetic political activity of a year in which there was a constitutional crisis and two general elections. The following year was quieter as the Pankhursts had declared a truce. In this context constitutional action could become more prominent. In Cardiff a woman tried to gain a municipal seat for the first time; the Liberal *South Wales Daily News* had advocated this course as far back as 1908. Standing for the City Council with its much wider powers was a greater challenge to established norms than was standing for the Board of Guardians, of which there were usually women members in Cardiff by this time. Janet Price stood for the Cathays Ward as an Independent backed by a committee of women's organizations. She claimed not to have any political objectives, which was true only in the narrowest of party terms. She supported a clear women's issue, the creation of a municipal hostel for women (about which there was considerable debate in Cardiff at the time). Cathays was a railwaymen's quarter, and one of the more strongly organized wards for Labour in the city. It had long been a stronghold of Liberalism, and had a radical reputation. In a hotly contested election she came bottom of the poll, but her showing was far from disastrous.[47]

Gradualism and militancy existed side by side in the period, and militants also used peaceful techniques like public meetings. When Mrs Pankhurst toured north and mid Wales in 1911 she attracted a large, mainly female, audience to a meeting at the Coliseum at Aberystwyth. The local Liberal press expressed support for votes for women, yet it attacked the 'foolish, nagging policy of the WSPU' claiming that local inhabitants had been annoyed by advertisements and slogans chalked on pavements.[48] The year 1912 saw an explosion of militant actions in Wales, as part of the WSPU's reaction to the defeat of the Conciliation Bill. On 18 May Lloyd George's speech in favour of disestablishment at the Pavilion in Caernarfon was interrupted by a woman demanding 'votes for women'. After further incidents, male and female protesters were ejected. The women were treated very harshly, their clothing torn and their hair ripped out. They were beaten with hats, sticks and umbrellas. Later at the National Eisteddfod at Wrexham, Lloyd George was again the object of attack. The scenes at Caernarfon were repeated. A man in the crowd was heard to say: 'They are amongst the Ancient Britons and we'll show them how to deal with suffragettes.' Lloyd George made comments which were unbecoming for a Cabinet minister: 'I remember little eisteddfodau at which prizes were given for the best hazel walking-stick. One of those sticks would be rather a good thing to have now.'[49]

Two weeks later came the most famous incident when Lloyd George returned to his native Llanystumdwy to open the village hall. The local branch of the NUWSS appealed in vain for him to be allowed to speak in peace. No sooner had he started than he was interrupted by the inevitable cry of 'Votes for women!' The interrupters were fiercely attacked by the crowd and again clothing was torn and hair pulled; pieces of both were given out as souvenirs. One woman was stripped to the waist before she was rescued. Another was almost thrown over the bridge to be dashed on the rocks in the River Dwyfor; this would almost certainly have been fatal. It was a media event, for trouble had been anticipated and the national press were out in force. The *Daily Mirror* and the *Illustrated London News* each devoted a full page to photographs of the incidents. The Welsh press poured scorn on English women who had dared to challenge one of the heroes of Wales, but also felt that the violent behaviour of the crowd had tarnished the image of peaceful, Nonconformist, chapel-going Wales. One woman, remembering the violence she had witnessed as a child, was clearly horrified. Lloyd George claimed that suffragettes would not show their faces in Wales again, but a Cricieth suffragette emphasized that they would maintain their campaign. In November 1912 Ben Evans, a solicitor's clerk, was charged with assaulting Mrs Watson of London and with obstructing the police. The case was dismissed because of conflicting testimonies, lack of evidence, and alleged provocation.[50]

Both the militant and the non-militant factions of the movement seemed to have suffered from these incidents. Mrs Gladstone Solomon established a branch of the National League for Opposing Women's Suffrage in Bangor in 1912 which held meetings in the surrounding area in the summer of 1913, establishing branches in Anglesey. At a debate with the NUWSS at Penmaen-mawr the new body carried the day. It claimed over a hundred members within a short period. In April the NUWSS placed an advertisement in the *North Wales Chronicle* denouncing the work of the WSPU and other militants. The Bangor branch rewrote its constitution to limit its actions to orderly propaganda and public discussion; the word 'agitation' was left out. Local activists drew on the support of the wider movement in the north-west to hold a range of meetings in May. One at Holyhead which tried to win more support from men was held at the Seamen's Club. Another was aimed at teachers, and both of these gained resolutions in favour of their object. The meetings continued into the summer and one drew a speaker from Norway — Fru Anker — who spoke on 'How Women got the Vote in Norway — and Used it'.[51]

In the remaining time before the outbreak of war the NUWSS spent its time in north Wales organizing educational and propaganda campaigns. Many local branches took part in the march to London in July 1913. About twenty-eight members from Bangor, Caernarfon, Cricieth, Pen-y-groes and Pwllheli left Bangor on 2 July travelling to Penmaen-mawr by bicycle, car or brake where a meeting was held. The next day at Conwy they were joined by members of the

Llandudno branch and meetings were held there and at Colwyn Bay. As they proceeded to Abergele, 200 cheering quarrymen greeted them, and insisted on discussing the suffrage issue. The women felt there was an affinity between their cause and that of labour. However, at Rhyl there was violent opposition to their meeting and the women had to be escorted to their lodgings by police. The next day they walked to Prestatyn, their last objective in Wales. Mrs Price White said that their purpose had been to show the country the difference between the methods of the militant and non-militant factions. Some went on to join the four armies of women that converged on London on 26 July.[52] There they would have been part of the same crowd as their sisters from south Wales. The latter contingent left Cardiff on 7 July.[53]

Militants continued to make an impact in south Wales. In 1912 when the Home Secretary was visiting Llandaff with the King and Queen he was confronted by Helen Craggs who denounced him: 'Mr McKenna, you are a traitor to all the women in the country.' The procession was held up while she was arrested. No action was taken against her, though news of 'A Suffrage Attack on Mr McKenna' was prominently displayed on billboards in Cardiff. In February 1913, in a meeting at Cory Hall in Cardiff, Mrs Pankhurst accepted full responsibility for the attack on Lloyd George's home the night before, and when asked why they had blown up the Chancellor, she replied, 'To wake him up'. In April there was a series of attacks on letter-boxes, in Bridgend and Newport, for instance, though none of the mail was seriously affected. In one box a note was found comparing the harsh treatment of Mrs Pankhurst with the leniency extended to Sir Edward Carson. At Llantarnam, near Pontypool, telegraph wires were cut three times. A notice pinned to the telegraph pole read, 'We won't be quiet until Mrs Pankhurst is let out of prison.' Between April and September hoax bombs were planted at Cardiff and Abertillery, and telegraph wires cut at Queen Street Station in Cardiff. Special precautions were taken at the National Eisteddfod pavilion at Abergavenny. Margaret Haigh became involved in the acts of violence committed by the Newport branch. She collected the material necessary to make firebombs for deposit in letter-boxes from London and hid it in her garden for a week while she plucked up her courage. She was convicted in a hearing at the Newport Police Court, which was besieged by suffragettes for the occasion. She declined to pay her £10 fine and was sent to prison at Usk where she went on hunger strike, before being released under the terms of the 'Cat and Mouse Act'. She did not return as her fine was paid for her after her release.

At about this time a militant suffragette interviewed by the *Western Mail* said that the repressive measures taken by the government would only stimulate further militancy. Socialist militants in the Rhondda came to feel an affinity, at least in tactics, with the WSPU. In 1913 the WSPU conducted a series of meetings in association with the Rhondda branches of the NUR, and George Barker, Miners' Agent, wrote a laudatory account of the 'Martyrdom of Miss Emily Davison'. He had been in London on the day that she had thrown herself under the King's horse in the Derby, and complained that more concern had been expressed about the horse than about her. Lewis Jones's later dismissive comment that Lord Cwmardy (i.e. D. A. Thomas) had made so much money that his daughter was able to advocate the cause of women's suffrage did not reflect contemporary attitudes to the WSPU in the Rhondda syndicalist movement.[54]

By 1914 a pattern had been established. The non-militant societies built up their presence steadily, partly benefiting from the public prominence and urgency of the issue established by the militants, and partly suffering from the bad publicity which the whole of the movement got as a result of violent action. Certainly roots were being put down. The NUWSS held one of its summer schools in Tal-y-bont in the Conwy Valley in 1913, and north Wales women were amongst those to benefit from the training in public speaking that was given. Training in public speaking was also given in Cardiff. After Lloyd George had claimed that women's suffrage was not a popular cause it was shown that 10 per cent of the population of Cricieth belonged to the suffrage society and a petition in favour of women's suffrage was signed by all the members of Pwllheli Town Council, more than 90 per cent of the Men's Liberal Executive and the Women's Liberal Committee, by all the clergy approached and by seven out of ten professional men. Similar figures were recorded at Nefyn, Cricieth and Caernarfon.[55] In south Wales there were signs of working-class involvement with the movement through the work of the Women's Co-operative Guild. The first guild in the Rhondda was established at Tonpentre in 1914. Elizabeth Andrews, Labour Party Women's Organizer for Wales from 1919 to 1948, was the first secretary of the Tonpentre Guild and an active member of the NUWSS. She remembered a hostile response — from the Young Liberal League — when the local ILP branch invited a prominent suffragette to speak.[56]

The outbreak of war disrupted this pattern as so many others. The factions of the movement united to aid the war effort and engage in voluntary work. In Bangor propaganda work was put aside and collections made for war casualties. Firm support was given to Mrs Fawcett against branches in England which argued for pacifism. Discussions centred on economy in wartime and refugees, though the suffrage issue was not abandoned. It remained on the agenda for post-war action and there were current suggestions to be considered.[57] In Cardiff a Women's Advisory Council was created from all women's organizations working in social and relief work, so that co-operation and co-ordination could be improved. It was particularly concerned with moral questions, especially when there were large numbers of soldiers in town and they attracted young girls to their camps and to parks. A club was established for 'Girls and their Soldier Friends' but there was an obvious concern that unless this were well regulated it might serve the purposes of prostitutes. A patrol of women was organized, a course of action rejected at Bangor. The Cardiff and District Suffrage Society also turned to relief work at the outbreak of war. By 1916 all its political activities were in abeyance, though it did try to improve the conditions of war service for women. It may have turned back to politics in 1917, as other Welsh societies did, but we have found no record of its work in 1917–18.[58]

Suffrage was a prominent issue in the Llangollen society. Its suffrage supporters backed Mrs Fawcett in the debates over the war, did charitable work related to the war effort, and established a League of Honour, but from 1916 political concerns made a comeback. They protested against the pro-Labour stance of the NUWSS and sent out a stream of resolutions on proposals to amend the franchise. In 1917 a petition with eighty 'influential and representative' signatures in favour of women's suffrage was sent to its MP, Sir Herbert Roberts. They also conducted a study circle on international relations and congratulated Mrs Fawcett on her seventieth birthday in 1917; their hope that that year would see the victory of their cause was not fulfilled.[59]

Relief work helped keep the movement together during the war, though the Welsh branches had particular difficulties in maintaining their membership. The branches exerted pressure from below which contributed to the push for a limited female franchise in 1918. The

NUWSS accepted this to win the principle, when sticking out for complete equality might have led to another disappointment. The Bangor branch of the NUWSS virtually gave up the ghost at this point. Its minute book peters out in February 1921. Llangollen dissolved itself, though it bequeathed its heritage, funds and banner to the local branch of the National Union of Women Workers. By contrast, the Cardiff society found plenty to do after 1918. It worked to secure the election of women to local government office; in 1919 and 1920, Janet Price — now Mrs Janet Price Williams — stood unsuccessfully as a non-party candidate for the city council. In 1921 the society decided that its original objects had been largely attained and it reconstituted itself as the Cardiff and District Women's Citizenship Association. This aimed as fostering a sense of citizenship amongst women, campaigning on civic, political and economic questions and securing adequate representation for women. Miss Helen Fraser came in 1923 to discuss 'The Future of the Women's Movement', but in Cardiff it clearly still had a role in arranging meetings with candidates in local and parliamentary elections. By 1924 there were two female councillors. In 1927 the voting records of the city's three MPs on women's issues were probed; the national society informed it that 'they are all in need of conversion'. Pioneer members died or retired in the 1920s but satisfaction could be taken at the formal civic reception given to Mrs Fawcett in 1924, in contrast to her first visit to Cardiff in 1908 when she had needed police protection. In 1928 equal voting came, and in Swansea there was a Victory Dinner. The Tory *Western Mail* blamed the 'flapper vote' for Labour's success in the 1929 general election. Amongst the celebrants in Cardiff were the Splott Women's Section of the Labour Party, complete with prams and banner.

One struggle for women had been resolved, but many more were on the agenda. Women's Citizenship Associations survived in south Wales until at least the 1940s, as direct descendants of the women's suffrage campaign. In 1943 there were branches at Abertillery, Ebbw Vale, Newport and Cardiff organized into a South Wales Area Group. They engaged in war work (with familiar concerns for law and morals) and campaigned for women police officers. Predictably, the Chief Constable of Cardiff was against this innovation. In a few areas of Wales, at least, the women's suffrage movement had put down deep roots and continued its activities. Political traditions could endure. An early memory of Eirene White, one of only four women to sit for a parliamentary seat in Wales, is of wearing her mother's NUWSS sash. Her mother, Eirene Lloyd, was secretary of the Barry branch before 1914. In 1950 the Cardiff society gave the banner made by Mrs Henry Lewis to the National Museum of Wales. It was the end of an era.[60]

How then, did Wales respond to the women's suffrage movement? The question is put in this way as it seems obvious that the stimulus came from elsewhere. Wales was following rather than leading, but clearly by 1914 women's suffrage was on the agenda of Welsh politics. Militant suffrage activity hit the headlines, but the patient work of the non-militants is harder to uncover. There is certainly more to be unearthed than has been done here. It is misleading to judge Welsh response to the issue by focusing exclusively on the violence against the WSPU. Firstly the militants tried many people's patience in 1910–14 (including the NUWSS), and there were equally hostile responses in England. Old Testament fervour was not confined to the Welsh. Opposition to the suffrage movement provided an excuse for violating the persons of middle-class women, something not normally condoned in Edwardian life. The constant attempt to strip and the invasion of private places like waiting rooms indicate the exercise of domination over such women that the people who composed the crowds could not normally exercise. It was, as some feminists have argued, a collective symbolic rape, analogous to the aggressive male behaviour that women had sometimes encountered in their charitable activites. In taking to the streets in pursuit of political power, women were presenting a much greater challenge to the conventional idea of what was their appropriate role, and some men seem to have thought that this made them legitimate targets for bodily and verbal abuse.[61]

Secondly, responses in Wales were conditioned by the intrusion of the especially upper middle-class WSPU, the majority of whose 88 branches were in the south-east of England. There were only five in Wales, all in the south.[62] The prominence of Lloyd George in the government made him a natural target, particularly as he could be harangued for hypocrisy. He had become a national institution to be defended in Wales, as was revealed by the public campaign to support him during the Marconi scandal. When he was attacked while speaking at another national institution on a cause dear to Welsh radicalism for half a century, it was to be expected that tempers would fray. This was particularly the case for those who had despaired of gaining disestablishment at the turn of the century and now saw it back on the agenda. Women's suffrage could also be seen to be competing for parliamentary time with disestablishment. Irish nationalists abandoned it as they feared it would destroy the government and their cause with it. There was also particular sensitivity over village halls. They were established in Edwardian Wales as attempts to preserve the values of rural society as it teetered under the effects of the haemorrhage of population to urban centres. The opening ceremony was to be a celebration of a community and a holiday. For all its celebratory activity, Victorian and Edwardian Wales was easily wounded and could readily take offence. Sexist violence was fuelled at least partly by national pride as well as patriarchal values.[63]

Thirdly, suffrage activists recognized that there was potential in linking their cause to the traditions of liberty that Wales liked to celebrate. This was expressed in many ways, from the red dragon on the banner made by Mrs Lewis for the Cardiff NUWSS to the Welsh costume that some Welsh activists wore on their demonstrations in London. Suffragettes tried to appeal to these traditions in Haverfordwest in 1908. No doubt some of this was an attempt to deflect hostility, but local feminists frequently made this appeal. After the failure of the first Conciliation Bill, Welsh suffragists joined together to form the Cymric Suffrage Union, the majority of whose members later left to form the Forward Cymric Suffrage Union. This was another attempt to 'go native'. Welsh branches of the NUWSS remained unusually loyal to the Liberals when the parent body developed its Labour alliance after 1912. This too was an expression of Welshness. It was peculiarly difficult to maintain a balance of feminism and Welshness when the conflicts of 1906–14 pitted the militants — and even the constitutionalists — against the Liberal Government and Lloyd George in particular. Some allowance has to be made for the way that Wales became a flashpoint for conflicts in the struggle, an arena in which broader forces met head on. The issue in Wales proved to be a victim of the failure of women's suffrage to embed itself in the party system as a Liberal cause. The growth of anti-suffrage activity was very late and steep — only two branches of the National League for Opposing Women's Suffrage in April 1912 had grown to seventeen in number a year later — suggesting that militancy expressed against a Liberal Government may have been the crucial factor. Suffragettes beginning the 1910 election campaign in

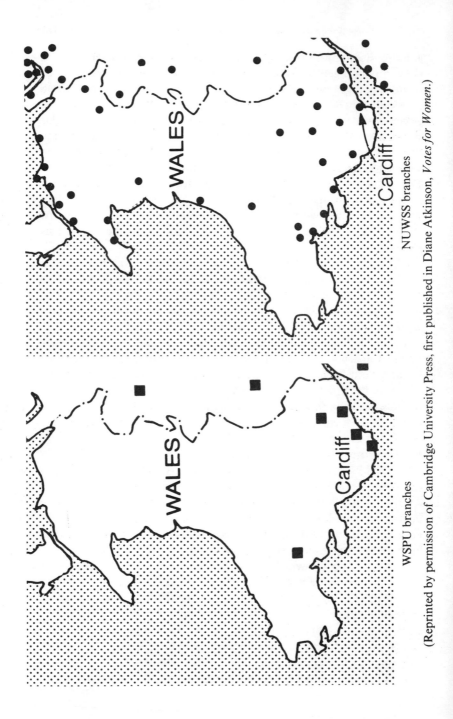

WSPU branches

NUWSS branches

(Reprinted by permission of Cambridge University Press, first published in Diane Atkinson, *Votes for Women*.)

December 1909 explained their election policy to a puzzled reporter. They stressed that they were not simply against ministers like Lloyd George, but against anti-suffragists likely to be Tory Cabinet ministers. Had the peak of suffrage agitation coincided with a Tory government, the story in Wales might have been different. The first impact of the suffrage campaign had not produced any particular hostility in Wales. Indeed from the 1870s to the 1890s it seemed to be another expression of a general Liberal commitment to human progress; Cymru Fydd embraced it in that way. With the Tories in government it seemed an unambiguously Liberal cause; with a Liberal government things were less clear-cut. In 1908 the *South Wales Daily News* published a cartoon commenting on the Pembrokeshire by-election (see p. 161). It showed a man and woman driving side by side in the Liberal car of progress. Their road was blocked by an unholy alliance of a plutocratic tariff reformer, a brewer and a suffragette. We have been too aware of Liberal opposition to the 'bell-ringing boisterous band' and too little aware of the Liberal car of progress which ran on Welsh roads.[64]

Emphasizing the non-militant movement will not make Wales into one of the centres of women's suffrage, but it will help to produce a better understanding of the response of Wales to women's questions. The impetus came from outside, but visiting speakers needed favourable local people to make the arrangements, and they left a good deal of commitment behind them. As the WSPU used a charismatic approach based on campaigns by 'stars', it was bound to leave an impression of external stimulus. The NUWSS built up a network of democratic organization, and Wales participated fully (see Map 1).[65] Yet the women in the movement themselves recognized that they had ground to make up; Cardiff's position as the largest non-metropolitan branch was essentially a false and temporary one. At a huge demonstration for women's suffrage in Hyde Park in 1912 Miss Wynne Nevison addressed the issue generally:

> Today they were told that their movement did not go forward as it ought to in Wales, a country which had stood out for its freedom, and she thought Welsh women ought to be as one with them. The reason they did not make much headway in Wales was that women in that country were better off than their Saxon sisters. What would the Welsh farmers do without their wives? In business the Welsh women were pre-eminent, as was evidenced by the fact that much of the draper and milk trades was in the hands of the Welsh.[66]

'Hear, hear,' responded her audience at the Cymric Suffrage Union's platform, but almost certainly they and she were wrong. What we now know of the social and occupational structure of Edwardian Wales suggests exactly the opposite interpretation. Wales was slow in taking up the issue because its women, in general, lacked economic power. This, rather than peculiarly Welsh patriarchal values, was the issue. This is not to deny the presence of strong patriarchal values in Welsh society. Rather, we would argue that patriarchy needs to be explored in connection with the virtual exclusion of women from waged work. Margaret Wynne Nevison pointed out two of the areas where women had an economic presence in Wales, and she might have added the professions too. Outside these spheres women were largely denied waged work and this limited the public impact which they could make. Feminist consciousness certainly existed in turn-of-the-century Wales but it could not resonate in the social and economic structure which so confined women. Opportunities were limited but the female suffrage movement made of them what it could.

*Bibliographical note*

There is an excellent study of women's activity in the major parties by Linda Walker (see n.16). An effective brief introduction to the suffrage campaign is Martin Pugh's pamphlet (n.23). The best overall analysis is by Sandra Stanley Holton (n.23). The Fawcett Library, City of London Polytechnic, Calcutta House, Old Castle Street, London E1 7NT publishes a document pack and a comprehensive bibliography.

On Wales, Peter Ellis Jones has produced a well-documented study of Caernarfonshire (n.24), and Dylan Morris gives an account (in Welsh) of the Llanystumdwy events (n.50). For those who do not read Welsh, Ann Holt's article (n.50) is useful for the latter topic. Ursula Masson's study of Swansea's suffragettes (n.21) is brief but helpful. Margaret Haigh's insider's account of the militant movement is indispensable — she wrote under her title Viscountess Rhondda (n.35).

*Notes to Chapter 7*

1. A comment made during the Pembrokeshire by-election of 1908: 'Is Pembrokeshire to be fooled by the petty antics of the bell-ringing boisterous band?', *South Wales Daily News* (*SWDN*), 9 July 1908.

2. This essay grew out of the enthusiasm of many Coleg Harlech students for Welsh women's history — Pamela Kneller and Gareth Owen in particular — and from Kay Cook's dissertation. We would like to thank Clive Hughes, Gwyn Jenkins, Bryn Parry, Lewis Lloyd, Ursula Masson, David Rubinstein and Chris Williams for help and references. Angela John's contribution extended far beyond editorial obligations.

3. Jihang Park, 'The women's suffrage activists of 1913', *Past and Present*, 20 (1988); Jill Liddington and Jill Norris, *One Hand Tied Behind Us: The Rise of the Women's Suffrage Movement* (London, Virago Press, 1978).

4. See above, Chapter 5.

5. M. J. Daunton, *Coal Metropolis: Cardiff, 1870–1914* (Leicester University Press, 1977); Neil Evans, 'The Welsh Victorian city: the middle class and national and civic consciousness in Cardiff, 1850–1914', *Welsh History Review (WHR)*, 12 (1985).

6. R. Merfyn Jones, 'The Liverpool Welsh', in D. Ben Rees and Jones, *The Liverpool Welsh and their Religion* (Liverpool, Modern Welsh Publishers, 1984).

7. See Chapter 3 above. *Cardiff Times (CT)*, e.g. 24, 31 January, 14 February 1880; 16 May 1885; 31 January 1891; *Western Mail (WM)*, 3 January 1880; 2 January, 11 December 1886. We should like to thank Joanne Cayford for the use of her notes on the *WM* and her unpublished paper '"The obscene and filthy boastings of quackery" — newspaper advertising in the late nineteenth century'.

8. *CT*, 14 February 1880; 12 March 1881.

9. Neil Evans, '"The first charity in Wales": Cardiff Infirmary and south Wales society, 1837–1914', *WHR*, 9 (1979); and 'Urbanisation, élite attitudes and philanthropy: Cardiff, 1850–1914', *International Review of Social History*, 27, 3 (1982).

10. Cardiff Dorcas Society, Annual Report, 1888; Queen Victoria Institute for Nursing, Cardiff, Annual Reports, 1887–1914.

11. *CT*, 14 February 1880.

12. Cardiff and District Women's Suffrage Society (CDWSS), Annual Report, 1912–13, 9. At Tonpentre Miss Naylor predicted that white slavery would end soon after women gained the vote: *Rhondda Leader (RL)*, 4 December 1909. Similar comments were made by Mrs Earp at Penmaenmawr, *North Wales Observer (NWO)*, 4 July 1913; F. K. Prochaska, *Women and Philanthropy in Nineteenth-Century England* (Oxford University Press, 1980).

13. D. Emrys Evans, *The University of Wales: A Historical Sketch* (Cardiff, University of Wales Press, 1953), 52–3; J. Gwynn Williams, *The University College of North Wales: Foundations, 1884–1927* (Cardiff, University of Wales Press, 1985), 54–5; E. L. Ellis, *The University College of Wales, Aberystwyth, 1872–1972* (Cardiff, University of Wales Press, 1972), 55, 85; *Young Wales (YW)*, 2 No.17 (May 1896).

14. *YW*, 2 Nos.17, 18 (May, June 1896); *Christian Commonwealth (CC)*, 8 (February 1900).

15. University of Wales Association for the Furtherance of Social Work,

Annual Reports 1900–14. Conversation with Baroness White of Rhymney, 29 June 1990; *Common Cause*, 6 March 1914.

16. Martin Pugh, *The Tories and the People, 1880–1935* (Oxford, Basil Blackwell, 1985), 133–5; *Caernarfon and Denbigh Herald (CDH)*, 4 July 1913; Linda Walker, 'Party political women: a comparative study of Liberal women and the Primrose League, 1890–1914', in Jane Rendall (ed.), *Equal or Different: Women's Politics, 1800–1914* (Oxford, Basil Blackwell, 1987).

17. *YW*, 2 No.13 (January 1896).

18. Aberdare Public Library, PY 2/2 Aberdare Women's Liberal Federation (WLF) Minute Book, 1891–1907, 26 November 1891 to 17 February 1896; National Library of Wales (NLW), MS 21971B, Letters of Well-Known Women to Leonora Phillips.

19. *SWDN*, 18, 19 April 1895; *Cambrian News (CN)*, 19, 26 April 1895; *CDH*, 15 September 1893; 21 February 1896; *YW*, Jan., May, June, Oct. 1896; Feb. 1897; Emyr W. Williams, 'Liberalism in Wales and the politics of Welsh home rule 1886–1910', *Bulletin of the Board of Celtic Studies*, 37 (1990).

20. *YW*, 2 No.17 (May 1896); University College of North Wales (UCNW), Bangor MS 26003, Margaret Williams, 'A few reasons why women should *not* vote — why women's suffrage would be a national danger'; MS 5471, Papers of William Jones MP, Circular Letter from Lord Cromer, 15 December 1909.

21. Aberdare WLF, Minutes 1900–7; *Welsh Leader*, 12 May 1905; Cardiff Central Library (CCL), Cochfarf Papers, Handbill for Women's Liberal Association Social, 10 November 1911, advertising an address on disestablishment; *South Wales Daily Post (SWDP)*, 2 October 1908; *SWDN*, 12 May 1908; Ursula Masson, 'The Swansea suffragettes', in Luana Dee and Katell Keineg (eds.), *Women in Wales: A Documentary of Our Recent History, Vol. 1* (Cardiff, Womenwrite Press, 1987), 67–76; *CDH*, 17 October 1913.

22. Aberdare WLF, Minutes, 14 April 1899; CCL, Cochfarf Papers, Gertrude Steward to Edward Thomas, 25 April 1895; Miss W. Watt to Edward Thomas, 15 May 1908; *SWDN*, 18, 19 April 1895, 12 May 1908; *Cambrian News (CN)*, 19, 26 April 1895; Gwyneth Vaughan in *CC*, 8 February 1900. In the copy in her unlisted papers, Gwynedd Archives Service (GAS) XD85, the printed words 'equal legal rights' are amended to 'equal political rights'.

23. Martin Pugh, *Women's Suffrage in Britain, 1867–1928* (London, Historical Association, 1980); Sandra Stanley Holton, *Feminism and Democracy: Women's Suffrage and Reform Politics in Britain, 1900–1918* (Cambridge, Cambridge University Press, 1986), *passim*.

24. *North Wales Chronicle (NWC)*, 5 October 1906; *Llandudno Advertiser*, 14 January 1907; Peter Ellis Jones, 'The women's suffrage movement in Caernarfonshire', *Transactions of the Caernarfonshire Historical Society (TCHS)*, 48 (1987), 88. This is a pioneering article to which we are much indebted throughout for information, references and ideas.

25. Keith Kissack, *Victorian Monmouth* (Monmouth Historical a9

Educational Trust, 1986), 36–7; Pugh, *Women's Suffrage*; Helen Meller, *Leisure and the Changing City, 1870–1914* (London, Routledge and Kegan Paul, 1976).
26. *CDH*, 31 January, 7 February, 4, 11 April 1874.
27. *Rhyl Advertiser*, 1 November 1878.
28. *NWC*, 18 June 1909.
29. *SWDN*, 12, 13 May, 23 October 1908.
30. *Women's Franchise*, 28 May 1908.
31. Ibid.
32. *WM*, 3, 10 July 1908; 27, 28 December 1928; *SWDN*, 18 September 1908; Roger Lee Brown, *The Lewis' of Greenmeadow* (Tair Eglwys Press, Tongwynlais, 1984); Brian Harrison, *Separate Spheres: The Opposition to Women's Suffrage in Britain* (London, Croom Helm, 1978). See above, Chapter 2.
33. *WM*, 21 June 1908; *SWDN*, 3, 7, 18 September, 2, 23 October 1908; Antonia Raeburn, *The Militant Suffragettes* (London, Michael Joseph, 1973), 11; Viscountess Rhondda, *This Was My World* (London, Macmillan, 1933), 118.
34. *Haverfordwest and Milfordhaven Telegraph*, 15 July 1908; *SWDN*, 6, 7, 8, 9, 10, 11 July, 1908; *Votes for Women (VW)*, 9 July 1908.
35. Viscountess Rhondda, op. cit., 121–3.
36. Ellis Jones, op. cit., 88.
37. *NWC*, 28 January 1910.
38. Ellis Jones, op. cit., 86–8; *CDH*, 14, 21 January 1910.
39. Ellis Jones, op. cit., 92, 94.
40. UCNW, Bangor MS 25800, Minute Book of the Bangor and District Women's Suffrage Society, Meetings of 28 November 1912 to 6 June 1914; MS 5471 (6), Edward Greenly to William Jones, 29 March 1913; Peter Ellis Jones, *Bangor 1883–1983: A Study in Municipal Government* (Cardiff, University of Wales Press, 1986), 257–8.
41. CDWSS, Annual Reports, 1912–13; 1913–14.
42. Ibid; *RL*, e.g. 17, 24 April, 1 May, 12 June 1909; Glamorgan Record Office (GRO), D/DX 158/6 (i), Minute Book of the Penarth Women's Suffrage Society, 1910–14; *Rhondda Socialist*, 6 January, 20 July, 12 October, 23 November 1912; *South Wales Worker (SWW)*, 6 December 1913; Caroline Rowan, 'Women in the Labour Party, 1906–1920', *Feminist Studies*, 12 October 1982; Holton, op. cit., Chs. 3 and 4.
43. *WM*, 28 May, 14 July 1909.
44. NLW, D. A. Thomas Papers, circulars from the WSPU about conduct at demonstrations, and a petition taken by Sybil Thomas to the House of Commons; GAS, XM/4595/90, unidentified cutting [*CN? c.*1956]; *The Guardian*, 12 November 1987; 6 March 1988; *The Independent*, 5 February 1988.
45. *WM*, 18 November 1909.
46. Viscountess Rhondda, op. cit., 139–44.
47. *SWDN*, 3 November 1908; 12 October 1911; *WM*, 3 November 1911.
48. *CN*, 21 April 1911.
49. *Welsh Coast Pioneer (WCP)*, 19 September 1912; Raeburn, op. cit.,

180.
50. *WCP*, 26 September, 21 November 1912; *Standard*, 24 September 1912;
    Ellis Jones, op. cit., 100–2; Ann Holt, 'The Battle of Llanystumdwy',
    *New Society*, 18 September 1987; Dylan Morris, 'Merched y screch a'r
    twrw: yr WSPU yn Llanystumdwy', *TCHS*, 46 (1985); GAS Oral
    History Interviews, XM/T/159 and XM/T/222.
51. *NWC*, 17 January, 14 March, 11 April, 23 May, 26 June 1913; *CDH*, 27
    June 1913.
52. Ellis Jones, op. cit., 104–6; *NWC*, 11 July 1913.
53. *WM*, 7 July 1913; *SWDN*, 14 July 1913.
54. *The Times*, 20 February 1913; *WM*, 3, 7, 23, 24, 25, 26, 28 April, 9, 12
    May, 12 July 1913; *SWDN*, 19 July 1913; Raeburn, op. cit., 176;
    Viscountess Rhondda, op. cit., Ch. 12; *VW*, 29 March 1912; *SWW*, 7, 21
    June, 30 August 1913; Lewis Jones, *Cwmardy* (London, Lawrence and
    Wishart, 1978), 240.
55. *NWC*, 15 September 1913; 13 February 1914; Ellis Jones, op. cit., 106.
56. Elizabeth Andrews, *A Woman's Work is Never Done* (Ystrad, Rhondda,
    Cymric Democrat Publishing Society, n.d. [1956]), 7–8. The meeting is
    possibly one reported in *RL*, 4 December 1909.
57. Bangor MS 25800, Meetings of 1 September 1914 to 10 February 1921.
58. *WM*, 27 November 1914; CDWSS Annual Reports, 1914–15, 1916;
    GRO D/DX 158/1, Minutes of the Sub Committee for Organising the
    Club for Girls and their Soldier Friends, 1915.
59. NLW, MS 22636B, Minutes of the Llangollen Branch NUWSS, 1914–
    18.
60. Minutes, cuttings and annual reports of the various organizations are in
    GRO D/DX 158/1; 158/2/1; 158/3 (ii); Baroness White, 29 June 1990;
    *SWDP*, 20 October 1928; *WM*, 1 June 1929.
61. Martha Vicinus, *Independent Women: Work and Community for Single
    Women, 1850–1920* (London, Virago Press, 1985), 262–8.
62. Pugh, *Women's Suffrage*, op. cit., 25.
63. Neil Evans, 'Gogs, Cardis and Hwntws: region, nation and state in
    Wales, 1840–1940', in Evans (ed.), *National Identity in the British Isles*
    (Coleg Harlech Occasional Papers in Welsh Studies, No. 3 1989). Some
    of the arguments in this section are paralleled in Morris, op. cit.
64. Lisa Tickner, *The Spectacle of Women: Imagery of the Suffrage
    Campaign, 1907–14* (London, Chatto and Windus, 1987), 128–9; *VW*, 9
    July 1908; 30 June 1911; A. J. R. (ed.), *The Suffrage Annual and Women's
    Who's Who* (London, Stanley Paul, 1913); Bangor MS 5471, Circular
    from Cymric Suffrage Union; *CDH*, 24 December 1909; E. W. Williams,
    'Liberalism in Wales'; Holton, op. cit., 79–80; Harrison, op. cit., 122;
    Brian Harrison, 'Women's suffrage at Westminster, 1866–1928', in
    Michael Bentley and John Stevenson (eds.), *High and Low Politics in
    Modern Britain* (Oxford University Press, 1983); *SWDN*, 11 July 1908.
65. Holton, op. cit., 41.
66. *SWDN*, 15 July 1912.

# 8

# Munitionettes, Maids and Mams: Women in Wales, 1914–1939

## DEIRDRE BEDDOE

It is essential to set the history of women in Wales within the broader context of events which shaped the lives of women in Britain as a whole. This is particularly true of the period covered by this chapter, 1914–39, embracing as it does the Great War and the two troubled decades which constitute the inter-war period.[1]

The First World War, 1914–18, created an unprecedented demand for women's labour.[2] Women in all areas of Britain were required to fill civilian jobs vacated by men who had been called upon to serve 'King and Country', and they were needed too in the factories which produced the machinery and ammunition of war. Women swept chimneys and roads, dug graves and fields, drove trams and buses, laboured in shipyards and engine sheds, assembled aeroplanes and tanks and manufactured shells and bullets. They donned uniforms too. Many took up the traditional female calling of nursing and joined such bodies as Queen Mary's Army Auxiliary Corps or Voluntary Aid Detachments whilst others put on entirely different uniforms and joined branches of the newly formed women's military services — the WAAC, WRNS and WRAF. It was a splendid contribution and everybody said so. Industrialists, press barons and even some male trade unionists lavished praise upon the work done by 'our gallant girls'. Feminists, delighted that women, once given the chance, had proved their worth so handsomely, looked forward to a rosy future in which women would build upon their wartime gains in employment. This was not to be. When the war ended women were expected to down tools and to return quietly to the home to fulfil their 'natural' roles as mothers, wives, sisters and daughters. If women persisted in wishing to take up paid employment, the only job deemed

suitable for the vast majority of them was in somebody else's home —
as domestic servants.

A powerful array of forces came into operation to make sure that
women returned to the domestic sphere: these included a media 'hype'
projecting the image of the housewife and mother as the only
desirable role for women, a press outcry against women who took
men's jobs, national insurance legislation which coerced women into
domestic service by making it virtually impossible for them to claim
unemployment benefit, and finally the introduction of marriage bars
in the professions to eject women from well-paid employment.
Women in Britain were told loudly and clearly that their only place
was in the home. In Wales this message operated within the context of
traditionally low female economic activity rates and very limited job
opportunities in the industrial areas.

Yet women in Wales in the inter-war years also reaped certain
benefits in common with women in the rest of Britain. They gained
the vote in parliamentary elections in two stages: those over thirty in
1918 and those over twenty-one in 1928. The Sex Discrimination
(Removal) Act of 1919 had in theory, if not in practice, opened the
door to the professions, and other legislation granted women
divorces on the same terms as men (1923), granted sex equality with
regard to the guardianship of infants (1925) and introduced widows'
pensions. It is against the backdrop of these national events and
trends that we must see the history of women in Wales in the period
1914–1939. I have chosen to look at just two aspects of Welsh
women's lives in these years. They are employment and home life.

*Employment*

A great deal of research has yet to be undertaken to give us a full
picture of female employment in Wales in the period under review.
There is plenty of evidence, however, for reconstructing the role
played by Welsh women in the Great War, for charting their ejection
from the work-force when it ended and for examining their
experience in the only employment sector which they were
encouraged to enter — domestic service.

The Great War revolutionized women's work in Wales, just as in
other areas of Britain.[3] The shortage of men available for
employment became acute particularly after the introduction of
conscription in 1916. The absence of men opened up employment

Funeral procession of a woman munition worker, August Bank Holiday, 1917. (Imperial War Museum.)

opportunities for women in a whole range of occupations which we would today assume to be 'women's work' but which were certainly not so regarded at the time of the First World War. Women were taken on throughout Wales as clerks and as shop assistants in grocery stores and shoe shops, hitherto largely male preserves. Even public libraries advertised for female assistants.

The employment of women in such sectors as public transport and the post office was considered to be extremely newsworthy and newspapers present full accounts of the introduction of women staff to the tram-cars and to sorting offices. The Cardiff Tramway Corporation first proposed employing female conductors in the spring of 1915 and met considerable opposition from the union, the Cardiff Tramways Association. The union pulled no punches and went on record as emphatically protesting 'against the employment of females on the Cardiff cars and more especially the employment of married women whose husbands are in regular work'.[4] The men threatened to refuse to work with the women but a compromise agreement was reached and the company was able to go ahead with the employment of women as conductors. Surprisingly there was less friction when women took on jobs as tram-drivers, which they did by 1917. Perhaps this was because women tram-drivers accepted that they were doing this work purely as a wartime measure and would relinquish it when the men came back. One woman tram-driver interviewed in the *Western Mail* in May 1917 stated: 'We shall yield up the positions of women drivers but I do not think men will ever again take up conductorship.'[5] Women took up driving all sorts of other vehicles too. Private grocery stores and the 'Co-op' (Co-operative Society) employed women to drive delivery vans throughout Wales, and in Cardiff the first woman taxi-driver took to the road in 1915.

In the post office women took over a wide range of functions previously done by men. They were employed as clerical workers, sorters, telephone and telegraph operators as well as post-women, collecting and delivering mail. In several of these jobs women were required to work nights, thus temporarily breaking down another barrier which had previously been used to exclude women from these posts.

Welsh women were employed in munitions too.[6] There were several factories in Wales engaged in various aspects of explosive and shell manufacture and many young Welsh women also went to work in munitions factories in England. Amongst the Welsh depots there were establishments in Blaenafon, Swansea and Newport in the south and Caernarfon and Queensferry in the north. Queensferry, for example, which became fully operational by May 1915, produced TNT and gun-cotton whilst Newport, operational from June 1916, was a National Shell Factory, making shell casings, heads and noses. Large numbers of women workers were employed in these two factories, with women forming by far the larger group working on the factory floor. At Queensferry over 70 per cent of the production workers were female and at the Newport Shell Factory, by 1918, women constituted 83 per cent of the work-force. Contemporary accounts pay handsome tributes to the patriotic fervour of women munition workers, whilst almost always overrating the wages and underestimating the dangers. It was of course very unhealthy and dangerous work. TNT workers were exposed to acid burns, eye injuries, industrial dermatitis and the possibility of being blown up. Amongst the Imperial War Museum's collection of photographs of women at war is a poignant image which depicts the funeral of a Swansea 'munitionette' killed on duty. The funeral which took place on August Bank Holiday Monday, 1917, paid military honours to the dead woman: her coffin was draped in the Union Jack and beside the hearse women munition workers in uniform formed a procession of pall-bearers.

In November 1918 the Great War ended and within a year of the Armistice some three-quarters of a million women in Britain had left their posts. The immediate problem facing women workers at the beginning of the inter-war period was unemployment. By March 1919 half a million women in Britain were officially admitted to be unemployed. Lady Rhondda painted an even more depressingly realistic picture when she wrote to the *Daily News* in a letter of 15 February 1919:

> Sir, There are over half a million women workers at present receiving unemployment allowances, *and there are probably an additional million of industrial women at present out of employment.*[7]

In some areas such as office work (but not the Civil Service) women did hang on to their jobs. The Cardiff women tram-conductors were still there in 1920 when complaints that 'women are being kept on to the detriment of ex-servicemen who are walking the streets' prevailed.[8] Just across the water in Bristol ex-servicemen attacked the vehicles of the Tramways and Carriage Company and demanded that the women — who they said could easily get jobs as servants — be dismissed.[9]

Women ex-war workers were entitled to collect an 'out of work donation' of 25 shillings for thirteen weeks, first payable in December 1918. In order to qualify for this benefit they had to attend the labour exchange daily and be available for work. The policy operated by labour exchanges was to offer women work as domestic servants, the most hated of all work. When women refused these posts, which were usually way below the level of their dole money, they were struck off the list of those entitled to benefit.[10] The press launched a full-scale attack on women who had the effrontery to collect benefit and turn down jobs in domestic service. Almost overnight 'our gallant girls' and 'our Amazons' of wartime were renamed 'Slackers With State Pay', 'Hussies' and 'Pin Money Girls'. In Wales the *Western Mail* echoed the tone of the London dailies when it commented in January 1919 on women living it up on their 25-shilling donations and tried to drive home to these women that the only answer was for them to go into domestic service.

> In the case of women, however, the hope of meeting the demand for 'suitable' employment seems hopeless, chiefly because these women war workers were, prior to 1914, either employed in domestic service, to which they will not return at the wages offered to them, or were at home with their parents. During the war they have had artificially inflated high wages, and they have not a sufficient grasp of economic factors to appreciate that the country's post-war industries, now in a state of flux, cannot absorb them on the old abnormal wage terms. Human nature being what it is they decline to accept anything offered to them as 'suitable' and stick to the 25 shilling a week donation, on which they continue to enjoy their holiday . . . Thousands of young Welsh women from the South Wales areas went to the large munition districts. Now they have returned and claimed the donations, and unless new industries are established or old industries extended and developed these women cannot possibly be absorbed and the time is approaching when they must realize that domestic service, which they were originally engaged in, must again be their main source of livelihood, that is if they want to do anything at all. Seaside places and other holiday centres throughout the country are said to be now reaping a harvest from young women who are out for a good time on their savings as munition workers, and their donations.[11]

All of this must be set against the background of an acute shortage of domestic servants in the immediate post-war period. This servant shortage, or the 'servant problem' as the middle classes termed it, loomed large in national British papers and also in Welsh newspapers. As one letter from a 'Constant Reader' of the *Western Mail* put it,

> ... I have just advertised for a domestic help in a Cardiff evening paper for 6 days specifying any requirements as to expertise, etc., but with no response whatsoever. I find that I am by no means the only sufferer in this respect. Most women and girls can do some domestic work and there must be hundreds of Cardiff householders who would be glad to get unskilled help. It seems evident that most of the 2000 women in Cardiff now in receipt of the unemployment donation prefer to remain as they are.[12]

Young Welsh women, like their English counterparts, were determined not to return to the long hours, low pay, personal restrictions and indignities of service, but did they have any choice?

It is worth pausing here to look at the chief characteristics of the Welsh female work-force. John Williams's and Dot Jones's invaluable study 'Women at work in nineteenth century Wales' shows a picture of the female work-force in Wales from 1851 to 1911 characterized by low economic activity rates (considerably lower than in England), with even fewer job opportunities in industrial south Wales than in rural west Wales.[13] This work-force was mainly young and mainly single and the waged work performed by women was concentrated in the sections of domestic service and dress. In the inter-war years these dominant characteristics continued. Women in Wales continued to have lower economic activity rates than in England. In 1921 the Welsh rate was 23 per cent and in 1931 it was 21.52 per cent. This compares with 32.3 per cent and 34.2 per cent for England and Wales as a whole. We do not have separate figures for these years with regard to the age and marital status of the female work-force in Wales alone or for their occupational distribution, but in England and Wales as a whole the work-force remained predominantly young and single in the inter-war years.[14] Although domestic service did not command quite such numbers as it had in the very early part of the century, it remained the largest single employer of women in England and Wales in both 1921 and 1931 and right up until the outbreak of the Second World War. In 1921 33 per cent of all working women were occupied in some sort of personal service and by 1931 that figure had risen to 35 per cent. That increase was partly the result of government policies and partly due to the lack of other job opportunities for women.

Throughout the inter-war period domestic service was regarded as the only fit work for working-class women and as the sole solution to female unemployment. Any training provided by government agencies for unemployed women was almost exclusively domestic.[15] The Central Committee for Women's Employment (CCWE), set up in the First World War, was granted half a million pounds in 1920 to train women in such varied fields as journalism, horticulture, hairdressing and domestic service, but by 1921 the committee's grant was tied exclusively to domestic training. Throughout the 1920s the Central Committee and the Ministry of Labour were in conflict about the type of courses on offer, but the financial upper hand of the Ministry dictated that whatever body organized the courses, they would be in domestic service. 'Homecraft courses' were introduced in 1921: they ran usually for thirteen weeks in residential centres and women entering them had to give a written undertaking to enter service. The CCWE even put on 'Home-maker courses', which were not intended to produce servants but to keep up the morale of unemployed women and make them better housewives. The Ministry of Labour would only fund courses to increase the supply of servants; between 1924 and 1939 it funded Home Training Centres organized by the CCWE. Yet another way in which women were 'helped' into domestic service was through the 'Outfit Scheme', which enabled women to make or purchase a servant's uniform.

Women in the depressed regions, of which south Wales was one, were encouraged to attend training centres in domestic service with a view to taking up posts in Britain's more prosperous regions. In 1931, for example, non-residential courses were on offer in south Wales at Aberdare, Cardiff, Hengoed, Maesteg, Merthyr Tydfil, Neath, Pontypool, Pontypridd, Swansea and Ystrad Rhondda.[16] The records of the Ystrad Rhondda Training Centre for 1929 show that the young Welsh girls trained there (mainly 16–19 year olds) took up positions as domestics in houses and in hospitals not only in Cardiff and Bristol but in Islington, Peyton, Hendon, Basingstoke and Brighton: in 1929 some of them were paid as little as seven shillings a week.[17]

Welsh women formed a vast migrant army of cheap labour in the affluent south and south-east of England. They were driven to this expedient by lack of job opportunities at home, especially in the areas of heavy industry like the south Wales coalfield where, when jobs were available, they were for men. Yet the story of the women who were forced to leave their homeland and work amongst strangers remains untold. Only an urgently needed oral history rescue operation can salvage tales of their experiences.

Oral testimony, where it exists, often informs us about relations between classes, nationalities and individual human beings. Ex-servants' reminiscences frequently reveal a picture of young Welsh girls feeling alienated amongst English people and often not getting even enough to eat from their employers. Two extracts make this point clearly. The first is from an interview by Hywel Francis with a young Maerdy woman in Croydon in the 1920s.

> And they just received me from this girl and in I went; I felt awfully nervous and then she took me to my bedroom which was right up in the attic and told me to change into my afternoon uniform and to come down to make tea. Well if I hadn't been to this training centre, I wouldn't know the difference between afternoon tea and high tea, because we didn't have that kind of thing at home . . . They were both widows, the daughter had two sons, the older son which I called Mr Eric and the younger was Master Kenneth. They were supposed to be very religious people and I suppose they were. Anyway evening times we used to have a cooked meal and I would take my place and have whatever was going. I never really had enough you know but I would never ask for more. I was too frightened to ask for more . . . I didn't feel I was part of the family at all. I felt I was the servant then you know and I was there to do my work and that was that . . . they didn't converse much with me at all, and when they did it was just to run the Welsh down . . . You wouldn't say that they were gentry because I met gentry after that and I found that they were far better, nicer people than they were.[18]

The second extract, from an interview by Anne Jones with a Rhondda woman who was in service in London in the 1930s, paints an even more appalling picture of deprivation. The woman was employed firstly in a bug-infested house and secondly in one where they starved her.

> At one place I was only there one night . . . it was alive with bugs . . . when I went to bed I lit the candle and oh my goodness I picked up the

pillow like that and without a word of a lie they were there scattering
. . . I had never seen them before, I couldn't sleep on the bed so I spent
the night on the boards . . . When it came to daylight I went downstairs
. . . and I told her. Oh she said, you must have brought them with you
. . . I left that place and went to my brother's . . . I was all lumps, oh I
was in a terrible state. I couldn't even look for another job until all
these had cleared . . . but then I went from the frying pan into the fire . . .
I was starved to death there. She [her employer] locked everything up
and gave me 3 lumps of sugar for one day and I had a small pat of
margarine . . . and for my dinner every day I had half a bag of potato
crisps for 3 weeks . . . and yet I was cooking for them but being what-
do-you-call being slow, I suppose in those days I wouldn't think of
taking anything. That's one thing that was always drummed into us . . .
don't you ever take anything that doesn't belong to you . . . She said her
daughter was dieting . . . and she wouldn't diet if I ate . . . [19]

Other Welsh girls were, as the National Vigilance Association
(NVA) delicately put it, exposed to moral dangers. The records of the
Association make harrowing reading and show that job advertisements often turned out to be very misleading when the girl arrived
to take up her post. One girl from south Wales arrived at a bachelor's
home in the Midlands to find only a see-through partition separating
her 'bedroom' from his and a nude photograph on her side of the
partition.[20] NVA workers often had to rescue girls from exploitative
households and send them home by train from Paddington in the care
of the guard. The girls were often naïve and innocent and above all
they were very young. The *Vigilance Record*, the journal of the
Association, frequently referred to very young Welsh girls going up to
London — sometimes only fourteen years of age. That journal offered
advice and practical assistance:

> We have repeatedly drawn attention in the columns of the VIGILANCE
> RECORD to the very significant and disturbing migration, which has
> been in process for some years past, of Welsh girls coming to London
> to take up employment. The problem is not confined to Welsh girls,
> but it extends also to girls coming from the North-Eastern coalfields. It
> is, however, particularly obvious where Welsh girls are concerned, any
> visit to Paddington Station when the excursion trains come in will
> convince any of our readers.
>     It is difficult to argue that girls should not go out into the world to
> earn their own living, particularly when family circumstances at home
> render their means of livelihood precarious in the extreme. But clearly

there should be some limit of age, and desirably some limit of occupation. The National Vigilance Association, apart from its station work, which is of greater value from the preventive point of view than is commonly recognised, lays stress on two points. Firstly girls coming to London should assure themselves beforehand that the situation to which they are proceeding is a safe and desirable one, second, since many social workers exist for the purpose of helping these girls, it is desirable that those social workers should do something more than offer through the printed word to assist them. Personal contact should be established by means of friendly visits. We have made enquiries for many years past, and an experiment in the manner of paying visits is now in process, since the names and addresses of a number of such girls are regularly given to the Central Council for the Social Welfare of Girls and Women in London and the London Welsh Girls Friendly Aid Society.[21]

Lest too depressing a picture is painted, it must be added that not all employers were exploitative villains. One Rhondda girl in service at a Clapham Common Welsh dairy — and there were strong links between Wales and London dairies — was taken by her employers to see plays: because she was in the service of other Welsh people she did not experience the full rigour of class differences.[22] The women themselves had their own circles of friends and contacts. Although time off was very limited, they often spent it together. One woman said that she and other Welsh women domestic servants used to meet up on their day off outside a London Woolworth and others would go on a Sunday evening after chapel to the Welsh corner in Hyde Park. Another factor which acted as a support was that women often came from the same village. Several young girls from Aberfan went to Sutton in Surrey.

A new development in the inter-war years was that domestic service went public. Not only did girls go into service in private houses but increasingly they went to hotels and hospitals. The hours and workloads in such places seem to have been no better than in houses. As one Welsh woman in a nursing home in Bristol recounted:

> I had to get up at 6.30 a.m. and clean the grates and lay the fires, take early morning tea, help cook prepare breakfast, scrub the steps and all these kinds of jobs had to be done before breakfast.[23]

She was one of only two domestic workers, who had to attend to seventeen people.

Conditions were frequently very bad. The women were far from home and many felt isolated. So why did they enter service? Quite simply they had no choice: there was no work at home and to have stayed would have put an extra burden on their families. Of some sixty women interviewed by Anne Jones, all sent money home. This was the only way in which these women could contribute to the support of their families in Wales.

Other areas of women's work in inter-war Wales await investigation. There has not as yet been, as far as I know, any study of women shop workers in Wales, although this was one of the few alternative occupations open to them. Industrial work was very limited for women. Wales did not profit from the boom in light industries witnessed by the south-east of England and the Midlands, although some Welsh women migrated to England to take up factory work there. Although many firms in England, engaged in producing processed food and electrical goods, introduced new conveyor-belt technology, it tended to be the less progressive, English-based manufacturers who recruited women from Wales and other depressed areas to work in their factories. Biscuit manufacturer Huntley and Palmer of Reading was slow to take up new technology and preferred instead to employ the cheap labour of Welsh girls: my mother went from Barry, South Glamorgan, to work there in the early 1930s. Industrial estates, with job opportunities for women, came to south Wales only at the end of the inter-war period. Finally, with regard to employment much work has yet to be done on Welsh professional women — those who became doctors, civil servants and, above all, teachers. Since marriage bars operated in all these careers, this would be a study of single women.

*Home life*

Most women in Wales were not, however, single women. The great majority of Welsh women were housewives and the home was a very important part of their lives. It is therefore essential to look at both housing and women's day-to-day home lives.

Housing in Wales, as in the rest of Britain during this period, was characterized by shortages, appalling conditions and high rents; this situation was further exacerbated by the fact that no new houses had been built during the First World War. Investigations highlighted the problems of housing. Evidence given to the Sankey Commission on coal-mining (1919) by Mrs Elizabeth Andrews, Labour Party Women's organizer for Wales, stressed shortages, high rents and poor conditions. She stated:

> Women acquiesce in bad housing in Wales because they have no alternative, under the present circumstances, due to the extreme shortage of houses, a shortage which was very acute in industrial areas long before the war.[24]

Elizabeth Andrews went on to describe overcrowding in the Rhondda, where the average occupancy per house was 5.8 persons and where a further 1,500 to 2,000 houses were urgently needed. Overcrowding remained a serious problem throughout the 1920s and 1930s. A government survey published in 1936 showed that 1,066 working-class families in Merthyr and 1,453 in Cardiff lived in homes which were officially designated as overcrowded.[25] These figures represent overcrowding percentages of 6.4 per cent and 3 per cent respectively. But this was not solely an urban problem. In fact rural Wales suffered far more serious difficulties. Anglesey, with a rate of 9.5 per cent, was the third worst county in the whole of England and Wales. Caernarfon, Denbigh, Flint, Montgomery, Pembroke, Glamorgan and Merioneth all figure in the top twenty in the county table of overcrowding for England and Wales.[26] The state recognized the existence of severe deficiencies with regard to rural housing: there was concern about the dilapidated condition of many houses in country areas as well as about cramped and inadequate living space. In 1937 the Ministry of Health, then responsible for housing, published *Rural Housing: Second Report of the Rural Housing Sub-Committee of the Central Housing Advisory Committee* and in 1944 *Rural Housing: Third Report etc.* The 1944 report devoted a special section to Wales and 'exceptional housing conditions in Wales'. 'Exceptional' meant exceptionally bad and the committee stated:

> In many parts of rural Wales housing conditions are much worse than is generally the case in rural England, that less progress was made up between the wars, and in consequence far more leeway remains to be made up before they will conform to modern standards.[27]

They blamed this state of affairs in Wales upon the laxity of the Welsh local housing authorities but more especially upon the poverty of rural Wales.

Bad housing particularly affected women who spent so much time in the home. When Megan Lloyd George made her maiden speech in the House of Commons in 1930, she spoke on housing and women's health. Referring to a report made some years earlier in her own constituency of Anglesey, she said it was shown that the death rate from tuberculosis among women was the highest but one on the list for the whole of the administrative counties of England and Wales, and yet the death rate of the men came only twenty-second on that very black list. 'The greater risk to health', she said, 'was for the woman who spent the greater part of her life in those squalid, dark, ill-ventilated cottages . . . '[28] When an investigation was made into tuberculosis in Wales and Monmouthshire at the end of the 1930s, it showed that Caernarfonshire had the highest mortality rate from tuberculosis in England and Wales and it drew an appalling picture of housing in that county. Many houses were damp and overcrowded, many had no lavatories but only buckets in an outside lean-to; these buckets were normally emptied into streams.[29]

The lack of the most basic amenities in the house greatly increased women's workload. Indeed, housing was increasingly regarded as a 'woman's issue'. During the First World War the government set up the Women's Committee on Housing to advise on house design, and the Women's Co-operative Guild made housing one of its key campaigning points. In 1923 the Guild held a conference on housing calling for the government to tackle the problem on a nationwide basis and setting forth what they regarded as essential amenities in a working woman's home. The Welsh Housing Association, an organization in which women played an important part, clearly set out the demands of working women for better housing. They asked for houses not to be built in rows but to be semi-detached or in blocks of four; separate bathrooms and separate WCs; an efficient supply of hot water to the sink and bathroom; a minimum of three bedrooms and generously proportioned living rooms.[30] For most women these demands remained only an unfulfilled dream.

Progress was nevertheless made in these years in trying to tackle the housing problem. Addison's Housing and Town Planning Act of 1919 had placed the responsibility for remedying housing shortages on the local authorities and in 1924 the first Labour Government passed Wheatley's Act which gave a major boost to council-house building. Conservative governments, however, encouraged building in the private sector and halted the progress of the local authority building programme; in fact, in 1932 the National Government abolished all subsidies for council building. In Wales 146,471 new houses were built between 1919 and 1940, 34.2 per cent of these by local authorities and 65.8 per cent by private enterprise.[31]

Although this was a step in the right direction we have seen from the overcrowding survey of 1936 that a major problem still remained and the third *Rural Housing Report* (1944) commented that the record of Welsh Housing authorities 'in all spheres of housing compares in general unfavourably with that of the majority of English authorities'.[32] In short, the vast majority of people in Wales continued to live in old houses.

In turning to look at the day-to-day lives of women in the home I have chosen to concentrate on the south Wales valleys and particularly the Rhondda Urban District. This area, which had experienced boom conditions in the late nineteenth century with the rapid expansion of coal-mining, suffered great distress and wholesale unemployment in the inter-war years: the long-drawn-out General Strike of 1926 and the Depression of the late 1920s and the 1930s hit this area hard, reducing its people to extremes of poverty.

Even in relatively good times, life was tough for women in the home. In houses which lacked the basic amenities of hot water supplies, bathrooms and indoor WCs, housework was a never-ending round. One woman in Caerffili, the mother of five, reported to a survey into women's health that she was on her feet for sixteen and a half hours per day and about 'leisure' she wrote:

> After my children go to bed, I gets two hours rest, if (I can) call it rest, I am mending my children's clothes and tidying in those few hours I get.[33]

The fact that south Wales was a coal-mining area added greatly to women's workload. The houses were built as close as possible to the pits and, as Mrs Andrews reported to the Sankey Commission, 'the women who live in those houses before they can think of washing clothes have to go out to find which way the wind is blowing, because if it blows in a certain way, there is no point in hanging out the clothes'.[34] Husbands and sons, who were coal-miners, came home black with coal dust. The women had to heat the water on the open fire and fill a tin bath in front of the fire. 'It meant that a woman who has two sons and a husband working, that if they were on different shifts her life is nothing but slavery.'[35] Another miner's wife said:

> We had to bring a tub or tin bath, whichever we had, into the same
> room as we lived, and heat the water over our living room fire in a
> bucket or iron boiler, whichever we possessed. So you can imagine the
> life of a miner's wife is no bed of roses. We had also to do our weekly
> wash in the same room, so our one room was not much to look at. By
> the time we had done our daily clean, it was looking all right until
> hubby came home. Then after he had bathed and his clothes put to dry,
> and turned from time to time, there is a nice film of coal dust all over
> the room, and it means you want the duster in your hand continually.[36]

Inside these houses there were no coppers (boilers) to heat the water
and heating it in a bucket on the fire was dangerous. Mrs Smith of
Porth, quoted above, wrote sadly, 'No wonder so many little children
are scalded to death in Wales.'[37] Not only was there the danger of the
bucket on the fire but also of children falling into the hot bath water.
It is easy to see why pit-head baths were a priority with miners' wives.

Despite all the difficulties of keeping the houses clean, or perhaps
*because* of them, women in the mining valleys took an enormous
pride in keeping their houses spotlessly clean. They followed strict
routines — Monday: wash, Tuesday: ironing and bread-making,
Wednesday: upstairs rooms, Thursday: mats beaten, Friday: parlour,
Saturday: shopping. Cleanliness was next to godliness and people
could say proudly, 'we were poor but we were clean'. Women's
triumph over adverse circumstances was reflected in polished surfaces
and conveyed to neighbours by shining door-knockers and scrubbed
doorsteps. One woman, interviewed by Rosemary Crook, used the
phrase 'scrubbed white' no less than seven times in half an hour's
conversation. Another's testimony to her industry echoes with
personal satisfaction:

> I used to wash the path . . . from the back door right down to the toilet
> . . . And then the front, flagstones was in the front them, and I used to
> wash the pavement from the front door, right past the window, right
> down to the drain. The pavement, I used to wash all that. Beautiful,
> lovely.[38]

These women were, in their own language 'tidy women', a term that
implied far more than good housekeeping: it connoted respectability.
A 'tidy woman' adhered to a received moral and behavioural code,
itself shaped by Nonconformity and policed by women themselves.
Those who fell by the wayside and slipped from the highest standards

of cleanliness, religious observance or morality could not be condoned. They were perceived as a threat to all women. And yet some women under the deadening pressure of unemployment and poverty did fall. The Pilgrim Trust's Report, *Men Without Work* (1938), refers to women who had 'lost all pride in personal appearance and the appearance of the home'.[39] It paints a bleak picture of women 'whose outings extended little beyond the small shops at the corner of the street', to which they 'slipped-down' without washing and who thought that there was little point in washing the children since they only got dirty again. Oral history preserves the record only of those who bravely carried on in the face of adversity: those who succumbed to the bitterness of defeat are marked only by their absences.

The incredible resilience of most women during the hard times of the General Strike and the Depression of the 1930s commands our admiration.[40] Theirs was the responsibility of feeding the family and managing the household on a pittance. One woman, speaking of the 1926 strike, said:

> I can always remember my father coming home from work after the afternoon shift, putting his pay on the table and saying there you are Mag — £2.12*s*. — there you are Mag, that's the last you'll get for a while. We got poorer and poorer because my mother only had this 10*s*. food note to keep us, which she put in the shop across the road, you know, also we used to have 10*s*. worth of tick, say 10*s*. worth of tick every week.[41]

Women had to feed their families on the small amount provided by means-tested public assistance. Debt fell on the woman's shoulders and she had to adopt strategies to handle it including pawning anything that would raise a few shillings. Women did what they could to bring in any extra money.

> We used to have the sacks from the grocer's shop, he used to sell potatoes out of, and we used to take the bags up the tip, fill them with coal, and bring it down. Sometimes we'd sell a bag for 18 pence and the rest we used to use ourselves.[42]

Other women sold cheap food and drink such as faggots, and small beer made from nettles. But although these measures helped they were never enough. Women were the first to go without. A health visitor, recalling 1926, said:

Puerperal mortality rates: rates per 1,000 births

|      | Wales | England and Wales |
|------|-------|-------------------|
| 1928 | 5.79  | 4.25              |
| 1929 | 5.58  | 4.16              |
| 1930 | 5.30  | 4.22              |
| 1931 | 5.13  | 3.94              |
| 1932 | 5.91  | 4.04              |
| 1933 | 5.75  | 4.32              |
| 1934 | 6.61  | 4.41              |
| 1935 | 5.89  | 3.93              |

Source: *Report on National Mortality in Wales*, 1937

> Very often I visited a miner's home where the mother wasn't able to
> have anything for dinner, as I say, it was very terrible to see the miners'
> wives — the anxiety they had, because one must admit it was on the
> mother that all these problems were put on her shoulders.[43]

Women bore the brunt of the hardship. The Pilgrim Trust's survey
found, not surprisingly, that men and children suffered the effects of
malnutrition far less than women in the depressed areas.

Health standards were shown to be directly related to income. Poor
health was a perennial problem for women on low incomes. In 1939
the Women's Health Enquiry published its findings, which showed
that whilst 17 per cent of women in the income group with 10s. per
head per household member had very bad health, the percentage of
women so categorized in the income group of 4s. housekeeping per
head was a staggering 46 per cent. As we saw in Chapter 5, one
particularly appalling feature which relates to the health of Welsh
women was the high rate of maternal mortality. This remained the
case during the Depression years. Puerperal mortality rates (that is,
deaths directly related to pregnancy and childbirth) in Wales were
consistently higher than those for England and it is a shocking fact
that the death rates rose for much of the inter-war period. The table
below shows the horror of this story.

It will be clear to many readers that the type of woman I have been
writing about in the second part of this essay is the stereotypical
'Welsh Mam', the cherished image of womanhood which prevailed in
south-east Wales. She was the wife of a miner and the mother of sons

who were miners; she was scrupulously clean, scrubbing her husband's coal-black back and her front-door step with vim and vigour; she scrimped, saved and did without herself; she was pious, devout and a chapel-goer; she was the moral custodian of the home, tolerating no intemperance, bad language or immorality. She is, in the words of Gwyn Williams, one of 'two archetypical and quasi-mythical figures [who] loom through the mist of our memory of Wales'.[44] She is indeed a mixture of reality and myth. She is real in all the features listed above and there were thousands and thousands of such women, who were loved and respected by their children. The 'Mam' was an icon, venerated like the Angel-Mother, who features so regularly in Victorian school anthologies. The myth concerns her powers. Her sphere of influence was confined to the home: the public sphere remained a male domain. Some nostalgic historians have written of Wales's industrial valleys as being matriarchal societies, but this could not be further from the truth. The 'Mam', although enfranchised politically in 1918, (*if* we assume she was over thirty), had little say in public affairs in Wales; she was economically dependent on men and she even lacked, in those days of only very sketchy birth control information, control over her own body.

The nineteenth century was the heyday of the 'Mam': in the 1920s and 1930s, when an entrenched domestic ideology and a lack of job opportunities for women kept her at home, her resilience and self-sacrifice added to her sanctity. Now, she is a figure of the past. In a Wales where there is more work for low-paid, part-time, working-class women workers than for coal-miners, she has slipped into history.

*Bibliographical note*

Very little has been written on women in Wales in these years. Note the following: D. Beddoe, 'Women between the wars', in G. E. Jones and T. Herbert (eds.), *Wales Between the Wars* (Cardiff, University of Wales Press, 1988), 128–60: R. Crook, '"Tidy women": women in the Rhondda between the wars', *Oral History*, 10, No.2 (1982), 40–57: Angela V. John, 'A miner struggle? Women's protests in Welsh mining history', *Llafur*, 4 No.1 (1984), 72–90.

For a general book on women in Britain in the inter-war period, see D. Beddoe, *Back to Home and Duty: Women Between the Wars 1918–1939* (London, Pandora, 1989).

## Notes to Chapter 8

1. See D. Beddoe, *Back to Home and Duty: Women Between the Wars 1918–1939* (London, Pandora, 1989).
2. For a very useful study of women's work in Britain during the First World War see G. Braybon, *Women Workers in the First World War* (London, Routledge, 1989).
3. I am very grateful that I am able to draw on Joanna Wilmot's unpublished work. J. Wilmot, 'Women workers in South Wales in the First World War' (Polytechnic of Wales BA dissertation, 1988).
4. *South Wales Echo*, 25 April 1915.
5. *Western Mail (WM)*, 23 May 1917.
6. The details are taken from J. Wilmot's work.
7. D. Beddoe, op. cit., 49.
8. Ibid., p.49, taken from *WM*, 17 February 1920.
9. *The Vote*, 7 May 1920.
10. D. Beddoe, op. cit., 50–3.
11. *WM*, 20 January 1919.
12. Ibid., 29 March 1919.
13. L. J. Williams and D. Jones, 'Women at work in the nineteenth century', *Llafur*, 3 No.3 (1982), 20–32. See also Chapter 5 above.
14. D. Beddoe, op. cit., 56–7.
15. Ibid., 63–4.
16. Ibid., 64.
17. Ibid.
18. H. Francis, 'The secret world of the South Wales miner', in D. Smith (ed.), *A People and A Proletariat: Essays in the History of Wales* (London, Pluto, 1980), 169.
19. Oral interview conducted by Anne Jones with Mrs E. D., Rhondda, 1983.
20. D. Beddoe, op. cit., 64.
21. *The Vigilance Record*, January 1930.
22. H. Francis, op. cit., 169.
23. D. Beddoe, op. cit., 62.
24. *Reports and Minutes of the Royal Commission on the Coal Industry* (Sankey Commission), CMD 359, 360 (1919), Evidence of Mrs Elizabeth Andrews.
25. *Housing Act 1935: Report on Overcrowding Survey in England and Wales* (London, HMSO, 1936), table IX, p. xvii.
26. Ibid., table X, p. xviii.
27. *Rural Housing: Third Report of the Rural Housing Sub Committee of the Central Housing Advisory Committee* (London, HMSO, 1944), 50–1.
28. *The Vote*, 11 April 1930.
29. Ministry of Health, *Report of the Committee of Inquiry into the Anti-Tuberculosis Service in Wales and Monmouthshire* (London, HMSO, 1939), 152–3.
30. *Welsh Housing Association Year Book* (Cardiff, 1921).

31. J. Williams, *Digest of Welsh Historical Statistics* (Welsh Office, HMSO, 1985), I, Housing Table 7, p. 88.
32. *Rural Housing*, op. cit., p. 52.
33. M. Spring Rice, *Working Class Wives* (1939, reprinted London, Virago, 1981), 110.
34. Op. cit.
35. Ibid. See Chapter 5 above.
36. Mrs F. H. Smith, 'In a mining village', in M. Llewelyn Davies (ed.), *Life As We Have Known It* (1931, reprinted London, Virago, 1977), 67.
37. Ibid., 70–1.
38. R. Crook, '"Tidy women": women in the Rhondda between the wars', *Oral History*, 10 No.2 (1982), 41.
39. Pilgrim Trust, *Men Without Work* (Cambridge, 1938).
40. See Angela V. John, 'A miner struggle? Women's protests in Welsh mining history', *Llafur*, 4 No.1 (1984), 72–90.
41. Documentary film, *Women of the Rhondda* (1973).
42. Ibid.
43. Ibid.
44. See Chapter 5 above; also G. A. Williams, 'Women workers in Wales, 1968–1982', *Welsh History Review*, 2 No.4 (1983), 530–48; D. Beddoe, 'Images of Welsh women', in T. Curtis (ed.), *Wales: The Imagined Nation* (Bridgend, Poetry Wales Press, 1986), 227–38.

# Index

*Index*